GANGSTERS AND REVOLUTIONARIES

GANGSTERS AND REVOLUTIONARIES

The Jakarta People's Militia and
the Indonesian Revolution 1945–1949

ROBERT CRIBB

UNIVERSITY OF HAWAII PRESS

Honolulu

Published in North America by
University of Hawaii Press
2840 Kolowalu Street
Honolulu, Hawaii 96822

First published in 1991 by
Allen & Unwin in association with
The Asian Studies Association of Australia

Library of Congress Cataloging-in-Publication Data:

Cribb, R. B.
    Gangsters and revolutionaries: the Jakarta People's Militia and
the Indonesian revolution, 1945–1949 / Robert Cribb.
        p.   cm.
    Based on research for the author's dissertation carried out at the
School of Oriental and African Studies, University of London.
1979–1984.
    Includes bibliographical references and index.
    ISBN 0-8248-1395-2
    1. Indonesia—History—Revolution, 1945–1949. 2. Lasykar
Rakyat Jakarta Raya History. 3. Hoodlums—Indonesia—
Jakarta—History
    4. Jakarta (Indonesia)—History. I. Title.
    DS644.C73   1991   90-27543
    959.803'5   CIP

Typeset by Vera-Reyes Inc., Manila
Printed by Fong & Sons Printers Pty Ltd, Singapore

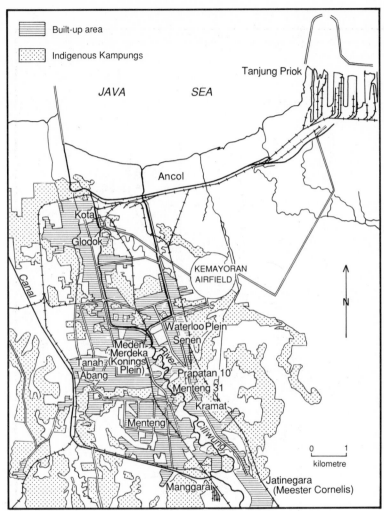

Map 1 Jakarta

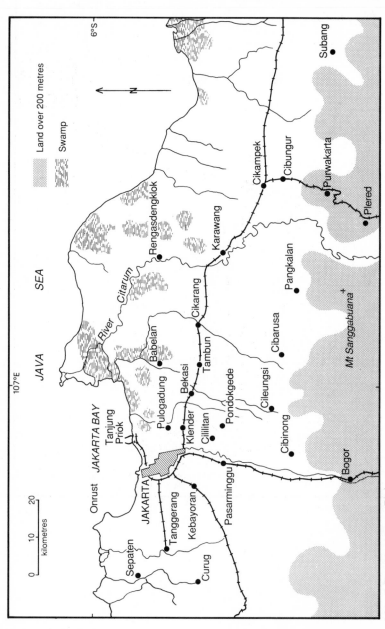

Map 2 The Karawang Plain

Contents

Acknowledgements

This book has accumulated a long train of personal and professional debts of gratitude. It has grown out of research for my doctoral dissertation, 'Jakarta in the Indonesian Revolution 1945–1949,' which I carried out as a student in the Department of History at the School of Oriental and African Studies in London during 1979–1984. I should like first, therefore, to record my indebtedness to my supervisor, Ruth McVey, for her encouragement and careful criticism of my work. Her advice and guidance, often at a great distance, was invaluable.

At various stages of my dissertation research, Sue Abeyasekere, Cees Fasseur, Kenichi Goto, Wim Hendrix, Audrey Kahin, Jacques Leclerc, Anton Lucas, Onghokham, John Smail, Wardiningsih Soerjohardjo, Ulf Sundhaussen and Heather Sutherland offered valuable advice, information and insights. Since then, Jim Alvey, Leonard Blussé, David Bourchier, Tom Cribb, Petra Groen, Ranajit Guha, John Ingleson, John Legge, Tony Reid, David Schak, Tony Stockwell, Heather Sutherland, Greg Weichard, Michael Williams, Ron Witton and an anonymous reader for Allen & Unwin have read parts of the manuscript and provided important comments on it. Colleagues in the School of Modern Asian Studies at Griffith University and the Research School of Pacific Studies at the Australian National University have commented usefully in seminars.

I owe an even greater debt to the many individuals, mainly in Indonesia and the Netherlands, who took time to tell me of their experiences during this period. Many have preferred that their names not be mentioned, but I would like to thank them all for their contributions.

I should like to express my special thanks to the members of the family of Dr Mohamad Tarekat, whose hospitality made my stay in Jakarta so easy and enjoyable. The bulk of my doctoral research was supported financially by the Shell Company of Australia, to whom I am grateful, both for their generosity and for the readiness with which they acceded to my complicated research programme. I should also like to thank the School of Modern Asian Studies at Griffith University for supporting the additional research work needed to turn the thesis into a book and the Department of Pacific and Southeast Asian history at the Australian National University for providing a congenial environment in which to complete the writing.

I must also record my gratitude for the assistance and, where necessary, the permission to publish given to me by the Algemeen Rijksarchief, the Centraal Archievendepot of the Ministry of Defence, the Ministry of Foreign Affairs, and the Rijksinstituut voor Oorlogsdocumentatie in the Netherlands and the Arsip Nasional, the Arsip Jayakarta, and the Perpustakaan Angkatan '45 in Indonesia. I should further like to thank the Southeast Asia Program at Cornell University, the Institute of Southeast Asian Studies in Singapore, and the Lembaga Ilmu Pengetahuan Indonesia in Jakarta for their formal sponsorship of my research in their respective countries.

I should also like to thank the late Lt-Col. K. Bavinck for permission to publish his photograph of the surrender of Panji and to record my thanks to Ian Heyward of the Cartography Section in the ANU's Research School of Pacific Studies for Preparation of the maps.

Responsibility for errors and omissions remains my own.

Abbreviations and Glossary

AFNEI	Allied Forces, Netherlands East Indies
AILO	Afdeling Intelligence en Loyaliteitsonderzoek, Intelligence and Loyalty Investigation Section
ALFSEA	Allied Land Forces, South East Asia
Alg.Sec.	Algemene Secretarie, General Secretariat
ALRI	Angkatan Laut Republik Indonesia, Navy of the Indonesian Republic
AMACAB	Allied Military Administration, Civil Affairs Branch
API	Angkatan Pemuda Indonesia, Youth Generation of Indonesia
APWI	Allied Prisoners of War and Internees
ARA	Algemeen Rijksarchief, General State Archives, The Hague
badan ekonomi	Economic organization; trading company attached to an armed unit
badan perjuangan	Struggle organization; armed irregular group
Bambu Runcing	Bamboo Spears
Benteng Republik	Republican Fortress
BERI	Badan Ekonomi Rakyat Indonesia, Economic Organization of the Indonesian People
Beruang Merah	Red Bears
Betawi	Batavian Malays, the oldest ethnic group in Jakarta
BKR	Badan Keamanan Rakyat, People's Security Organization

bupati	'regent', regional administrative rank, below resident, above wedana
camat	sub-district head, beneath wedana
CMI	Centrale Militaire Inlichtingendienst, Central Military Intelligence Service
CORO	Corps Reserve Officieren, Reserve Officers Corps
dalang	puppeteer for the wayang puppet play
DOBIN	Dagelijks Overzicht Belangrijkste Inlichtingen, Daily survey of most important intelligence information
DST	Depot Speciale Troepen, Special Troops Depot
DPJB	Dewan Perjuangan Jawa Barat, West Java Struggle Council
FO	Foreign Office
FP	Field Preparation
HAMOT	Hare Majesteits Ongeregelde Troepen, Her Majesty's Irregular Troops
Hizbullah	Army of God
HKGS-NOI	Hoofd Kwartier van de Generale Staf, Nederlands Oost-Indië, Headquarters of the General Staff, Netherlands East Indies
jimat	charm, amulet
kabupaten	'regency', administrative division ruled by a bupati
KL	Koninklijke Landmacht, Royal [Netherlands] Army
KNI	Komite Nasional Indonesia, Indonesian National Committee
KNIL	Koninklijk Nederlands-Indisch Leger, Royal Netherlands Indies Army
KRIS	Kebaktian Rakyat Indonesia Sulawesi, Indonesian People's Loyalty Organization of Sulawesi
lasykar	militia, armed irregular band
LRJB	Lasykar Rakyat Jawa Barat, People's Militia of West Java
LRJR	Lasykar Rakyat Jakarta Raya, People's Militia of Greater Jakarta
Minog	Ministerie van Overzeese Gebiedsdelen, Ministry of Overseas Territories
MvD/CAD	Minister van Defensie, Centraal Archievendepot, Ministry of Defence, Central Archival Depot

NEFIS	Netherlands Forces Intelligence Service
negara	state, here commonly a constituent state of the proposed Indonesian federation
NICA	Netherlands Indies Civil Administration
OBB	Officiële Bescheiden betreffende de Nederlands-Indonesische Betrekkingen, 1945–1949, Official Documents on Dutch-Indonesian Relations, 1945–1949
ommelanden	'lands around', the countryside around Jakarta
particuliere landerijen	private estates
Pepolit	Pendidikan Politik, Political Education [Staff]
PETA	Pembela Tanah Air, [Volunteer Army] of Defenders of the Homeland
PID	Politieke Inlichtingendienst, Political Intelligence Service
PKI	Partai Komunis Indonesia, Indonesian Communist Party
PP	Persatuan Perjuangan, Struggle Union
PRJB	Pemerintah Republik Jawa Barat, Republican Government of West Java
Proc.Gen.	Procureur-Generaal bij het Hooggerechtshof van Nederlands-Indië, Attorney-General of the Netherlands Indies
resident	regional administrative rank, below provincial governor, above bupati
RVD	Regerings Voorlichtingsdienst, Government Information Office
SP88	Satuan Pemberontakan 88, Rebellion Unit 88
SPKI	Sekitar Perang Kemerdekaan Indonesia, On the Indonesian War of Independence
TKR	Tentara Keamanan Rakyat, People's Security Army
TNI	Tentara Nasional Indonesia, Indonesian National Army
TRI	Tentara Republik Indonesia, Army of the Republic of Indonesia
VPSONI	Verkort Politiek Situatie-Overzicht van Nederlandsch-Indië, Brief survey of the political situation in the Netherlands Indies
wedana	district head
Wehrkreise	military regions
WO	War Office

Introduction

Gangsters are an ancient feature of the social landscape on Java. Three hundred years ago, the island was still sparsely populated and the forests which enclosed the settled regions of the river valleys offered, as in other parts of the world, a safe refuge for men beyond the laws of settled society. The early chronicles speak thus of brigands who preyed upon travellers as they passed by forests and mountains, and early states measured their power in part by their success in suppressing them. It was typically in time of war, rebellion or economic crisis, when the state was under threat, that brigands conducted their activities with the greatest boldness, plundering not just individual travellers but whole villages.

Brigandry in old Java, however, was also a matter of perspective. The depredations of the brigands were sometimes not so very different from those of rulers. In the Hinduistic philosophy which governed traditional Javanese society, the crime of the brigand was perhaps less against the victim than against the cosmologically-sanctioned social order. The brigand (always male, to my knowledge) was guilty of hubris, of stepping outside his appointed place in society. The dividing line between brigandry and rebellion, therefore, was often a fine one, particularly since, as far as we can tell, brigands tended to be drawn from those who were fleeing life under one or other ruler. Brigands frequently took part in, and even led, rebellions. Ken Angrok, founder of the kingdom of Singosari, began his career as a bandit, as did numerous powerful regional chiefs.

Many successful rulers, moreover, overcame the problem of gangsterism not by suppression but by incorporation. In exchange for acknowledging the ruler's broad authority and promising to regularise his depredations, a brigand leader often received official recognition as local headman or governor.[1] Rarely, however, was such an arrangement stable and, with the ebb and flow of state authority, the status, power and independence of such figures rose and fell. To this day, relations between gangsters and the state have oscillated between these poles of recruitment and suppression. Gangsters, for instance, were employed to considerable effect in the 1982 general election campaign in Indonesia as participants in rallies, as bully boys and as occasional *agents provocateurs*. Yet in 1983–84 the government waged a sustained campaign of extermination against them, several thousand being murdered in what were known somewhat ingenuously as the 'mysterious killings'.[2]

The ambiguity of the relationship between state and criminality has always been most pronounced in times of political struggle, for then not only are the stakes high and the involvement of the gangsters may elevate them to the role of almost-respectable power-brokers, perhaps crucial to the outcome, but the identity of the state also becomes blurred, so that ruler, challenger and ally are no longer clear categories. This was particularly the case during the Indonesian national revolution (1945–49), when the fate of Indonesia appeared to lie in the balance. At issue was not only the question of whether Indonesia should obtain independence from the Dutch but what political form that independence should take. In this struggle, a coalition of Jakarta gangsters with young left-wing nationalists played a significant role. This coalition, which reached the height of its power as the People's Militia of Greater Jakarta, was for a time one of the most powerful irregular armed forces involved in the struggle. Despite partially successful efforts by both the Republic and the Dutch to suppress and to incorporate it, the coalition survived not only to the end of the revolution but beyond it.

Aside from telling the turbulent history of that coalition, this study has two aims. The first—and this is the principal topic of the opening chapters—is to shed light on the social basis of revolution in Indonesia. There is a broad scholarly consensus today that the Indonesian revolution was essentially an artefact of Dutch colonial rule, that it was the product of social, economic and intellectual changes wrought by colonialism in the Indonesian archipelago. This transformation gave society and politics a new form and new problems to which people sought new solutions, one of the more important of which was independence, in the form of the Indonesian Republic. Many have suggested that independence as it was ultimately obtained may not have been as much of a solution as was originally expected, but the assumption remains that the revolution was, or at least could have been, a new phenomenon in Indonesian history. This study suggests, however, that we should bear in mind ways in which the

revolution drew upon older styles of rebellion. The revolution which
the Jakarta underworld joined in 1945 was a different kind of affair
from the small-scale local revolts which had been common in the
colonial era, but the national struggle in the Jakarta countryside drew
on very much the same kinds of social organisation which underlay
these earlier risings.

Second, this study examines the evolving relationship between the
People's Militia of Jakarta and the new Republican state during the
revolution. In part this is a story of growing Republican competence.
In the early stages of the revolution, the Jakarta underworld formed
an important element in the defence of the Republic and in the
picture of a nation united against the return of colonialism. As state
institutions grew stronger, the need for the Jakarta underworld
diminished and it was discarded. In part, however, it is also a story of
growing Republican self-confidence. The Republic came into existence wanting both to inherit the status and prerogatives of the
colonial state and to draw a sharp line between colonial domination
and independence. One of the more difficult problems it faced was in
the area of law. At independence it adopted a formula under which
all colonial law was preserved insofar as it was consistent with the
constitution, a formula which seems increasingly imprecise the more
one considers it. Legal means—trials, regulations and the like—had
been a central element in the colonial repressive apparatus and
nationalist leaders had been strongly aware in'turn of the tactical
importance of choosing between legality and illegality. Despite the
formal difference in status which the declaration of independence
gave them—all acts and regulations of the post-war Netherlands
Indies government became illegal as far as the Republic was
concerned—the nationalist leaders did not shed their respect for
Dutch law, and they commonly described, for instance, underground
work in Dutch occupied regions as 'illegal activities'. Not quite
certain of the Republic's future for most of the revolution, some of
them at least, therefore, remained respectful of the naive and vigorous nationalism of the Jakarta Militia. The need both to release and
to control the energies of the Jakarta underworld bedevilled Republican decision-making throughout the revolution, and the story of
changing Republican attitudes to these 'irregular' forces is a major
theme in this study.

This work is based on research which I conducted at the School of
Oriental and African Studies in London for a doctoral dissertation on
the history of Jakarta during the Indonesian revolution. That study
commenced as an examination of nationalists in occupied Jakarta and
their attempts to contribute effectively to the national struggle under
the restricted conditions of Dutch occupation. I first met the gang-

sters, figuratively speaking, in Mochtar Lubis' *Road with No End*. He describes a visit by a young Jakarta nationalist, Isa, to Bekasi, a town east of Jakarta and one of the headquarters of the gangsters in the early revolution. There he met Ontong, a tough from the market area of Senen in Jakarta.

> His face was coarse and almost square, his eyebrows narrow and his hair straight and coarse as root fibre. His lips were thick and protruding, his eyes fiery and bloodshot. He was wearing only coarse black cotton shorts and an old striped sailor shirt. The flesh of his huge flat thighs was thick with grime and filth. A red kerchief was bound around his head, and at his waist was a machete.[3]

It was not a particularly felicitous meeting, neither for Isa nor for me, and I viewed Ontong and his like primarily as opportunists who used the chaos of the revolution for their own personal profit. It was only after visiting Indonesia and having the opportunity to talk to surviving members of the Jakarta revolutionary underworld (none of whom, incidentally, resembled Ontong), and to some who had been closely associated with them during the revolution, that I realised that another interpretation of their role might be possible.

My hope that this reinterpretation might be worth making has been reinforced by recent research challenging the standard received view of traditional Javanese rural society. In that view the village is a self-possessed, self-enclosed community dealing with the outside world suspiciously, unwillingly and as a unit. Within this established view, gangsters are peripheral figures, inconvenient and disruptive but not a structural feature of rural life. Jan Breman has argued, however, that this view of the village may itself be a colonial artefact, created in order to enable the tighter control of labour by colonial authorities.[4] Onghokham has described the importance of patron-client relations extending down as far as the individual household in pre-colonial and early colonial Java, an arrangement inconsistent with the true village republics of the established view. He has also pointed out the importance of a wide variety of spies and hit-men in sustaining local power structures, conclusions echoed in the writings of Bill O'Malley and Henk Schulte Nordholt.[5] The work of James Rush on the techniques of social control used by the holders of opium monopolies in nineteenth century Java has reinforced this point.[6] In this revised interpretation, gangsters appear as a significant element in the structure of rural society and one worthy of closer study. At the same time, the work of Sartono Kartodirdjo and Michael Williams has indicated the role which gangsters may play not in sustaining but in challenging the social order.[7] Anton Lucas, too, has studied the role of an individual gangster, the lenggaong Kutil of Tegal, in the revolution itself.[8]

The Jakarta region is not Java. As explained in Chapter 1, Jakarta has its own history and its own distinctive ethnic, social and economic character. One should be as wary of extrapolating from the whole to the part as from the part to the whole. Nonetheless, as part of a revolution which swept Java and Sumatra in the mid-1940s, the revolution in Jakarta was not just a local phenomenon. By studying the region and its gangsters, one may hope to learn a little more about the revolution as a whole.[9]

1. Soemarsaid Moertono, *State and Statecraft in Old Java: a Study of the Later Mataram Period, 16th to 19th Century* (Ithaca, N.Y., 1968), 85–6. Sartono Kartodirdjo and Anton Lucas, 'Banditry and political change in Java', in Sartono Kartodirdjo, *Modern Indonesia: Tradition and Transformation* (Yogyakarta, 1984), 3–4.
2. J. M. van der Kroef, '"Petrus": Patterns of Prophylactic Murder in Indonesia', *Asian Survey* 25, 7 (1985), 745–59.
3. M. Lubis, *A Road with No End* (Singapore, 1982), 82. Lubis has since treated gangsters more sympathetically in his short story, 'Bromo-corah' published in M. Lubis, *Bromocorah: Dua Belas Cerita Pendek* (Jakarta, 1983).
4. J. Breman, *The Village on Java and the Early Colonial State* (Rotterdam, 1980).
5. Onghokham, 'The Inscrutable and the Paranoid: an Investigation into the Sources of the Brotodiningrat Affair', in R. T. McVey, ed., *Southeast Asian Transitions: Approaches through Social History* (New Haven and London, 1978), 112–57; and Onghokham, 'The *Jago* in Colonial Java, Ambivalent Champion of the People', in A. Turton and S. Tanabe, eds, *History and Peasant Consciousness in South East Asia* (Osaka, 1984), 327–43.
6. J. R. Rush, 'Social Control and Influence in Nineteenth Century Indonesia: Opium Farms and the Chinese of Java', *Indonesia* 35 (1983), 53–64. W. J. O'Malley, 'Criminals, Society, and Politics in Java', in Ron May, ed., *Goons, Raskols and Rebels* (Bathurst, forthcoming). H. Schulte Nordholt, 'De Jago in de Schaduw: Misdaad en "Orde" in de Koloniale Staat op Java', *De Gids* 146, 8/9 (1983), 664–75.
7. Sartono Kartodirdjo, *The Peasants' Revolt of Banten in 1888* (The Hague, 1966); M. C. Williams, *Sickle and Crescent: the Communist Revolt of 1926 in Banten* (Ithaca, N.Y., 1982).
8. A. Lucas, 'Lenggaong, Kyai, Guru: Three Revolutionary Biographies from North Central Java', in R. Hatley *et al.*, *Other Javas: Away from the Kraton* (Clayton, Vic., 1984), 43–4.

9. Note on Spelling: In accordance with contemporary custom, all terms and proper names in the Indonesian language have been spelt according to modern conventions (e.y.d.).

I
THE MAKING OF A REVOLUTIONARY ALLIANCE

1

The Jakarta
Underworld

Tropical rains erode twenty centimetres' depth of soil and rock every century from the string of volcanic mountains which form the spine of the island of Java. Rock and soil washes down on one side into the currents and depths of the Indian Ocean and on the other into the shallow and more placid waters of the Java Sea.[1] At the start of the Quaternary era, after the end of the last ice age, the low waves of the Java Sea lapped close to the foothills of these peaks and the island did not take its present shape until sedimentation over many centuries had pushed the coastline away to the north, especially towards the western end of the island's coast, forming an alluvial coastal plain. Dissected by meandering rivers and dotted with shallow lakes and swamps, this plain grew to average fifty kilometres in breadth from the coast to the mountains and stretched 250 kilometres from what is now Banten to Cirebon. In prehistoric times, the plain was thickly forested with tropical jungle and was the habitat of rhinoceros and tigers. The mangrove swamps which fringed the coast were home to saltwater crocodiles, while the somewhat less savage freshwater variety inhabited the lakes and inland swamps. Despite the fertility of the soil, therefore, the plain offered a hostile environment for the human inhabitants of the region, and they found it easier to settle on the better drained volcanic slopes to the south.

The shadowy sixth century kingdom of Taruma was centred on these foothills, perhaps near the modern town of Bogor.[2] We know little about it, except that its ruler employed Hindu cosmology to reinforce the majesty of his rule and that he presided over irrigation works, presumably implying a hydraulic society of the kind found elsewhere in Java.[3] Perhaps fugitives from Taruma sporadically sought shelter in the lowland jungles, creating small communities of

9

outlaws, but we are unlikely ever to find a trace of them. We know virtually nothing about Taruma's society below elite level, though one would assume that it had its poor and its criminals like everywhere else. Trade routes from Taruma, however, and from its successor state Pajajaran, followed the rivers to the coast and small settlements gradually appeared on the plain. These communities of fishermen and forest product collectors, predominantly Sundanese from the West Java uplands, were joined later by agricultural and trading communities, but the plain remained a wild area, where tigers continued to be a major hazard and travellers found rivers and the well-beaten tracks of rhinoceros offered the easiest paths through the jungle.

In the fifteenth and sixteenth centuries, the political geography of this part of Java was transformed by the rise of trading states along the north coast. New states, both Islamic sultanates, arose around the ports of Banten and Cirebon, situated at opposite ends of the plain. The countryside around both kingdoms was extensively colonised by ethnic Javanese in this period. By seizing control of the river mouths which were Pajajaran's link with the outside world, Banten supplanted it as the major power in the region and it was to Banten that the first major European trading expeditions came when they arrived at the start of the seventeenth century.[4]

The Dutch East India Company (VOC) established its first permanent foothold on the coast in 1610, when it purchased a small area of land on the east bank of the river Ciliwung, close to the mouth and opposite an existing local settlement called Sunda Kalapa or Jakatra, whose ruler was a vassal of the Sultan of Banten. In 1618, the redoubtable fourth Governor-General of the Netherlands Indies, Jan Pieterszoon Coen, built a fort there which successfully resisted an attack from Banten in the following year and which was given the name Batavia, after the prehistoric inhabitants of the Netherlands.[5] Although at first largely a coastal entrepot, it soon became the administrative centre of the growing Dutch trading empire in the east. During the eighteenth century, Batavia moved a few kilometres inland and a few metres uphill. The swampy coastal strip where the city lay was notoriously unhealthy, its inhabitants plagued by malaria and dysentery, and the uphill retreat was largely governed by the need for a healthier environment. Dutch economic interests, too, focussed increasingly on the control of agriculture in the interior, and less on the management of coastal ports, and the move inland reflected this change in mood and purpose. At the beginning of the nineteenth century, the governor-general Marshal Daendels constructed a postal road along the north coast of Java, giving Batavia its first reliable overland link with the rest of the island. He also sponsored the construction of a new European town, Weltevreden ('Well content'), at the heart of which were two extensive open areas, which after the defeat of Napoleon were to become Koningsplein ('King's Square') and Waterlooplein ('Waterloo Square'). Government offices, churches, company headquarters, the museum, educational institutions and the like faced for the most part onto one or other of these squares, while Europeans lived a little behind them in the leafy districts of Menteng and Tanah Abang with their wide shady streets and large houses with broad verandas.[6]

As the city flourished, the market gardens along the canal and main road linking Batavia and Weltevreden gave way to suburbs and then to commercial buildings, creating a single metropolis. The city later lost some of its importance in the flight of government offices still further inland and uphill. Increasing congestion in Batavia and the improved road system encouraged the Governors-General to shift their residence to Buitenzorg ('Free from care'), now Bogor, on the cooler foothills beneath Mt Salak, and by the 1920s the Dutch colonial army and some government offices had made the move even further uphill to Bandung. In the early twentieth century, however, Batavia was booming again and travel writers enthused about its charms. In 1930, on the eve of the Depression, the combined populations of Batavia and the former up-river settlement of Meester Cornelis (now Jatinegara) exceeded half a million and the city was a major administrative, cultural and economic centre of Dutch life in the archipelago.[7] 'It is the home of the Dutch residents', wrote a British commentator early this century,

> in a far more real sense than any town east of Suez can be said to be the home of the Englishman, and very naturally they have endeavoured to make it as attractive and cheerful a home as possible. . . . Weltevreden is indeed in many respects the 'Queen of the East'.[8]

Batavia, of course, was home to far more than its Dutch inhabitants. No trace, it is true, remained of old Jakatra: not a single pre-colonial building had been left standing and the physical structure of the city was that created by the Europeans. Parts at least of the colonial capital, however, were the acknowledged home of non-European minorities. The *oude stad* or old city, for instance, which had been the original hub of the colonial administration, came to be dominated by those whom the Dutch called 'foreign orientals' (*vreemde oosterlingen*). These were predominantly Chinese with a sprinkling of Arabs and Indians, and they were classified, in a rudimentary form of apartheid, as legally distinct from both the 'natives' (*inlanders*) and the Europeans. The Chinese of Batavia formed the largest Chinese community on Java, and were concentrated especially in the Glodok area, from which they dominated medium-scale trade in the city.[9] At the southern end of the city, in Meester Cornelis, were the military barracks with their garrison communities of Ambonese, Menadonese and a small number of Timorese; these were outer islanders, predominantly Christian, who formed the mainstay of the Dutch military presence in the city. Ethnically, culturally and religiously different from the majority of Indonesians in Batavia, socially isolated by their military existence, and representing the coercive power of the colonial regime, these soldiers formed a distinct military caste within the city and had little to do with the other Indonesians who comprised the vast majority of the inhabitants of Batavia.

The vast majority of Indonesians lived in the *kampungs*, cluttered areas of less permanent housing away from the main streets, tucked behind the solid commercial and residential buildings of Batavia and Weltevreden. The British observer cited earlier noted of Weltevreden:

> The suburb has been well-planned, it is kept scrupulously clean, and while the natives in their bright coloured clothes, quietly making their way hither and thither, give the required picturesque touch to the life in the streets, the absence of the crowded native dwelling houses prevents the occurrence of those objectionable features which so often destroy the charm of the towns in the Orient.[10]

Like the city itself, these inhabitants had little connection with old Jakarta. From its first days as an armed trading post, Batavia had drawn its Asian population from all over the Indonesian archipelago and beyond and its inhabitants consisted largely of outsiders: Japanese, Chinese, Pampangans (from Luzon), Ambonese, Bandanese, Buginese, Timorese, Balinese, Malays, Indians and others. The proportion of the different ethnic groups varied dramatically over the centuries, partly in response to the changing economic circumstances of the city and changing conditions elsewhere in the archipelago, partly because the chronic unhealthiness of urban life and the perennially high mortality rate necessitated repeated replenishment of the population from outside. It can be argued, for instance, that for much of the seventeenth century and for the first half of the eighteenth Batavia was 'basically a Chinese colonial town under Dutch protection'.[11] In the seventeenth and eighteenth centuries, somewhere between an eighth and a quarter of the population consisted of the so-called Mardijkers, the descendants of freed slaves whose ancestors were predominantly Indian and whose culture was a mestizo blend of Portuguese and Asian customs.[12] The city's racial diversity quickly gave it a colourful history of ethnic mixing and cultural hybridisation. *Kroncong* music, for instance, a blend of Malay melodies and Western instrumentation, developed in the city. By early in the nineteenth century, moreover, when the population of Batavia was perhaps 50,000, it was possible to recognise a distinct Batavian ethnic group, the *orang Betawi* (people of Batavia), largely eastern Indonesian in ethnic origin, Muslim in their religious affiliation though not renowned for their piety, and speaking a dialect of Malay heavily influenced by Balinese, Hokkien and other languages. The Betawi presence in the city was, however, diluted from the beginning of the twentieth century by major immigration from Java itself, which brought the population to the half million mark by 1930.[13]

The physical segregation of Batavia's ethnic groups reflected a social segregation. Batavian society was plural, a society, in Furnivall's words, 'comprising two or more elements or social orders which live side by side, yet without mingling, in one political unit'.[14] Each ethnic group tended to occupy, or at least to dominate, particular economic niches, and the economic bases of each group in turn moulded its internal political characteristics. Politics in European colonial society, thus, was dominated by the so-called colonial troika of bureaucracy, army and big business,[15] while it was businessmen who ruled Chinese politics. Much has been written, too, about the development of politics in indigenous Indonesian societies, in particular the preservation and then transformation of traditional elites co-opted into the colonial order,[16] and the rise of a modern, professionally and technologically oriented elite in the twentieth century in response to the demands of the evolving colonial system,[17] but both these phenomena left the Indonesian population of Batavia largely untouched. Betawi society had no traditional aristocratic elite. Most immigrants came to Batavia to occupy fairly humble service positions in the European city and their own traditional elites had no role there. Batavia itself offered little opportunity for the development of an elite. Education, government office and military command were the prerogatives of Europeans until the beginning of the twentieth century, while economic power was shared between Europeans and Chinese. Even when the colonial system began to open to Indonesians in the early twentieth century, the positions available in Batavia went largely to members of extra-regional elites, not to Batavians. Thus the first *bupati* (regent) of Batavia, appointed in 1924 to bring the region administratively into line with the rest of Java, was a Bantenese, Ahmad Jayadiningrat.

In 1905, the Dutch established the municipality (*gemeente*, later

stadsgemeente) of Batavia as part of their programme of administrative decentralisation. In time the municipality received not only a
mayor and an executive council (*college van burgemeester en
wethouders*), but also a municipal council (*gemeenteraad*), elected on
a limited franchise, with separate electorates for the different races.
Dutch representatives outnumbered those from the Indonesian,
Chinese and Arab communities, however, and the council acted, as it
was intended to act, as a municipal council for European Batavia,
giving little attention to the kampungs. The municipality offered a
political and administrative training ground for some of the Indonesians who were to run the Republican municipal administration after
the declaration of independence in 1945, but these were members of
the broader modern Indonesian elite whose involvement in administration, politics or the professions had brought them to Batavia, and
few had any direct links with the people of the city.[18]

Politics in Indonesian society in Batavia was shaped therefore by
the fact that most Indonesians worked in some sense or other as
labourers for the colonial establishment. The key figures in local
Batavian politics thus were the labour bosses, who coordinated the
otherwise structureless Indonesian society of the city with the fluc-
tuating demands of its service industry. In exchange for a hefty slice
of their clients' incomes, the bosses found work for them, ensured
that they were paid enough to survive, provided accommodation in
dormitories and hostels, and sometimes even organised for them to
return home for important family occasions or if there were no work
in the city. The mobile population and constantly changing economic
profile of Batavia demanded middlemen of this kind. New migrants
to Batavia found it easier to make their way in their new surround-
ings with the assistance of others from their own ethnic group and
district and were thus natural recruits to the broad entourage of the
labour bosses. Employers for their part found it easier to deal with
established suppliers of labour than with individuals who might never
arrive for work or who might, for their own reasons, return to their
villages or move to another part of the city. The labour bosses
frequently had ties with home regions and could organise circular
migration of workers as demand fluctuated.[19] Particular areas of the
city and particular occupations, therefore, became dominated by
migrants from different regions. In the 1930s the port area of Tanjung
Priok was dominated by migrants from Banten and Tanggerang.
Bogor and the Priangan were most strongly represented in Weltevreden, while the central Javanese were most concentrated in Weltevreden and Meester Cornelis, especially around the Manggarai workshops. Laundrymen came from Bogor, bread-sellers from nearby
Peuteuy, female servants from Tanggerang or Tasikmalaya.[20]

The operations of these labour bosses required organisation, and thus each boss was typically not just the coordinator of a clientele of workers but also leader of a more narrowly defined gang of lieutenants, helpers, advisers and enforcers. The exact composition and character of these gangs varied according to the style of operations of the individual bosses, but for most of them the enforcers were a particularly prominent element, necessary to discipline the workers themselves, to keep employers tractable and to preserve the boss's fief from encroachment by rivals. Although the control of labour itself was not formally criminal, this need for coercive power equipped the local bosses effectively for participation in a range of shady service industries such as prostitution and hired thuggery as well as directly criminal activities like armed robbery, extortion and pickpocketing.

The world of labour control in Batavia, therefore, shaded into a criminal and semi-criminal underworld such as one finds in most large cities. Labour bosses might, for instance, become involved in the sale or transport of stolen goods, perhaps through the mediation of itinerant puppeteers in the *wayang* puppet play. They might operate with Muslim religious leaders in arranging pilgrimages to Mecca in exchange for guarantees of labour from the pilgrims after they returned. They might be employed by a Chinese or Arab trader to smash the property of a competitor or to intimidate his customers. They might run their own protection rackets. Many of these enterprises drew the bosses into shorter or longer term cooperative arrangements with other bosses, thus modifying the antagonism and suspicion which existed between them and creating an invisible network of power and authority, cooperation and alliance, antagonism and competition between the groups, always in flux and having no formal public or institutional manifestation of its presence. This network seldom extended above the lower levels of society, but it ensured that what was done by one group did not happen in isolation. It was a network standing outside the hierarchy of government authority, antagonistic to it yet not overtly hostile. Except to the extent that lower officials were under the control of the bosses or, more rarely, were local bosses in their own right, the network sought not so much to rival the official hierarchy as to circumvent or at least ignore it. In some respects at least, the criminal underworld even enjoyed an almost symbiotic relationship with the forces of law and order. To the authorities it provided, of course, a multitude of bribes, kickbacks and other benefits in exchange for overlooking a wide variety of misdemeanours. It was also a source of information and intelligence which enabled the authorities to keep tabs on the level of crime in order to maintain it at an acceptable level. And from Batavia the network stretched on via trading ships to Singapore and, by a multitude of connections, to the other cities of Java and into the countryside around the capital.

The world of the Betawi did not end at the boundaries of the city but spread out into the surrounding countryside, known since early in the Dutch occupation as the *ommelanden* ('lands around'). When the Dutch first occupied Batavia they forced people to leave the surrounding countryside in order to create an empty buffer zone. The Company was still more or less at war with Banten and with the central Javanese state of Mataram, and it preferred to create a *cordon sanitaire* around its fort. In succeeding, more peaceful times, this area was settled by immigrants who had passed through the city. Much of the original work of clearing the jungle seems to have been conducted or at least organised by Chinese,[21] and well into the twentieth century the region was dotted with settlements of so-called *peranakan* ('native') Chinese engaged in agriculture and fishing. Though they retained their Chinese names and religion, these Chinese spoke Malay and were often virtually indistinguishable from the ethnic Indonesians of the region.[22] Aside from these Chinese, the rural population within a thirty to fifty kilometre radius of Batavia consisted of Betawi. Beyond this area were Sundanese and Javanese, the Sundanese predominating towards the hills of the Priangan, the Javanese along the coast in both directions, towards Banten and Cirebon.

Settlement gradually transformed the land. The jungles were thinned for firewood and building materials and cleared for agriculture. The lakes and swamps were drained and rudimentary irrigation works were put in place. At the beginning of the nineteenth century, Daendels' postal road between Batavia and the eastern end of Java cut through the region, abruptly broadening its horizons. A railway line appeared later in the nineteenth century. The social transformation of the ommelanden under colonialism was even more dramatic. The Betawi settlers of the region were not permitted to become freehold farmers or to form collective village communities but rather were placed under the control of the notorious private estates (*particuliere landerijen*). These estates dated from as early as 1620, when the VOC had begun to grant parcels of land in the ommelanden to its servants, friends and supporters. Initially these lands were granted only within the protected vicinity of the city, but as Dutch rule became secure the system was extended to cover much of the coastal plain of West Java. In the flat country around Karawang the estates produced mainly rice, with some fruit and vegetables. Further south, in the foothills which stretched from Cibarusa to Purwakarta and Subang, the landscape was dominated by rubber plantations interspersed with a few teak forests.

The scope of the business operations of these estates varied widely. Those within the expanding fringes of Batavia became the gardens of urban dwellings. A few of the largest estates came into the hands of Western companies and were turned into major agricultural enterprises. The English-owned Pamanoekan-en-Tjiasem-Landen, or P. & T. Lands, around Subang were a massive operation, running from the hills down to the coast and growing rice, rubber, tea, sisal, cinchona and tapioca as well as maintaining experimental gardens, three hydro-electric stations, a network of narrow-gauge railways, a large staff and achieving an impressive annual turnover.[23] The Dutch-owned Michiels-Arnold-Landen in Cibarusa operated on a similar scale. The majority of the lands, however, were much smaller affairs, frequently owned by Chinese landlords and concentrating on a smaller range of crops.

With the possession of this land came various taxation and corvee rights over the peasants who tilled it, so that in fact a kind of feudalism existed. Peasants were obliged, for instance, to provide *kompenian* ('company service') to their landlords amounting to sixty days unpaid labour a year, to be served at a time convenient to the landlord. Peasants delivered a fifth or more of their rice harvest to the landlords and paid further tax on household crops, trees and buildings. By ommelanden custom, moreover, they were obliged to obtain the permission of the landlord to harvest their own crops, and this was given only when they had paid all taxes due to him. Before the harvest, of course, the peasants had no money or goods to pay, and so they were driven into the hands of extortive money-lenders, often working in collusion with the landlords.[24]

The estates were almost mini-states—Dutch legal specialists in the early twentieth century described them as 'sovereign'—comparable to the plethora of indirectly ruled states and principalities in the rest of the archipelago, and the landlords, although having no diplomatic pretensions, were responsible for education, health and other social services within their domains. Since most estates, however, were small, badly undercapitalised affairs, the landlords were generally in no position to provide any of these services effectively. The landlords had little to gain from educating their subjects, and the simple agricultural work demanded on the estates could survive relatively high levels of illness. In consequence, the vast majority of the inhabitants of the region were illiterate, while standards of health and hygiene appalled those who penetrated beyond the main lines of communication. Enough investigators did in fact penetrate the region to draw the attention of the colonial government to the conditions there. The creation of new private estates ceased in 1855, and in the early twentieth century the dominant 'Ethical' policy line of the

Indies government included an ambitious plan to buy back the estates
from the landlords and to put their inhabitants on the same legal
footing as the remaining population of West Java. The repurchase
programme began in 1912 and important repurchases took place,
particularly in the prosperous 1920s. With the onset of the Depression, however, repurchases came to an abrupt halt. In 1935, the
government established a semi-official company, the NV Javasche
Particuliere Landerijen Maatschappij, or Java Private Estates Co,
which purchased estates on the open market and managed them with
itself as landlord. The charter of the company obliged it to reduce the
burden on the local people and to use the profits from the estates to
improve local infrastructure so that the estates could eventually be
handed over to the government without placing an immediate drain
on the treasury. Progress with repurchase therefore was slow and
large tracts of land remained in private hands when the Japanese
arrived in 1942.[25]

Lying on the fringes of both Sundanese and Javanese cultural
regions, and with its substantial immigrant groups from elsewhere,
Indonesian rural society in the ommelanden had the rough and
chaotic character of a frontier society rather than the order and
hierarchy commonly attributed to rural Java. In many parts of the
region, there was no formal structure of village government, and
even where lurah (village chiefs) could be found, they were often a
recent innovation with no deep roots in their villages. In general,
rather, the landlords and their henchmen held sway with a mixture of
coercion and intimidation. The estates, however, tended to be as
weak in the control of their subjects as they were in providing more
benevolent social services. The colonial authorities did not leave law
and order entirely in the hands of the landlord, but the sheriffs
stationed at Karawang were wholly inadequate for the job. Forbidding though the landlord's henchmen might be to peaceable peasants,
they were unable to prevent the emergence of other men of violence
in the form of powerful gangs of brigands who operated throughout
the region.

Brigandage in the ommelanden went by the name rampok, a term
which originally meant tiger-baiting, which had been, to modern
minds at least, one of the less attractive spectator sports of old Java.
The brigands themselves went by many names, but perampok (or the
Dutch rampokker) and garong were common. As in the labour
control networks of urban Batavia, the central feature of the rampok
gang was its boss, or jago (literally 'fighting cock').[26] These bosses
were at the same time part of that underworld network in Batavia,
coordinating with bosses there the supply of labour and produce to
the city, and having their own connections with a similar local

network of Arab traders, itinerant dalang, bush lawyers (*pokrol bambu*), Muslim teachers and leaders of other rampok gangs based in kampungs in the swamps of the marshy coastline north of Karawang and in the forests of the southern foothills.[27] In 1919 and 1920 a total of 170 'rampokpartijen' (incidents involving rampok gangs) were reported from the district of Meester Cornelis alone.

Like the rest of Indonesian society in the ommelanden, this criminal world was rather loosely structured, with a large number of individual criminals and semi-criminals grouped around locally pre-eminent *jago*. The followers of a jago formed a cluster around him, a few loyal followers having the status of *anak buah*, literally 'fruit children', the rest following at a greater distance from the jago, sharing his protection and patronage, learning some of his skills, and then perhaps moving on to other patrons. Thus, although they often formed definable gangs, choosing romantic or bloodcurdling names, the followers of the jago were essentially ephemeral groupings, changing with the ebb and flow of life in Batavia and never forming the institutionalised criminal structures of the secret societies of China.[28]

Chinese gangs apparently existed in the regions where peranakan Chinese were permanently settled. Van Hogendorp's short story, 'Korporaal Rampok', contains a brief but intriguing description of a well-armed Chinese gang in the Tanggerang region, the principal activity of which seems to have been the large-scale forging of copper coinage.[29] It is not possible to know how much this literary reference reflects reality, though it could be expected that secret societies existed as an element in local Chinese communities. Both Chinese and Arab gangs remained part of the criminal geography of the region until 1945, and the Karawang area was terrorised in 1942 by two clearly Chinese gangsters, Oey Soe Peng and Tan Goan Kiat. It is striking, however, that no evidence appears to exist of mixed indigenous and Chinese gangs. This contrasts with conditions in the Netherlands, where powerful gangs plundering wide areas of the countryside in the late eighteenth century were composed of similar numbers of Jews and Christians.[30]

The ommelanden jago was typically an individual who had mastered some skill which enabled him to survive on the fringes of society. Most commonly this skill involved one of the martial arts (*silat*), which might be as complex as judo or as simple as hitting people over the head. Their repertoire often also included more magical skills. Many jago were magicians (*dukun*), who could produce charms (*jimat*) which would bring the bearer strength, safety or success. There were also charms and rituals to increase sexual power and attractiveness, and a dukun whose charms had a reputation for success could live comfortably on the contributions he received from his clients. Other dukun and jago employed magic to destroy their enemies or those of their clients. Particularly common, however, were charms and rituals designed to reinforce skill in the martial arts, and it was these especially which enabled the jago to maintain the loyalty of his followers.

It was not uncommon, for instance, for jago and their followers to visit Mount Jatibening in Banten, where they would undergo a ritual to confer invulnerability. The suppliant would be drenched in holy water while incense was burnt and passages from the Qur'an were recited. The ritual would conclude with an unsuccessful attempt by the officiating dukun to hack the suppliant into little pieces with a razor-sharp sword, thereby demonstrating that the charm had worked. Other rituals were available to confer invisibility and inaudibility. In a similar way divination, or the discovery of auspicious times and places, for criminal acts played a major role in the activities of gangsters. Using complex numerological formulae, a gangster could calculate not only whether an operation was likely to be successful but what time he should depart and from which direction he should approach his target.[31] These skills might enable the jago to hire out his services, or they might simply enable him to pursue his criminal activities relatively undisturbed.

The principal criminal activity of the rampok gangs was robbery. The railway line and main road passing through the region offered many opportunities for plunder. Some gangs operated as pickpockets on trains, others staged hold-ups on the roads. The substantial residences of landlords and of traders in the towns were always tempting targets if they were not heavily enough guarded. The serfs of the estates probably suffered relatively little from the gangs because they possessed little that could be stolen. Indeed, for the immediate community in which a gang dwelt there might be a number of advantages, including protection and the probable flow of plundered goods into the community. The gangsters, it appears, often felt a close attachment to one community and hoped eventually to retire there on the proceeds of their activities, perhaps after establishing their respectability by making the pilgrimage to Mecca.

As in urban Batavia, however, the jago often enjoyed a close working relationship with the forces of law and order. Unable or unwilling to employ a full police force, the landlords often found it convenient to come to terms with the jago. Gangsters often acted as a kind of informal police force of hired toughs who could and did enforce the will of the landlords. Even those unfortunate enough to get caught by the authorities did not necessarily end up in jail. When the eponymous hero of 'Korporaal Rampok' was captured by troops in a fierce battle with a gang, he escaped prosecution by joining the army.[32] This ambiguity of their relationships both to Batavian society and to the colonial state gave the gangsters the opportunity to survive in the interstices of colonial society, the strong and the quick-witted becoming major local power brokers, the weak and slow disappearing rapidly into the Dutch prisons of Cipinang and Glodok or perishing at the hands of their more clever colleagues.

1. See K. Helbig, *Am Rand des Pazifik: Studien zur Landes- und Kulturkunde Südostasiens* (Stuttgart, 1949), 65–6.
2. On the geology and prehistory of the region, see J. Hardjono, *Indonesia, Land and People* (Jakarta, 1971), 13–35, 94–101, 119–23. On Taruma and its historical setting, see G. Coedès, *The Indianized States of Southeast Asia* (Canberra, 1968), 53–4; O. W. Wolters, *Early Indonesian Commerce: a Study of the Origins of Srivijaya* (Ithaca, N.Y., 1967), 205–22; and I. C. Glover, 'The Late Prehistoric Period in Indonesia', in R. B. Smith and W. Watson, eds., *Early South East Asia: Essays in Archaeology, History and Historical Geography* (Kuala Lumpur, 1979), 171, 179–81.
3. See N. C. van Setten van der Meer, *Sawah Cultivation in Ancient Java: Aspects of Development during the Indo-Javanese Period, 5th to 15th Century* (Canberra, 1979).
4. On the early history of the the region, see F. de Haan, *Priangan: de Preanger-Regentschappen onder het Nederlandsch Bestuur tot 1811* 4v. (Batavia, 1901–1912).
5. S. Abeyasekere, *Jakarta: a History* (Singapore, 1987), 7–12; J. L. Cobban, 'The City on Java: an Essay in Historical Geography' (Ph.D. dissertation, University of California, 1970), 67–9; and F. de Haan, *Oud Batavia: Gedenkboek Uitgegeven naar Aanleiding van het Driehonderd Jarig Bestaan van der Stad in 1919*, 2v. (Batavia, 1922–1923).
6. On the historical geography of cities in Southeast Asia in general and of Jakarta in particular, see Abeyasekere, *op.cit.*; N. Keyfitz, 'The Ecology of Indonesian cities', *American Journal of Sociology* 66, 4 (1961), 348–54; D. W. Fryer, 'The "Million City" in Southeast Asia', *Geographical Review* 43, 4 (October 1953), 474–94; W. F. Wertheim, *Indonesian Society in Transition* (The Hague, 1964), 171–94; H. J. Heeren, 'The Urbanisation of Djakarta', *Ekonomi dan Keuangan Indonesia* 8, 11 (1955), 698–701; P. D. Milone, *Urban Areas in Indonesia* (Berkeley, 1966), 11–41 and her doctoral dissertation, 'Queen City of the East: the Metamorphosis of a Colonial Capital' (Ph.D. dissertation, University of California, 1966); Abdurrachman Surjomihardjo, *Pemekaran Kota Jakarta/The Growth of Jakarta* (Jakarta, 1977). An extremely detailed geographical study of Batavia is available

in K. Helbig, *Batavia: eine Tropische Stadtlandschaftskunde im Rah-men der Insel Java* (doctoral dissertation, University of Hamburg, 1931). For contrasting accounts of Batavia by visitors in different centuries, see T. S. Raffles, *The History of Java* (Kuala Lumpur, 1965 [first published in London, 1817]), I, 33; II, 246 and appendix i–xii; and D. M. Campbell, *Java: Past and Present* (London, 1915), I, 459.

7. Netherlands Indies, Departement van Landbouw, Nijverheid en Handel, *Volkstelling 1930, deel I: Inheemsche Bevolking van West-Java* (Batavia, 1933), 7. Quantified but not necessarily reliable information on changes in Jakarta's population after the census of 1930 is contained in Heeren, *op.cit.*, 703–28.

8. A. Wright and O. T. Breakspear, eds., *Twentieth Century Impressions of Netherlands India: its History, Peoples, Commerce, Industries, and Resources* (London, 1909), 442.

9. *Indisch Verslag 1939, II: Statistisch Jaaroverzicht van Nederlandsch-Indië over het Jaar 1938* (Batavia, 1939), 4; L. Blussé, 'Batavia 1619–1740: the Rise and Fall of a Chinese Colonial Town', in L. Blussé, *Strange Company: Chinese Settlers, Mestizo Women and the Dutch in VOC Batavia* (Leiden, 1986), 73–96.

10. Wright and Breakspear, *op.cit.*, 442.

11. See Blussé, *op.cit.*, 74.

12. *Ibid.*; J. G. Taylor, *The Social World of Batavia: European and Eurasian in Dutch Asia* (Madison, Wisc., 1983), 47–9.

13. Abeyasekere, *op.cit.*, 19–31; Lance Castles, 'The Ethnic Profile of Djakarta', *Indonesia* 3 (1967), 153–204. The total number of Betawi in West Java was about one million in 1930; see *Volkstelling 1930*, I, 14.

14. J. S. Furnivall, *Netherlands India: a Study of Plural Economy* (Cambridge, 1939), 446.

15. J. A. A. van Doorn and W. J. Hendrix, *Ontsporing van Geweld: over het Nederlands/Indisch/Indonesisch Conflict* (Rotterdam, 1970), 53.

16. H. Sutherland, *The Making of a Bureaucratic Elite: the Colonial Transformation of the Javanese* **Priyayi** (Singapore, 1979); R. T. McVey, 'Introduction: Local Voices, Central Power', in R. T. McVey, *Southeast Asian Transitions: Approaches through Social History* (New Haven and London, 1978).

17. R. van Niel, *The Emergence of the Modern Indonesian Elite* (The Hague, 1960).

18. See S. Abeyasekere, 'Colonial Urban Politics: the Municipal Council of Batavia', *Kabar Seberang* 13–14 (1984), 17–24; Milone, *Urban Areas of Indonesia, op.cit.*, 18–22, 25–35; Satyawati Suleiman, 'The Last Days of Batavia', *Indonesia* 28 (1979), 64. On more purely administrative arrangements, see The Liang Gie, *Sedjarah Pemerintahan Kota Djakarta* (Jakarta, 1958), 31–2, 62–6.

19. The extent of pre-war circular migration is assessed in *Volkstelling 1930*, I, 33–4. Contemporary circular migration is discussed and brief mention made of labour brokers in L. Jellinek, 'The pondok system and circular migration', in L. Jellinek, C. Manning and G. Jones, *The Life of the Poor in Indonesian Cities* (Clayton, Vic., 1978).

20. *Volkstelling 1930*, I, 29, 36. Ethnic specialisation continued well past independence; see G. F. Papanek, 'The Poor of Jakarta', *Prisma* 3 (1976), 43.
21. Blussé, *op.cit.*, 84–5.
22. See, for example, Go Gien Tjwan, *Eenheid in Verscheidenheid in een Indonesisch Dorp* (Amsterdam, 1966), 163–72 and *passim*; Memorie van Overgave of the Resident of Karawang, 1929, published in *Memori Serah Jabatan 1921–1930 (Jawa Barat)* (Jakarta, 1976), 39; and J. E. Tideman, 'De Bevolking van de Regentschappen Batavia, Meester Cornelis en Buitenzorg', *Koloniaal Tijdschrift* 22 (1933), 149–51.
23. See 'Back to the "P. & T." Lands', *Java Gazette* 1, 5 (Mar. 1948), 117.
24. See 'De beteekenis der particuliere landerijen voor de economische en politieke verhoudingen in West-Java', *Nefis Periodiek* no. 2 (27 February 1946), 10–11, *Alg.Sec.II* I–21–1.
25. See C. Lekkerkerker, 'Het Krawangsche Oproer van Mei 1832', *De Indische Gids* 54, 2 (1932), 577–8; 'Toestand op Particuliere Landerijen', *Tijdschrift voor Economische en Sociale Geographie* 5 (1914), 36; 'Liquidatie der Particuliere Landerijen', *Bestuursvraagstukken/Soalsoal Pemerintahan* 1, 3 (1949), 351–3. 'De beteekenis der particuliere landerijen', *loc.cit.*, Interviews: H. Moh. Damsjik, Bekasi, 17 January 1983; K. H. Nurali, Babelan, Bekasi, 17 January 1983.
26. On the jago as a social institution, see P. M. van Wulfften Palthe, *Over het Bendewezen op Java* (Amsterdam, 1949); J. R. W. Smail, *Bandung in the Early Revolution 1945–1946: a Study in the Social History of the Indonesian Revolution* (Ithaca, N.Y., 1964), 88–89; B. R. O'G. Anderson, *Java in a Time of Revolution: Occupation and Resistance 1944–1946* (Ithaca, N.Y., 1972), 5–9.
27. See Raffles, *op.cit.*, I, 47; P. H. van der Kemp, *Oost Indie's Herstel in 1816* (The Hague, 1911), 283–4; 'De Onveiligheid op de Particuliere Landen in West-Java', *De Indische Gids* 59 (1937), 532–37; Tideman, *op.cit.*, 148.
28. There is an extensive literature on Chinese secret societies. See particularly L. F. Comber, *Chinese Secret Societies in Malaya: a Survey of Triad Society from 1800–1900* (New York, 1959); and F. Davis, *Primitive Revolutionaries of China: a Study of Secret Societies of the Late Nineteenth Century* (Honolulu, 1977).
29. C. S. W. Graaf van Hogendorp, *Tafereelen van Javaansche Zeden: Vier Oorspronkelijke Verhalen* (Amsterdam, 1837), 236–39.
30. F. Egmond, *Banditisme in de Franse Tijd: Profiel van de Grote Nederlandse Bende 1790–1799* (Dieren, 1986), 57–8.
31. G. Quinn,'The Javanese Science of Burglary', *Review of Indonesian and Malayan Affairs* 9, 1 (1973), 33–54; P. M. van Wulfften Palthe, *Psychological Aspects of the Indonesian Problem* (Leiden, 1949), 28–9; interviews with visitors to Mt Jatibening.
32. Van Hogendorp, *op.cit.*, 240.

2

Political Initiations

The Jakarta underworld challenged Dutch authority not simply by its criminal activity. The gangsters were a major element in the Jakarta region's tradition of rural unrest and rebellion. Rebellions of varying seriousness peppered the decades of the nineteenth century in the area.[1] From early in the twentieth century, moreover, this traditional unrest became linked with growing nationalist agitation against the Dutch. This link led ultimately to the revolutionary alliance of young nationalists and the Jakarta underworld in 1945, and it is important therefore to explain both the nature of underworld participation in the unrest and the terms of its early association with nationalism.

I am not concerned here with explaining rural unrest as a phenomenon in the society of rural Jakarta. Sartono Kartodirdjo has comprehensively examined protest movements in the region in the early nineteenth and early twentieth centuries,[2] and he has identified a variety of reasons for rebellion. Many rebellions had a broadly millenarian character. They sought to realise a fundamental, spiritually-based change in the ordering of the world and they looked to a leader with allegedly supernatural characteristics. Yet this spiritual radicalism was often blended with a relatively conservative, or at most reformist, concern with the material conditions of life in the ommelanden. Other rebellions appeared to have more mundane motives such as protest against extortion or against disruptions to the established pattern of life in the region. There was a major outbreak of unrest from 1913 in response to the colonial government's new regulations on the private estates, introduced in 1912. These were intended to improve conditions on the estates by defining more closely the rights and duties of landlords and tenants. In practice, the

24

disruption to the status quo seems to have outweighed any immediate advantages for the peasants in the new system, and many risings were sparked off by attempts to implement the new regulations.[3] None of this, however, is novel in the literature on peasant rebellion, and our concern here is not to fit the Jakarta examples into one or other of the many persuasive arguments which have been presented on the topic,[4] but rather to examine the participation of a particular section of society—the underworld —in these actions.

It may be useful to consider a typical uprising such as that in Tanggerang in 1924. A Dutch official investigating the affair reported that the participants in the revolt came from relatively prosperous areas and were themselves relatively well-off; in speeches and when later questioned they did indeed cite particular economic grievances but, according to the Dutch report, although some of the grievances were fully justified they did not affect the participants. The official attributed this to the spirit of the age; the great Java railway strike had taken place a year before and economic grievances were an appropriate justification for opposition to Dutch rule. The leader of the uprising, called Kaiin, made a certain amount of propaganda against the Chinese, presumably because some Chinese were local landlords, although he himself was married to a Chinese woman and had been trained by a Chinese as a dalang. This training gave Kaiin the familiarity with Javanese mythology and prophecy required to declare himself Prince, Ruler of the World (*Prabu Rabul Alamin*) and other titles, as well as owner of the private estates in Tanggerang. The rebellion thus involved the usual combination of mundane and messianic motives.

More interesting in this context, however, is the social composition of Kaiin's supporters. He attracted a following of forty-two 'leaders', amongst them a dukun who was proficient in *ilmu kewedukan* (the science of invulnerability) and *ilmu keselamatan* (mystical Islamic practices) and whose pupils formed the bulk of Kaiin's followers. Protected by charms giving invulnerability, he and his followers drove out local Chinese and seized their lands. He then announced that he would march on Batavia to destroy it. On the way, however, he was met by Dutch forces and was killed in the ensuing battle, along with fourteen of his followers. Twenty-four others were arrested and the revolt came to an end.[5]

Kaiin's rising was in no sense a mass movement. The total number of people involved can hardly have been more than two hundred. Nor was it in any way a serious threat to Dutch rule. The fact, moreover, that Kaiin designated himself as ruler of the universe and owner of the private estates is indicative of a social conservatism, in spite of the movement claiming to address certain social grievances.

It does, however, provide us with a glimpse of the way in which an armed challenge to Dutch authority could be mounted. What made the revolt possible was the coming together of a leader, who provided a focus, a consciousness and a sense of direction, with a number of existing groups each already able to act as a more or less coherent unit. The revolt thus did not start from scratch by recruiting disaffected individuals but worked rather with larger social units. The gangs of the Batavia underworld, whose 'leaders' were described in the account above, provided the organisational basis for these risings and it is worth asking why, aside from any personal or local reasons which may have been operating, this should have been the case.

In the first place, the gangsters were uniquely qualified to participate in rebellion by virtue of their skills. Under a colonial regime which had effectively disarmed the indigenous population, gangsters were amongst the very few groups to possess the skills in using offensive weapons which were necessary for a credible revolt. The variety of supernatural skills which they claimed, such as the ability to become invisible, inaudible or invulnerable, were as valuable for rebellion as for criminality. The gangsters seem moreover to have been particularly receptive to the kind of revolutionary promises made by messianic leaders because their own sub-culture contained strong elements of what Hobsbawm has called social banditry.[6] Many stories tell, for instance, of gangsters defending the poor against the depredations of landlords and distributing their booty freely amongst the poor peasantry. Leaders of the Jakarta underworld liked to think of themselves as Robin Hoods, protectors and benefactors of the weak, engaged in a noble but vain struggle with the holders of power in society. The traditional *lenong* drama of Jakarta often features the gangster whose heart of gold lies concealed beneath grim black clothes and a forbidding expression.

This sympathy for the weaker sections of society was not, of course, an exclusively Jakarta phenomenon. Hobsbawm has described a wide variety of such 'social bandits' from many parts of the world. Hobsbawm's explanation of social banditry proposed that a bandit, or gangster, or brigand, need not simply be an individual breaker of law and disturber of order but rather could be a representative of the massive antagonism of peasant society towards its rulers. Gangsters are peasants who have been displaced from peasant life by poverty or other misfortune but who nonetheless retain their peasant values and use their newly acquired skills as men of violence to defend peasant interests.[7] When an outlaw, therefore, stole from the rich and gave to the poor, he was not merely like the Bad Baronet Murgatroyd in Gilbert and Sullivan's *Ruddigore*, who committed a crime every morning to ensure his survival and good deeds for the rest of the day to ease his conscience; he acted not just for his own sake but for that of the peasantry from which he had sprung. The social bandit, according to Hobsbawm, does in a regular way what peasants themselves would like to be doing much of the time but in fact only carry out in the occasional jacquerie. Thus the bandit's predation on the rich is a kind of peasant rebellion by proxy, and the peasants acknowledge this by providing the bandit with the shelter he needs to survive and the flow of information he needs to avoid capture.

The notion of social banditry has been attacked most comprehensively by Anton Blok, who, although not denying that occasional social bandits may have existed, argues that they were more a product of peasant wishful thinking than a real phenomenon and that bandits were most commonly oppressors of the poor. The benefits they may have given to their home villages were more than outweighed by their depredations on others, and they were more often than not basically hitmen and goons in the semi-employment of local elites. Although Blok's criticism may be read in part simply as a warning against over-enthusiastic application of Hobsbawm's ideas, against seeing a social bandit in every rural criminal, he basically shifts the bandit from the ranks of the peasantry to the side of the elite. Instead of possessing essentially peasant values, the bandit takes on, or at least upholds, those of the elite.[8]

Since Blok, however, something of a rehabilitation of the notion of social banditry has taken place, with scholars such as McQuilton, Cheah and O'Malley carefully pinpointing cases of socially conscious bandits who sprang from amongst the peasantry, or from similarly impoverished groups, and generally championed the interests of the oppressed against the authorities.[9] This rehabilitation, however, has thrown up rather fewer cases of true social banditry than Hobsbawm seems to have first envisaged, and the Jakarta region certainly appears to offer no likely candidates. Application of this revised social banditry thesis to the Jakarta underworld, moreover, is limited by the apparent looseness of the social connection between the underworld and the peasantry.

Gangsters are certainly reported as being more numerous and daring in times of economic hardship, but this may simply reflect the diminished capacity of the authorities to suppress them, rather than any increase in the number of recruits. What we know of recruitment to gangsterism suggests that this was a profession chosen fairly early in life as an alternative to the mundane existence of a peasant, rather than a desperate measure into which an impoverished peasant might be forced. Many of the better known gangsters who displayed a social conscience seem in fact to have been the sons of gangsters. There is no evidence of long-lasting gangster dynasties or of the criminal tribes reported from the Indian Subcontinent,[10] but it was widely believed that the gangsters of the ommelanden were descended from soldiers of Sultan Agung of Mataram, who had unsuccessfully attempted to capture Batavia from the Dutch in 1629.[11] One does not have to take this genealogy as a reliable claim to descent; the manufacture or adoption of appropriate ancestors is an established technique for political legitimation on Java.[12] What is significant is that the genealogies gave the gangsters an identity different from that of the peasants, and this suggests that the reasons for their occasional benevolence may not lie simply or primarily in peasant values.

A more important reason for the social sympathies of gangsters in the Jakarta region perhaps lies somewhat concealed in the story of a gangster who enjoyed the power of invulnerability and could reputedly catch bullets in his hand but who lost these powers when he used them to accumulate personal wealth. This story reflects at one level the Javanese traditional belief that power is greatest when exercised *tanpa pamrih*, without self-interest,[13] but it also reflects two of the practical realities of a gangster's life. First, property itself was never very useful to a gangster. He could carry little with him on his excursions and thus could not enjoy possession in the same way as could a stable householder. Possessions, moreover, were vulnerable: they could easily be stolen during the gangster's frequent absences. To avoid such ignominy, the gangster did better to distribute wealth to others, building up debts of obligation and gratitude which could be called upon in the future, than hold onto it. In any case, a gangster in full possession of his faculties could expect to take whatever he wanted whenever he wanted it, regardless of who owned it. Second, despite his power, the gangster who was not protected by one of the local powerholders, such as a landlord, was dependent for his survival on the consent and complicity of the peasants in whose midst he lived. He relied upon them at very least not to inform on him and not to turn on him themselves. Intimidation could guarantee these things in the short term, but the gangsters who survived and prospered, and whose names became well-known, were generally those whose deeds inspired some degree of affection and admiration as well as fear and respect. To achieve this, a gangster needed to organise a continual flow of favours to the society in which he lived.[14]

In important ways, too, the criminal ecology of the Jakarta region encouraged the development of social gangsterism. Different societies offer not just different definitions of crime but different opportunities for criminality. In our own society, for instance, we acknowledge the virtual disappearance of the criminal niches for bandits, pirates and robber barons by appropriating those terms to describe poker machines, copyright infringers and senior corporate executives. The outstanding opportunities for crime in the Jakarta countryside came from the post road, a rich artery of people and commerce, and from the existence of wealthy landlords. Both offered opportunities for crime of a kind to which the impoverished peasants of the region were not vulnerable: highway robbery and burglary targeted merchants and landlords, not peasants. Stealing from the poor of course was possible too, but the pickings were likely to be so small that robbing them required the kind of systematic and extended operation already mastered by the landlords and money-lenders, rather than the deliberately unsystematic and surprise springing of an ambush. The equanimity with which the poor of the region viewed these dangerous and lucrative criminal activities did not itself invest them with an air of social banditry, but it freed the bandits to take on a social conscience if this suited them.

Not only the social conscience of the gangsters but also the sub-culture of gangster life made the gangsters ready participants in rebellion. There was a sense amongst the gangsters that they had a duty and function in society, as well as an appropriate mode of behaviour. A gangster was direct and confrontationist; he was not interested in talk or compromise but in action. He was a fighter *par excellence* and his social prestige depended upon his martial exper-tise. As a dweller on the fringes of society, he valued the respect which his fearsomeness earned him, and he could only preserve that fearsomeness by demonstrating his prowess regularly. Thus he could not afford not to take part in any fracas which might happen to be taking place in his vicinity. This sense of the appropriate behaviour of a gangster was perhaps derived ultimately from Hindu ideas of *dharma* (duty) and manifested itself at times almost in a sense of fatalism. While hoping on one level of consciousness, as mentioned in chapter one, to break into respectability and to retire in peace, the gangsters often expected in practice that they would die in harness, and there was thus an element of self-sacrifice in their ethos which emerged particularly strongly during the revolution.

At the same time, that desire to break into the system was often supplemented by a more ambitious dream to become respectable by gaining a formal position in the government hierarchy. The division between brigands and pirates on the one hand and governors and princes on the other was traditionally rather blurred in the Indone-sian archipelago, and legends remained of the days when a capable brigand could hope to become king. In colonial Indonesia participa-tion in rebellion was a singularly ineffective channel for social mo-bility, but the ethos which made rebellion a plausible strategy did not become extinct. A well-managed revolt which demonstrated the power of a gang leader and thus the political wisdom of bringing him into the system would have been an eminently rational move if the Dutch had accepted the same ground rules and had not been able to quell rebellions with superior firepower and even to prevent them from developing by means of superior political intelligence services.

The frustration which attended the effectiveness of Dutch repression was probably amongst the factors which led the Batavia underworld to become interested in the emerging Indonesian nationalist movement in the early twentieth century. With the establishment of branches of the Sarekat Islam (Islam Union) in the Batavia ommelanden in 1913, resistance there had begun to take on modern political characteristics. These branches were ostensibly religious in orientation but quickly developed a hostility towards the local economic power of the Chinese landlords. In Bekasi, Sarekat Islam members organised what amounted to a strike for higher pay amongst peasants asked to plant rice fields belonging to Chinese. In Tanggerang, some even cooperated with the police in suppressing illegal gambling amongst the local Chinese community.[15] More commonly, however, Sarekat Islam simply provided the organisation for summoning the population to protest against real or rumoured oppressive acts by Chinese landlords or their agents.[16] In all these activities, the organisation needed recourse to violence from time to time, if only to defend itself from the hired thugs of the landlords, and, through the recruitment of local jago, it acquired its own access to thuggery. Although the programmes of Sarekat Islam in the Jakarta area were far from being politically sophisticated, they nonetheless began to draw the Jakarta underworld into the nationalist challenge to Dutch colonial rule.

The Indonesian Communist Party (PKI, *Partai Komunis Indonesia*) further strengthened awareness within the Jakarta underworld of the broader political issues of the day. From its founding in 1920, the party had sought to raise consciousness and to build a firm base of support in Indonesia's meagre proletariat. Batavia, however, was not an industrial city. Except for the railway workshop at Manggarai and the docks at Tanjung Priok there was nowhere for Indonesian labour to develop a strong union structure and the city never acquired the 'red' reputation of industrial Semarang.[17] The PKI was also less active in recruiting workers for unions in West Java, and workers in West Java accordingly took little part in the great railway strike on Java in 1923.[18] Even its limited contacts with workers and efforts to establish trade unions in the Batavia region, however, brought the PKI quickly into contact with the underworld. For the PKI, the gangs were an invaluable organisational base, giving its local branches access to networks of support, information and protection which could not easily have been created by the party on its own. The gangs also gave to the party a body of dynamic and enthusiastic supporters not easily intimidated by the colonial authorities; they added an already glowing ember of revolutionary fervour to the sometimes damp hesitance of other recruits. Amongst the few involved in the railway strike in the Jakarta region was a young local boss called Muhammad Arif from Klender, on the railway line east of Jakarta. Under the name Haji Darip, he was to play a major role in the revolution of 1945 in Jakarta.

After 1923, however, the party began to expand its activities in West Java, shifting its headquarters from Semarang to Batavia and commencing active organisation amongst sailors and waterside workers at Tanjung Priok. Under the influence of Alimin, whose work in Tanjung Priok had brought him into particular contact with the Bantenese gangsters known as *jawara*, the party made a conscious decision to recruit actively within the underworld. Aside from the elan which the gangsters could contribute, they offered the PKI a means of protecting itself against the activities of other gangsters in the pay of local officials or Islamic leaders who attempted to break up the PKI by force.[19] For the gangs themselves the PKI was attractive as the rising political force in Indonesia, the most plausible challenger to the Dutch. The PKI promise of social justice through revolution struck a chord not only with messianic inclinations but also with the ethos of social gangsterism.

The Batavia underworld for its part was also in need of allies. In order to control the lawlessness of the region, the Dutch turned to a force which they had first used in the fierce Aceh War (1837–1908). This was the Korps Maréchausseé, formed in 1890 as a counter-guerilla force in the Kutaraja district. It consisted of small units of indigenous, predominantly Ambonese and Javanese troops, each with a European or Eurasian commander. Units were based in the countryside, first in Aceh and later in other troublesome areas including the Batavia ommelanden, where they were first stationed in 1916. They were allocated a swathe of territory and were required to keep it clear of criminal gangs and armed resistance to Dutch rule. In order to do this, Maréchausseé units departed radically from the hierarchical, parade-ground tactics of the rest of the colonial army, stressing instead manoeuverability, individual independence and initiative, and the development of mutual trust between officers and men. They also managed to build an effective local intelligence service by learning the local language and cultivating extensive local contacts.[20] The Maréchausseé was supplemented moreover by units of the Veldpolitie (Rural Police), a semi-militarised organisation under civilian rather than military authority but organised along lines similar to those of the Maréchausseé.

The effectiveness of the Maréchausseé and the Veldpolitie,

together with the generally tighter administrative control which the
Dutch exercised in Indonesia under the so-called Ethical Policy,
tended to restrict the Jakarta underworld's freedom to manoeuvre.
Gang leaders became increasingly interested in the possibility of
improving their position by giving their support to challengers to the
colonial system. There were common elements, too, in the style of
the two groups. As opponents of a powerful and resourceful state,
both the PKI and the gangs were acutely aware of the need for
security and discipline. They were notably unsuccessful in maintaining either, the PKI, like the gangs, being riddled with informers and
racked with divisions. As early as 1924, however, the PKI began
preparing for illegal and underground activity, and the techniques for
working clandestinely which the party began to develop—techniques
for moving people and information secretly, for obtaining funds
illicitly and for establishing the credentials of visitors from other
regions—contributed to a shared sense of purpose between the left
and the underworld.[21]

The importance of this alliance in giving the anti-colonial movement the means to revolt emerged clearly in the abortive communist
uprising of 1926. The rising in Batavia in November was part of what
was originally intended as a colony-wide uprising but in the event,
however, it involved only a few PKI branches. The revolt in Batavia
was carried out by armed gangs who clashed sporadically with police
and watchmen and briefly occupied the telephone exchange. The
principal targets of the operation, however, were the jails at Glodok
and Cipinang. Although the jails were significant symbols of Dutch
authority and the local PKI may have been inspired in part by
memories of the importance of the fall of the Bastille, prisons were
hardly a major strategic objective for a revolution attempting to seize
control of the capital city of the Netherlands Indies. For the gangsters, on the other hand, many of whom must have seen the inside of
one or other institution, they were perhaps the single most important
focus of resentment. An attack upon them, moreover, offered them
an opportunity to build their strength by releasing imprisoned colleagues. In the event, however, neither operation was successful. The
attack on Glodok jail was repulsed, while that on Cipinang never
began, for although a crowd of five hundred had gathered to make
the attack, those instructed to lead the rising did not turn up. The
other disturbances were swiftly quelled and after some three hundred
arrests were made, Batavia returned to colonial peace and order.[22]

Dutch repression in the aftermath of the 1926 uprising was effective in destroying the Batavia PKI and in driving the city's gangs back
into the underworld. The incipient revolutionary consciousness of the
gangs, which grew from their brief alliance with the left, nonetheless

remained. The Dutch continued to report suspected communist activity in the region, including a shadowy group calling itself *Korban Diri* (Self Sacrifice) which was probably based on one of the local gangs. Sukarno's Indonesian Nationalist Party (PNI) quickly began to be active in the Karawang region alongside surviving Sarekat Islam branches and a few trade unions. Dutch political police investigations frequently mentioned the region as a site of expected disturbances in the late 1920s.[23] Links with the nationalist movement were reinforced in the late 1930s by activities of the Gerindo (*Gerakan Rakyat Indonesia*, Indonesian People's Movement), the most left wing of the legal nationalist parties in the closing years of Dutch colonial rule. Gerindo took a strong socialist and internationalist line and was an important field for clandestine activity by the now-illegal and underground PKI; its leaders included the lawyer Amir Syarifuddin, who had become a member of the PKI secretly in 1927.[24]

Gerindo activists, heavily limited by colonial political restrictions, re-established ties with the underworld of the ommelanden by such techniques as conducting literacy classes in the region. A West Sumatran lawyer, Muhammad Yamin, another leader of the party for a time, was particularly active in establishing a network of sympathisers and supporters in the region. He was a charismatic figure, full of pithy aphorisms and sharp assessments of the characters of his colleagues in the nationalist movement. This characteristic hardly endeared him to members of his own generation, but Yamin drew enthusiastic support from a group of younger nationalists such as Khaerul Saleh and Johar Nur. There is no evidence that these Gerindo activities were used directly as a means of recruiting members of the Gerindo for the PKI, though this may have taken place. Ahmad Subarjo, too, a former activist in the disbanded nationalist Partai Indonesia (Partindo), quietly recruited supporters amongst junior officials of the state railways and other government bodies. The contacts served, however, to encourage political awareness and, perhaps even more importantly, to develop personal ties between a younger generation of radical nationalists and the underworld of the ommelanden.[25]

For this later generation of nationalists, the appeal of the Jakarta underworld did not lie in its access to armed force. Unlike the PKI, Gerindo and Partindo had no immediate plans for rebellion and perhaps even nourished the germs of a feeling that armed force—the pillar of colonial rule—was not an altogether legitimate tool for political activity. The attractiveness of the gangsters lay rather in the vitality they represented. The failure of Sarekat Islam and the PKI had made it clear that a nationalist movement weakly rooted in society was vulnerable both to changes in popular mood and to repression. In the late 1920s and early 1930s, Sukarno attempted to drive nationalist conviction deeper into the hearts of the people by ceaseless campaigning and public speaking; Hatta and Syahrir attempted to build a resilient nationalist cadre in order to reach every level of society. When these leaders, however, were arrested in 1928–29 and arrested and exiled in 1933–34, the organisations they had sponsored withered and their removal from the political scene was largely unmarked by political disturbance. Dutch investigations in 1930, moreover, revealed that a great many followers of the nationalist parties had only a relatively sketchy idea of what the leaders claimed that they stood for.[26] Between the parties and their supporters' perceptions of them there is, of course, always some discrepancy, but the gap between the value systems of the indigenous elite and those of the mass seemed particularly distressing to nationalists still at liberty. The fact that all major nationalist groups soon reconciled themselves to playing according to Dutch rules in the official legislative assembly, or Volksraad, made them acutely aware of the need to keep in touch with the masses they sought to represent.

In these circumstances, a band of underworld leaders was an attractive partner. Untainted by capitalism or government service and quite rough in their social manners, local bosses, for all their shortcomings, seemed unambiguously men of the people (*rakyat*) and to suggest important potentials in Indonesian society—daring, self-reliance, dignity, determination. Although there was no longer a strong hope that cooperation with the underworld would lead anywhere in the short term, these contacts helped to reassure nationalist leaders of their own popular credentials.

Nor were the Maréchaussée and the Veldpolitie, those pillars of Dutch authority in the ommelanden, wholly reliable from the Dutch point of view. Lacking the orderly system of command and reward on which the regular army and police were based, they tended to attract resourceful and independently minded men, not so very different in character from the gangsters they were instructed to suppress. As in many countries, the social distinction between law enforcers and law breakers was not great, and the Dutch had to be vigilant in isolating their local Indonesian forces from the ideas of nationalism and revolution which might turn their allegiance. There was mild panic, for instance, when in 1929 the Bandung branch of the PNI managed to send two copies of its journal by post to the Veldpolitie unit in Karawang, and immediate steps were taken to see that no further issues would get through.[27]

Despite the relative ease with which the Dutch defeated the 1926 uprising, they found the gangs of the region no less intractable in the years which followed. With the onset of the Great Depression in

1932, the position of the gangs in fact appeared to become stronger. This was due largely to the austerity measures adopted by the colonial government, which led to a reduction in the number of Maréchausseé troops and Veldpolitie stationed in the region.[28] The rise of the gangs was also, however, partly a consequence of the Depression itself. As a consequence of Dutch emergency economic measures designed to protect their plantation industry, the fall in the guilder's purchasing power in the world market was felt most sharply by Indonesian wage labourers. These included the peasants who worked on the private estates, as well as the urban workers of Batavia. There were thus more instances of oppression, exploitation and hardship for which local populations wished to call on the ambiguous protection of the black-garbed gangsters with their rudimentary social conscience. There were more occasions, too, on which landlords and others had to call out their own toughs. In times of trouble, men of violence often prosper.[29]

1. *Encyclopaedie van Nederlandsch-Indië* (The Hague and Leiden) I (1917), 222; II (1918), 450; III (1919), 437; V (1927), 54; Sartono Kartodirdjo, *Protest Movements in Rural Java: a Study of Agrarian Unrest in the Nineteenth and early Twentieth Centuries* (Singapore, 1973), 22–3, 26, 33–8, 60 and *passim*.

2. Sartono, *op.cit.*, 64–105.

3. *Encyclopaedie van Nederlandsch-Indië*, III; 'De Onveiligheid op de Particuliere Landen in West-Java', *De Indische Gids* 59 (1937), 532–7.

4. Classics in the extensive literature on peasant revolt and millenarianism include N. Cohn, *The Pursuit of the Millennium* (London, 1970); M. Adas, 'From Avoidance to Confrontation: Peasant Protest in Precolonial and Colonial Southeast Asia', *Comparative Studies in Society and History* 23, 1 (1981), 217–47; J. C. Scott, *The Moral Economy of the Peasant: Rebellion and Subsistence in Southeast Asia* (New Haven, 1975).

5. Beets, 'Rapport van de Tanggerangsche Ratoe Adil beweging' (photocopy in John M. Echols Collection, Cornell University Library). Kaiin's movement is also discussed in Go Gien Tjwan, *Eenheid in Verscheidenheid in een Indonesisch Dorp* (Amsterdam, 1966), 249–53; and in Sartono, *op.cit.* 45–57.

6. On this phenomenon, see E. J. Hobsbawm, *Bandits* (Harmondsworth, 1972).

7. *Ibid.*, 24; F. Braudel, *The Mediterranean and the Mediterranean World in the Age of Philip II* (London, 1975), 734–45.

8. Blok's critique of Hobsbawm is expressed most clearly in 'The Peasant and the Brigand: Social Banditry Reconsidered', *Comparative Studies*

in *Society and History* 14 (1972), 494–503; his own empirical research on bandits was published as *The Mafia of a Sicilian Village, 1890–1960: a Study of Violent Peasant Entrepreneurs* (Oxford, 1974). For arguments leading to a somewhat similar conclusion, see Pino Arlacchi, 'The Mafioso: from Man of Honour to Entrepreneur', *New Left Review* 118 (November–December 1979), 53–72.

9. John McQuilton, *The Kelly Outbreak 1878–1880: the Geographical Dimension of Social Banditry* (Melbourne, 1987); Cheah Boon Kheng, 'Hobsbawm's Social Banditry, Myth and Historical Reality: a Case in the Malaysian State of Kedah, 1915–1920', *Bulletin of Concerned Asian Scholars* 17, 4 (October–December 1985), 34–51; Pat O'Malley, 'Social Bandits, Modern Capitalism and the Traditional Peasantry: a Critique of Hobsbawm', *Journal of Peasant Studies* 6, 4 (1979), 489–501.

10. See A. A. Yang, ed., *Crime and Criminality in British India* (Tucson, 1985).

11. Soeparno Soeriaatmadja, *Sedjarah kepolisian dari Zaman Klasik sampai dengan Zaman Modern* (Jakarta, 1971), 38.

12. For a more recent example, see C. L. M. Penders, *The Life and Times of Sukarno* (London, 1974).

13. See B. R. O'G. Anderson, 'The Idea of Power in Javanese Culture', in C. Holt, ed., *Culture and Politics in Indonesia* (Ithaca, 1972), 38–40.

14. There were exceptions to this, of course, such as the rapacious Entang Tolo, described in Sartono Kartodirdjo and A. Lucas, 'Banditry and Political Change in Java', in Sartono Kartodirdjo, *Modern Indonesia: Tradition and Transformation* (Yogyakarta, 1984), 6–7.

15. *Sarekat Islam Lokal* (Jakarta, 1975), 18–24, 30–1.

16. *Ibid.*, 11, 17, 38, 40; Sartono, *op.cit.*, 163–4, 167.

17. See the meagre tally of industries in Batavia Residency listed in *Indisch Verslag 1939*, II, 302–3.

18. See J. Ingleson, '"Bound hand and foot": railway workers and the 1923 strike in Java', *Indonesia* 31 (1981), 55, 75.

19. M. C. Williams, *Sickle and Crescent: the Communist Revolt of 1926 in Banten* (Ithaca, N.Y., 1982), 15–17; H. Sutherland, *The Making of a Bureaucratic Elite: the Colonial Transformation of the Javanese Priyayi* (Singapore, 1979), 95.

20. H. J. Schmidt and M. H. Du Croo, *Marechaussee in Aceh* (Maastricht, 1943), 31–34; G. Teitler, *The Dutch Colonial Army in Transition: the Militia Debate, 1900–1921* (Townsville, 1981), 10–12; *Encyclopaedie van Nederlandsch-Indië*, II, 675.

21. See J. Leclerc, 'Underground Activities and their Double: Amir Syarifuddin's Relationship with Communism in Indonesia', *Kabar Seberang* 17 (June 1986), 72–98; R. T. McVey, *The Rise of Indonesian Communism* (Ithaca, N.Y., 1965), 274; Williams, *op.cit.*, 15, 22.

22. McVey, *op.cit.*, 343–4, 488; J.-Th. P. Blumberger, *De Communistische Beweging in Nederlandsch-Indië* (Haarlem, 1928), 72–4.

23. H. A. Poeze, ed., *Politiek-Politioneele Overzichten van Nederlandsch-Indië: Deel I, 1927–1928* (The Hague, 1982), 63, 118, 145, 462–3, 489, *Deel II 1929–1930* (Dordrecht, 1983), 101, 206–49, 379.

24. On Gerindo, see D. M. G. Koch, *Om de Vrijheid: De Nationalistische Beweging in Indonesië* (Jakarta, 1950), 125–6; G. McT. Kahin, *Nationalism and Revolution in Indonesia* (Ithaca, N.Y., 1952), 96. On the underground PKI, see Leclerc, *op.cit.*; J. Leclerc, 'La Condition du Parti: Révolutionnaires Indonésiens à la recherche d'une identité (1928–1948)', *Cultures et Développement* 10, 1 (1978); H. Poeze, 'The PKI-Muda 1936–1942', *Kabar Seberang* 13–14 (1984), 169–71; A. E. Lucas, *Local Opposition and Underground Resistance to the Japanese in Java, 1942–1945* (Clayton, Vic., 1986).

25. B. R. O'G. Anderson, *Java in a Time of Revolution: Occupation and Resistance, 1944–1946* (Ithaca, N.Y., 1972), 457; interviews.

26. W. J. O'Malley, 'Second Thoughts on Indonesian Nationalism', in J. A. C. Mackie, ed., *Indonesia: the Making of a Nation* (Canberra, 1980), 607–8.

27. Poeze, *op.cit.*, Deel II, 161.

28. See S. Cohen, 'Herstel der Veldpolitie', *Koloniaal Tijdschrift* 27 (1938), 119–20.

29. 'Onveiligheid op de Particuliere Landen', *op. cit.*, On the Depression in Indonesia, see W. J. O'Malley, 'Indonesia in the Great Depression: a Study of East Sumatra and Jogjakarta in the 1930's' (Ph.D. dissertation, Cornell University, 1977), 60–88.

3

New Masters, New Opportunities

The Japanese occupation of Indonesia gave the Jakarta underworld its first taste of the opportunities offered by major political change. Japanese troops landed on the north coast of Java on 1 March 1942 and near Subang, at the western edge of the Jakarta region, the Netherlands armed forces surrendered unconditionally eight days later. Since the raid on Pearl Harbour, Ahmad Subarjo's network of followers in the region had been listening to Radio Tokyo and passing on what they described as instructions to the people. They seem to have had some effect, sowing panic amongst the small European community with reports that the Japanese were closer by and in much greater numbers than was really the case, and they were also able to thwart Dutch attempts to destroy local installations such as railway workshops by persuading the Indonesian workers, who had to do the actual job of laying the mines and dismantling buildings, to stay at home. When the Japanese arrived near Subang, local people presented them with food and threw up road blocks to hamper a Dutch counter-attack. The nationalist activists' hope, however, of being able to hand the region over to the Japanese in good order was quickly dashed by a massive outbreak of rural violence.

The retreat of the Dutch and other Allied troops and the advance of the Japanese was accompanied by a massive breakdown in law and order in much of the Jakarta countryside. The ommelanden gangs seized a brief opportunity for plunder, confident that the forces of official justice would have more urgent things to do than stopping or catching them. For some, the plunder probably had strategic overtones, creating the illusion of assisting the Japanese advance. One kyai on the north coast is said to have helped the Japanese forces by hypnotising the local Dutch defenders so that they exhausted their ammunition shooting at a blank wall, believing that the Japanese were in front of it.[1] For the most part, however, the gangs directed their attentions to the newly-vulnerable houses of landlords and merchants. One imaginative charlatan sold what purported to be Japanese safe-conduct passes, though these turned out to be written in a language which no-one, including the Japanese, could read. Gangs based south of Batavia found a rich harvest amongst panic-stricken Dutch and Chinese residents of the city who fled for the mountains or the south coast, while to the east the main victims were local Chinese. According to a Chinese report, three-quarters of the Chinese businesses in Karawang were looted. Chinese rice mill owners tried to pacify the looters by distributing large amounts of rice, but this seems unlikely to have mollified them.[2] The violence of March 1942 had a political tinge, as one might expect—a few Chinese landlords and their Indonesian agents were killed in parts of the region while the more senior indigenous government officials decided it was in their best interests to flee—but for the most part the plunderers were opportunists who were recognising a short-lived chance for self-enrichment rather than carrying out anything approaching a political programme. When the Japanese, therefore, announced their intention to restore law and order, the better-established bosses realised that the moment for plunder had passed and reined in their followers. Others who continued to run wild were rapidly crushed by the Japanese in a series of operations during late March and early April.

Expectations of social change in the ommelanden were raised briefly by the Japanese themselves when in May 1942 they issued Regulation no 17 of the military government, abolishing the private estates. The news prompted a minor outbreak of contrition on the part of the landlords, with one or two abolishing some of the categories of tax on their peasants. It provoked a somewhat more extensive wave of indiscipline amongst the peasants themselves, in the form of disregard for landlord privileges. On one estate, for instance, people cut down trees belonging to the landlord in order to repair their own houses. This mild insubordination ended, however, when the Japanese announced formally that although the estates were now government property there was to be no change in their mode of operations. The military government had inherited all the prerogatives of the landlords and these were to be exercised on its behalf by the landlords themselves. Production, the Japanese went on to announce, had to be increased and all stolen goods returned, though they conceded that those ashamed (*malu*) to return stolen goods openly could do so under cover of darkness. The unfortunate cutters of trees mentioned above were tried and sentenced to hard labour for periods from one to thirty days. The sole concession by the Japanese to peasant interests was to release them from the obligation to pay off their debts annually before harvesting their rice. Under the new order, they were permitted to do so after the harvest and were thus released a little from the clutches of the money-lenders. Moreover, with the Chinese-owned rice mills of Karawang closed for some months at the start of the occupation, farmers were no longer able to sell their rice in advance under the disadvantageous *ijon* system, while the need to husk the paddy manually expanded employment opportunities.[3]

For the rest, however, the Japanese occupation brought little relief. Having crushed the active gangs, the Japanese instructed their local Indonesian officials to deal with those responsible for the violence of March 1942. So many officials, however, had fled at an early stage in the unrest that they often had little more than rumours and tendentious reports to guide their investigations, and the subsequent wave of arrests swept in many innocent, or relatively innocent, people. One of Subarjo's followers, seeing the old bureaucracy restored to all its original powers, commented bitterly that the officials were extracting taxes so energetically that they were deliberately trying to make Japanese rule seem more oppressive than Dutch.[4]

More significant change in Indonesian society, both in urban Jakarta and in the ommelanden, came from Japanese endeavours to mobilise the Indonesian people directly for the war effort. To this end, they set up a wide variety of mass organisations. Some of these—the *Gerakan Tiga A* and the *Putera*—were overtly political and were not allowed to penetrate to village level, but others—the *Keibodan* (Auxiliary Police), *Djawa Hokokai* (Java Service Association), *Seinendan* (Youth Organisation) and towards the end of the occupation the *Barisan Pelopor* or *Suishintai* (Pioneer Brigade)—did reach the lower levels of society. The Seinendan, the Keibodan and the Barisan Pelopor maintained a quasi-military discipline and gave their members a quasi-military training, including at least some instruction in unarmed combat or combat with bamboo spears. At the same time the programme gave some Indonesians experience of quasi-military command, albeit at a low level.[5]

Especially important was the *rukun tetangga* or *tonari-gumi* (neighbourhood association), introduced in 1944 and modelled on similar organisations in Japan. Each rukun tetangga consisted of ten to twenty households, with an elected leader responsible for carrying out government policy as passed down through the hierarchy above it. It was responsible for tasks ranging from fire-fighting and funerals to education and the collection and distribution of goods, and was used as a local source of information for the government.[6] The significance of these organisations was not the creation of links from region to region across Java, for the upper echelons of all these organisations were firmly in Japanese hands. Rather, it was the strengthening of organisation at the grass roots. Within the limits of a year's operation, they reinforced the coherence of local groups by giving their members experience of organisational life.

To recruit for these organisations, the Japanese made use of prominent nationalist figures such as Sukarno. Inevitably, however, locally-based organisations of this kind became a power base for local forces, and many of the Keibodan and Seinendan in the Jakarta region became extensions of the local underworld. The Japanese in fact had no particular interest in challenging the position of the underworld. Like the pre-colonial rulers of Java, they recruited powerful gangsters as local police chiefs and towards the end of the war they sought actively to recruit selected underworld gangs in the Jakarta region for guerrilla warfare against an expected Allied invasion of Java. The gangsters for their part were happy to accept the status and implied protection that this official sponsorship brought.[7]

The Japanese, however, did challenge the position of the Jakarta underworld indirectly by constructing a rival institution. This was the PETA (*Pembela Tanah Air*, Defenders of the Fatherland). In 1943, worried by the reduction of Japanese military forces on Java caused by repeated withdrawals to the Pacific front, the Japanese decided to set up an Indonesian auxiliary army, armed with firearms and commanded by Indonesian officers up to the level of battalion commander (*daidancho*). The PETA was organised regionally, and battalion commanders were generally expected to be prominent local figures able to attract recruits and to provide a focus of loyalty but not to be involved in actual military command. This was left to the company commanders (*chudancho*) and even more to the platoon commanders (*shodancho*). It was between platoon commanders and their men that the strongest ties developed, reinforcing the tendency for social coherence to be strongest by far in small local groups.[8] Because it was locally based, relatively well-armed and trained, and organised with the same emphasis on group solidarity, the PETA had the potential to challenge the power of the local underworld as the Maréchaussee had done in the colonial period. The Japanese practice, moreover, of using platoon commanders to give basic training to Seinendan and Keibodan units enabled the junior officers to develop a broader range of contacts and allegiances beyond their units. The Japanese, however, did not intend the PETA to be a police force and they generally kept PETA units in their barracks, somewhat isolated from the rest of society except during supervised training sessions.

The PETA, moreover, suffered from its association with the increasing hardship of the Japanese occupation. During the latter part of the Japanese occupation, in particular, the Japanese made heavy demands on the population for produce and labour which they paid for, if at all, in rapidly depreciating occupation currency. Labourers (*romusha*) were assigned to military and strategic projects not only on Java but elsewhere in Southeast Asia and most suffered extreme hardship, stories of which gradually filtered back to their home villages. At the same time the Japanese neglected to maintain the physical economic infrastructure of Java, the roads, railways and irrigation works which had been the pride of the Dutch. This infrastructure had been built for the most part to serve the largely European plantation sector of the economy, but it had become equally essential for the cultivation and transport of food for the Indonesian population. Rice was rationed and families in the Karawang region were allotted only one litre for five days. They had to supplement their nutritional needs with potatoes and cassava, and there were numerous reports of poisonings which resulted from the incorrect preparation of cassava. The almost total cessation of importing consumer goods into Java compounded the difficulties, and the people of the island became increasingly impoverished and resentful.[9]

These economic difficulties, however, worked to the advantage of the Jakarta underworld leaders. The Japanese had brought to Java an ideology of economic control: they imposed a policy of economic autarky on Java, requiring each residency (*syu*) to be economically self-sufficient as part of preparation for decentralised guerrilla resistance on Java. Within each residency they established what was meant to be a centralised system of rice collection and distribution, with heavy penalties for those who did not conduct their rice transactions through official channels. Two fifths of the rice harvested in Karawang was required to be delivered to the Japanese produce offices at a price which, at the start of the occupation, amounted to around half the open market price. By the end of the occupation, inflation had pushed the market price to twenty times the official purchase price.[10] In practice the official infrastructure could not cope with so ambitious a programme, but since not dealing with the official hierarchy remained heavily punishable, those most accustomed to circumventing the law were best able to exploit the situation. The local bosses of Jakarta and Karawang who could use their contacts and organisations to evade these regulations were able to make significant profits which in turn strengthened their social positions.[11]

Perhaps most important of all for this study, the Japanese occupation also established the close relationship between the underworld and the younger generation of the nationalist movement which was the basis of a revolutionary coalition in 1945 and after. We have seen in previous chapters how contacts developed between the Batavia underworld and the evolving nationalist movement, based partly on shared antagonism to the Dutch, partly on their complementary skills. Command of violence and control of ready-made, if rudimentary, social organisations made the gangsters attractive partners for the nationalists, while the gangsters in turn saw in the political aspirations of the nationalist movement an opportunity to break into previously inaccessible realms of power and position. Before the arrival of the Japanese, this association of gangsterism with nationalism remained tenuous, having borne fruit only in the abortive Batavia uprising of the PKI in 1926. Under the Japanese, however, the alliance received its first institutional form.

Although the Japanese generally avoided allowing the nationalist elite to make any direct contact with the masses, they made an exception when they established a training course for young Indonesian political leaders in Jakarta in 1942. Some fifty trainees were selected for the programme from amongst students and members of the pre-war nationalist youth organisations, including a significant number of Yamin's protegés, including Khaerul Saleh and Johar Nur. The intention of this programme was not only to familiarise the coming generation with appropriate political concepts but to train them in basic organisational techniques. To this end the trainees not only received formal lectures from a range of nationalist leaders including Sukarno, Hatta and Yamın, but also were sent out with instructions to form trade associations amongst groups such as *becak* (pedicab) drivers. The purpose of these associations, of course, was not to promote the specific interests of the groups involved but to mobilise them within the context of the Japanese war effort. Nor is there any sign that these associations developed a life of their own. They did, however, reinforce that organisational contact between young nationalists of the centre and the underworld which was so important in the control of labour in Jakarta.[12]

As the war drew to a close, therefore, the basis was laid for a revolutionary alliance between the Jakarta underworld and the left wing of the Indonesian nationalist movement. This alliance rested not only on the historical experience of cooperation between the two groups but on their shared antagonism to the colonial authorities and their complementary skills. The young nationalists possessed an analysis, a programme and a broad scope of action which made effective resistance to the entrenched colonial authorities seem possible; the gangsters possessed an organisational base which the nationalists could use for mass mobilisation. At the close of the

Japanese occupation, however, the alliance was still dormant. It took the additional shocks of the Japanese surrender and the Allied re-occupation of Jakarta to make the alliance a reality.

1. 'De mystieke school als instrument der Republikeinsche ondergrondsche acties', n.d. [July 1948], *Alg.Sec.I* VII–3–10. Confidential interviews.
2. S. Suleiman, 'The Last Days of Batavia', *Indonesia* 28 (1979), 57; D. H. Meyer, *Japan Wint den Oorlog: Documenten over Java* (Maastricht, 1946), 30–31; *Gong Rong Bao*, 24 April 1942, cited in Twang Peck Yang, 'The Indonesian Chinese Business Minority in Transition, 1940–1950' (Ph.D. thesis, Australian National University, 1987), chapter 2; see also A. Reid and Oki Akira, *The Japanese Experience in Indonesia: Selected Memoirs of 1942–1945* (Athens, Ohio, 1986), pp. 42–3. Similar outbreaks occurred in other parts of Java; see B. S. Gifford and G. Hobbs, trans, *The Kenpeitai in Java and Sumatra* (Ithaca, N.Y., 1986), 25.
3. *Asia Raya* (Jakarta), 12, 19, 20, 22, 23 May, 2 June 1942; J. O. Sutter, *Indonesianisasi: Politics in a Changing Economy, 1940–1955, I: the Indonesian Economy at the Close of the Dutch Period and Under the Japanese* (Ithaca, N.Y., 1959), 158–9.
4. Confidential sources.
5. On these organisations, see G. S. Kanahele, 'The Japanese Occupation of Indonesia: Prelude to Independence' (Ph.D. dissertation, Cornell University, 1967), esp. 58–88; Aiko Kurasawa, 'Mobilization and Control: a Study of Social Change in Rural Java, 1942–1945' (Ph.D. dissertation, Cornell University, 1988), 476–505
6. On the rukun tetangga, see Kanahele, *op.cit.*, 142–45; Kurasawa, *op.cit.*, 275–98; S. Nishijima *et al.*, *Japanese Military Administration in Indonesia* (Washington, D.C., 1963), 187–8; Rochmani Santosa, 'Djakarta Raya pada Djaman Djepang (1942–1945)', Seminar Sedjarah Nasional II vol. VI (2), Yogyakarta, 1970, 7–8; I. J. Brugmans, ed., *Nederlandsch-Indiëonder Japanse Bezetting: Gegevens en Documenten over de Jaren 1942–1945* (Franeker, 1960), 161–4.
7. Warsa Djajakusumah, 'Api '45 Dari Masa Kemasa', *Aku Akan Teruskan* (Jakarta, 1976), 99–128; Meyer, *op.cit.*, 30, 60–1.
8. On the PETA, see B. R. O'G. Anderson, *Java in a Time of Revolution: Occupation and Resistance 1944–1946* (Ithaca, N.Y., 1972), 20–6; Nugroho Notosusanto, *The PETA Army during the Japanese Occupation of Indonesia* (Tokyo, 1979); and Kanahele, *op.cit.*, 116–32.
9. 'De beteekenis der particuliere landerijen voor de economische en politieke verhoudingen in West Java', *NEFIS Periodiek* 2 (27 February 1946), 12, *Alg.Sec.I* I–21–1. G. McT. Kahin, *Nationalism and Revolution in Indonesia* (Ithaca, N.Y., 1952), 128–9; M. A. Aziz, *Japan's Colonialism and Indonesia* (The Hague, 1955), 182–3; early issues of

the *Economic Review of Indonesia* (1947+), published by the Netherlands Indies Department of Economic Affairs; and A. Kurasawa, 'Social Changes in Javanese Villages, 1942–45: the Forced Delivery System and its 77–105). Interview: H. Moh. Damsjik, Bekasi, 17 January 1983.

10. 'De beteekenis', 12, 14–15, *loc.cit.*
11. Lea Jellinek has described a somewhat similar situation during the late Guided Democracy when a general breakdown of the national economy opened new opportunities to kampung dwellers. See L. Jellinek, 'Underview: Memories of Kebun Kacang, 1930s to 1980s', in S. Abeyasekere, ed., *From Batavia to Jakarta: Indonesia's Capital 1930s to 1980s* (Clayton, Vic., 1985).
12. Anderson, *op.cit.*, 41–2. Confidential interviews.

II
REVOLUTION

4

Social Revolution in the Ommelanden

News of the Japanese surrender on 15 August 1945 did not reach all Indonesians at once. The Japanese authorities in Jakarta were uncertain how to respond to the suddenly changed situation and they did not broadcast the news, though it rapidly became clear to the general public that something was happening. Precise information on the surrender was thus restricted to Japanese and to Indonesians with privileged or clandestine access to unsealed radios, and word of the surrender first became widespread amongst the nationalist elite of Jakarta. Within nationalist circles in the city there was intense debate over the correct strategy to be followed in the new situation. Older nationalist leaders such as Sukarno generally favoured a cautious approach, arguing that precipitate action might unnecessarily antagonise the Japanese and the Allies, leading to the destruction of the nationalist movement. Younger nationalists, on the other hand, argued for an immediate declaration of independence. A bold gesture of this kind, they contended, was not only necessary for Indonesian national self-respect but would attract to the nationalists such widespread support that neither Japanese nor the newly victorious Allies would dare to move against them.[1] Neither group thought at this stage in terms of a protracted revolution: at issue was simply the best way to step across the threshold to independence. None, therefore, paid any serious attention at this time to mass organisation or to making use of the Jakarta underworld.

This attitude persisted even though the younger nationalists discovered almost immediately the advantages of possessing a secure base outside the city. This base was provided by the PETA unit stationed at Rengasdengklok, a small town in the swamps of the Citarum delta. A local PETA company commander, Umar Bahsan, seized power in the town early in the morning of 16 August, disarming the few Japanese present and raising the red and white flag in the name of the yet-to-be-declared Indonesian Republic. It was to this secure base that a group of young radical nationalists brought Sukarno and Hatta, having kidnapped the two leaders in order to persuade them to declare independence immediately and in fiery terms. Sukarno and Hatta refused to do so unless they could be sure the Japanese would not move to crush them, but when an assurance of protection was received from Admiral Maeda, head of the Japanese naval liaison office in Jakarta, they were driven back to Jakarta to hammer out with their colleagues the exact terms of the declaration.[2]

Back in Jakarta, both older and younger leaders remained preoccupied with the question of the correct strategy towards Japan and the Allies. Sukarno and Hatta declared independence on the morning of 17 August and proceeded with their colleagues to establish the formal constitutional framework of a new Indonesian Republic. Their actions, however, remained heavily circumscribed by their wish to avoid provoking the Japanese and they refrained both from taking over government and from attempting to build any kind of non-government mass organisation. Instead, they issued soothing assurances that everything was under control and urged the Indonesian people to remain calm and inactive. Amongst the young radical nationalists there were many who disagreed passionately with this strategy, but they concentrated initially on attempting to persuade the older leaders to change their minds, rather than on building an organisation which could be used to carry out an alternative strategy. At the beginning of the revolution, consequently, there was no effective contact between the younger nationalists and the forces of social revolution which rapidly emerged in the countryside around Jakarta.

Word of mouth soon took news of the surrender through the Jakarta countryside, and within days the sullen calm of the occupation had disappeared. Japanese troops were still present, but their numbers were small and they could no longer rely on the backing of the rest of the occupation forces. The revolt of the PETA in Rengasdengklok had made the first breach in their authority, and it rapidly widened. Later, on 16 August, a PETA unit in the town of Karawang disarmed the Japanese there, and fighting took place between Indonesians and Japanese on the road out of Karawang. A somewhat conservative local nationalist alliance emerged in the regional capital, Purwakarta, between the PETA, the police and the Indonesian civil service, and, showing rather more daring than its counterparts in Jakarta, it attempted to take over the town from the Japanese. The coalition was shattered, however, by a Japanese counterattack in the town in which the regent and the chief of police were arrested. Despite this temporary success by the Japanese, the entire Karawang plain was soon submerged in an uncoordinated popular rising.

As had been the case in the days around the Dutch surrender in 1942, the forces responsible for public order suddenly seemed powerless, and a swelling wave of lawlessness swept the countryside, motivated by the twin desires for revenge and for plunder. Japanese, of course, were a target of pent-up resentment for their recruitment of romusha and their confiscation of rice crops, and those who did not flee were soon captured and were, for the most part, killed. The few who survived generally did so by offering their services to a gang leader as military instructors. Local Chinese, too, perennially the victims during disturbances in the region, suffered once more from murder and robbery. One informant recalled that it was difficult in those days to find a drink of fresh water in the Klender area, close to Jakarta, as most of the wells were stopped with the bodies of slaughtered Chinese. Numerous local officials and police were also deposed, and many were killed, along with the occasional corrupt pawnshop official. The local toughs often took new names with revolutionary connotations: Bubar (abolish, disperse, overthrow), Ribut (rowdy), Gembel (poor) and Belah (split).[3] The victims were generally those seen as the local political and economic power-holders the outbreak of violence seems to have been devoid initially of any open political content, though it is hard to know what was uppermost in the mind of Bekasi's 'political' gangster Camat Nata when he killed an overseer from the private estate at Kranji and added his wife to his harem. The killers and plunderers on the whole, however, had no political programme with which to follow up their actions; they were opportunists rather than social revolutionaries.

A political programme came, rather, from the local bosses. These, of course, were not averse to making the most of opportunities for revenge and plunder, but as well-established features of the local social landscape, they were interested also in the longer term. They wanted a congenial political order, rather than simple chaos, and they were not especially pleased that the disorder of late August and early September should give new rivals a chance to emerge. Although the breakdown of public order gave them the chance to expand their power bases, they also needed to protect their positions from interlopers. Those who moved most successfully into this power vacuum were those who tied their personal ambitions to the establishment of the Republic and adopted the rhetoric and even the substance of nationalist demands.

The old style rural gang with its lack of formal organisation and its reliance on the formal authority of a jago had major limitations as a power base. It could only expand so much before its size made it unwieldy and vulnerable to fragmentation. A declaration of allegiance to the Republic, on the other hand, which required nothing in terms of actual obedience to the current Republican authorities in Jakarta, immediately reinforced a boss's authority by the power of association. It also gave the bosses an opportunity to move into the lower levels of the government hierarchy in the countryside, just as their predecessors in pre-colonial times had done. The deposing of local officials, therefore, was not simply an act of revenge for their misdeeds under the Japanese but a move to clear the way for a more lasting power base, and it did not matter especially what the political orientation of those officials might be. The Japanese-appointed Resident of Jakarta, Sutarjo Kartohadikusumo, for instance, was a prominent nationalist and a member of the committee which had drafted the Republican constitution, but he was arrested and detained for a time by local gangster-nationalists in Rengasdengklok.[4]

Many small-time gangsters simply assumed official titles. Bubar in Karawang, for instance, declared himself bupati and occupied the kabupaten office in the centre of town. Others, like Haji Masum at Cilincing and Haji Eman at Telukpucung, took over the offices of the local private estates. Some of the better-established local bosses, by contrast, often preferred to create their own institutions, thereby not only bypassing the official hierarchy which had been tainted by its role under the Dutch and Japanese but also ensuring their own control of it. Typical of these larger bosses was the redoubtable Haji Darip, boss of Klender. Born around 1900, he was the son of a well-known local boss called Gempur (literally, 'pound' or 'attack'). At the age of about eleven, he had been sent to Mecca to study and spent three years in Arabia before returning to Klender, where he joined the local staff of the state railways and became a prominent local boss and trader. He was a religious authority and was believed to have the power to distribute talismans conferring invulnerability on his followers. As mentioned above, he had been involved in the 1923 railway strike, and now he drew on his extensive following in the underworld to create a fief which extended from his headquarters in Klender north to Pulogadung, east to Bekasi and west to Jatinegara. With his *Barisan Rakyat Indonesia* (Indonesian People's Brigade), Darip exercised a tight control over traffic on the main road west of Jakarta and successfully blended brigandage with patriotism by plundering only those whose skin was too light (Chinese, Eurasians and Europeans) or too dark (Ambonese and Timorese). Those more fortunately coloured had only to pay two guilders in Japanese occupation currency and shout 'Merdeka!' ('Freedom!') to be allowed past. Southeast of Jakarta, the Cibarusa area was controlled by one of the most prominent pre-war bandits, Pa' Macem ('Father Tiger'), who commanded a large band of experienced fighters. He sold amulets for invulnerability at the mystically determined price of *f*11.11 and subjected his fief to a mixture of plunder, terror and self-determination.[5]

In the Tanggerang area, massacres of Chinese, both landlords and peasants, took place when the Japanese surrendered, as they had in 1942. It was not long, however, before people also began to turn against the local government officials who had been upholders of the area's inequitable social order under the Dutch and the Japanese. These officials were doubly damned in the eyes of the local people for having failed to embrace the Republic either quickly or enthusiastically, despite the fact that the central government's delay in asserting itself against the Japanese had hardly given them a great deal of leadership in this matter. In the weeks following the declaration of independence, increasing numbers of village heads, police and local government officials were deposed, and in the township of Sepaten, northwest of Tanggerang, an assistant-wedana was killed. When the local Indonesian police reacted forcefully in an attempt to keep matters under control, the situation exploded.

From a kampung near Curug, southwest of Tanggerang, Haji Akhmad Khaerun, calling himself *bapak rakyat* (father of the people), coordinated a people's revolt on 18 October 1945, in which the entire remaining formal apparatus of government was swept away. As a haji, a veteran of the 1926 PKI uprising in the Tanggerang area, and an expert in *ilmu kebatinan* (mystical practices), Khaerun was well-placed to draw on several strands of the underworld network of Tanggerang. He drew particularly on Muslim elements; his followers included many haji and his armed followers were referred to as the *lasykar ubel-ubel* (from *lasykar*, meaning troop, and *ubel-ubel*, the turban worn by pilgrims to Mecca). He was also closely associated with a peranakan Arab, Syekh Abdullah, leader of an armed band known as the *Barisan Berani Mati* (Death Defying Brigade) or *Lasykar Hitam* (Black Troop). There was, however, no overt Islamic orientation in the government which Khaerun set up on 21 October in the house of the regent of Tanggerang, the regent himself having been wise enough to plead illness and flee to Jakarta. The local KNI was abolished and in its place Khaerun installed a four-man directorate presiding over a simplified administrative structure. Lower officials were elected directly by the people; Japanese, Chinese and Europeans were imprisoned, driven out or killed, and communications with Jakarta were cut. Tanggerang became, to all intents and purposes, an autonomous state and there was nothing that the central government, twenty-five kilometres away in Jakarta, could do about it.[6]

Brigandage was an important element in all these local revolutions, as it had been in earlier disturbances. The declaration of independence, however, and the local bosses' espousal of the Republican cause had added something. First it defined the enemy, so that the victims of the revolution in those areas were not simply those individuals who had the misfortune to meet Haji Darip's band of toughs on a lonely road, nor simply those who had participated in or been associated with local oppression, but anyone of suspect nationality who happened to be present or passing through. On 19 October, for example, eighty-six Japanese naval guards were massacred at Bekasi while on their way to be interned at Ciater. On 23 November, too, a party of British Indian troops was massacred after their Dakota had crashed near Bekasi.[7]

A clear distinction began to emerge between nationalist gangsters such as Darip and Macem, and sheer opportunists such as Bantir, who for a while controlled Tambun, just to the east of Bekasi and who reportedly plundered all passers-by regardless of race. The experience of controlling territory, moreover, was a new one for the bosses—previously they had been forced to exist in the interstices of ommelanden society as controllers of labour but not of land—this new experience was all the more precious because much of the land had been private estates within recent memory. Men such as Darip and Macem, therefore, became not only aware of having moved into a position of greater power and responsibility than before, but also conscious of the external dimension of their power, conscious that their own fate was tied to that of the Republic. They thus looked with interest and expectation to the leaders of the Republic in Jakarta, and they found it difficult to comprehend those leaders' calls for calm and restraint.

It was at this point that the young nationalists who had spearheaded the declaration of independence remembered their former associates in the Jakarta underworld. The young nationalists were frustrated with the older leaders' caution and hesitation because it seemed to ignore the potential of the Indonesian people to fight for their own independence. The younger leaders believed in this potential not just for general ideological reasons—Japanese political training during the war had emphasised the power which came from having the correct spirit—but also because they themselves had seen this potential at first hand in their practical work with the labour groups during the occupation. As Sukarno and Hatta persisted in their obdurate refusal to call the masses out into the streets, the younger nationalists began to think increasingly of doing it themselves, and they went back into the kampungs of Jakarta and into the ommelanden to renew contacts.

The young nationalists began by sponsoring an organisation called BARA (*Barisan Rakyat*, People's Brigade), which was led by Maruto Nitimiharjo, Syamsuddin Can, Sidik Kertapati and M. H. Lukman. BARA was given the task of 'mobilizing the population' in general, but its primary work was with the local bosses whom its leaders already knew directly or indirectly, especially in the kampungs of eastern Jakarta. Each boss was told of the aims of the revolution, urged to enrol his followers as a unit in BARA, and left to work out the details of defending his small patch of independent Indonesia. Can was particularly active on the eastern fringes of the city, encouraging local leaders to declare for the Republic and establishing a network of contacts in the area, based particularly on the long-standing ties which Muhammad Yamin and his proteges had established before the war. These contacts were strengthened by the arrival of four youth leaders from Jakarta, Wahidin Nasution, Manaf Roni, Sidik Kertapati and M. H. Lukman. All four had been arrested by the Japanese, but they had been able to escape and they now sought the relative safety of the countryside. Wahidin and Manaf Roni went to the Cibarusa area, where they immediately made contact with Pa' Macem. Sidik Kertapati chose Bekasi and Lukman went to Karawang.[8] Their impact on the world of the ommelanden gangs was small at first, though events in Jakarta were soon to send them numerous allies.

1. The policies of the nationalist leaders in this critical period are discussed at greater length in R. Cribb, 'A Revolution Delayed: the Indonesian Republic and the Netherlands Indies, August-December 1945', *Australian Journal of Politics and History* 32, 1 (1986), 72–85.
2. The events around the declaration of independence have been extensively reported and widely discussed. Most authoritative is the account in B. R. O'G. Anderson, *Java in a Time of Revolution: Occupation and Resistance 1944–1946* (Ithaca, 1972), 61–84.
3. A. Kurasawa, 'Mobilization and Control: a Study of Social Change in Rural Java, 1942–1945' (Ph.D. dissertation, Cornell University, 1988), 611–612. 'De beteekenis der particuliere landerijen voor de economische en politieke verhoudingen in West Java', *NEFIS Periodiek* 2 (27 February 1946), 13, 20, 21, *Alg.Sec.I* I–21–1.
4. O. Bahsan, *Tjatatan Ringkas tentang PETA ('Pembela Tanah-Air') dan Peristiwa Rengasdengklok* (Bandung, 1955), 9–11, 38–48, 55–8; Anderson, *op.cit.*, 74; '"Rengasdengklok" Akibat Perbedaan Paham', *Kompas* 16 August; 1975, in *Guntingan Pers Ibu Kota 30th Kemerdekaan R.I.: menungkap kembali semangat perjuangan 1945* (Jakarta,

1975), 24–5; 'Merah Putih Berkibar 16 Agustus 1945 di Rengasdeng-klok', *Violeta* 169 (175), *ibid.*, 175–6; A. H. Nasution, *Sekitar Perang Kemerdekaan Indonesia jilid 1* [hereafter *SPKI* I] (Bandung, 1977), 333–7, 39; Nasution, *SPKI* II, 527; Dinas Sejarah Militer Kodam V/Jaya [hereafter Semdam V/Jaya], *Sejarah Perjuangan Rakyat Jakarta, Tanggerang dan Bekasi dalam Menegakkan Kemerdekaan R.I.* (Jakarta, [1975]), 126. Interviews: H. Moh. Damsjik, Bekasi, 17 January 1983; K. H. Hasboelah, Klender, 19 October 1982; K. H. Nurali, Babelan, Bekasi, 17 January 1983.

5. Notes on 23 Ind.Div. *Weekly Intelligence Summary* 3 (23 November 1945), Public Record Office, London [hereafter *PRO*], War Office [hereafter *WO*] file 208/1699; 'Report on T.K.R.' (AHK-BSO), 4 January[1946], *Alg.Sec.I*, 1–13–1; 'De beteekenis', 13, 21, *loc.cit.*; Troepencommando, Mededeeling van gegevens, 22 November 1945, *MvD/CAD*, HKGS-NOI, Inv.nr. GG 1, 1945, bundel 158, stuk 1797; Semdam V/Jaya, *op.cit.*, 70–71, 129; Radjimin Moenawi, 'Pengalamanku selama 1945–1950', *Perpustakaan '45* no 636/XXXII; Soeparno Soeriaatmadja, *Sedjarah Kepolisian dari Zaman Klasik sampai dengan Zaman Modern* (Jakarta, 1971), 106–8; Nasution, *SPKI* I, 334–5, 337, 340; D. H. Meijer, 'Over het Bendewezen op Java', *Indonesië* 3 (1949–50), 182–3. Interviews: H. Asenie, Jakarta, 2 September 1982.

6. *Republik Indonesia Propinsi Djawa Barat* (Jakarta, 1952), 151–2; H. Rosihan Anwar, *Kisah-kisah Zaman Revolusi: Kenang-kenangan Seorang Wartawan 1946–1949* (Jakarta, 1975), 43; Nasution, *SPKI* II, 525–6; M. Sewaka, *Tjorat-tjaret dari Djaman ke Djaman* (Bandung, 1955), 81; Semdam V/Jaya, *op.cit.*, 87–9, 94; Anderson, *op.cit.*, 169–70. Uittreksel uit inlichtingenrapport van C-23 Ind.Div., 3 & 4 December 1945, *MvD/CAD*, HKGS-NOI, Inv.nr. GG 1, 1945, bundel 292, stuk 2227 & 2280.

7. Sukarno to Rear-Admiral Maeda, 24 October 1945, Rijksinstituut voor Oorlogsdocumentatie—Indische Collectie, Amsterdam, doc.no. 011240–242; 'Pertemoean dengan oetoesan Repoeblik Indonesia tentang perihal kedjadian di Bekasi', 25 October 1945, personal archive of Shigetada Nishijima. AFNEI [Allied Land Forces, Netherlands East Indies] to ALFSEA [Allied Land Forces, South East Asia], 25 November 1945, and AFNEI to WO, 1 December 1945, *WO* 208/1699. Semdam V/Jaya, *op.cit.*, 126, 130–1; Nasution, *SPKI* I, 334, 339–40; A. J. F. Doulton *The Fighting Cock: being the History of the Twenty-third Indian Division, 1942–1947* (Aldershot, 1951), 280; Mochtar Lubis, *A Road with No End* (London, 1968), 83–4, 86–7.

8. 'Titik-titik (saat-saat) bersama Syarif Alwahidin Nasution dengan Idris P. Siregar sejak zaman mahasiswa Ika Daigaku sampai kepada tahun 1950' (typescript, Jakarta, 1980). Interviews: Maroeto Nitimihardjo, Jakarta, 16 February 1983; Kusnandar Partowisastro, Bogor, 20 January 1983; Johar Nur, Jakarta, 11 October 1982; Alizar Thaib, Jakarta, 28 February 1983; Nur Achmad, Cileungsi, 12 February 1983; Sidik Samsi, Jakarta, 17 November 1982; Moh. Hasan Gayo, Jakarta, 1 March 1983; Abdul Muis, Cileungsi, 9 February, 1983; K. H. Hasboelah, Klender, 19 October 1982.

5

Terror in Jakarta

The weakness of the Japanese and the absence of other outside forces enabled local bosses in the ommelanden to seize power there with relative ease. In urban Jakarta, on the other hand, the obstacles to social revolution proved to be insuperable. Many Jakarta residents later looked back with nostalgia to the days of late August and early September as a time when the city might have fallen into their hands and the subsequent protracted war of independence might have been averted, but the reality was that the concentration of Japanese forces in the city made a repetition of the achievements of Haji Darip and his like impossible. Indeed, the tide of revolution in Jakarta quickly appeared to turn against the nationalists, and this diverted the revolution there along a path to urban terrorism.

When the Japanese surrendered, Lord Mountbatten, as Supreme Allied Commander in Southeast Asia, ordered Allied prisoners of war and internees in the Indies to remain in their detention camps. This command was couched in terms of concern for the safety of the detainees, but Mountbatten's principal worry was that emerging internees would be unable on their own to restore Allied authority in the region and to maintain security and order. Pending the arrival of Allied troops, therefore, he preferred to leave formal responsibility for the region with the Japanese, whom he instructed to maintain law and order, on pain of courts-martial, until the Allies arrived. Many detainees, however, found this all too subtle and ignored the instruction to remain behind barbed wire. Within a few days of the surrender, Dutch civilians and soldiers began to appear on the streets of Jakarta and by the end of August there was a sizeable Dutch community in resumed residence attempting to restore the pattern of pre-war life.[1]

57

On first hearing the news of the proclamation of independence the Dutch had generally reacted with disbelief and amusement.[2] When, however, the Republic proved to have more staying power than expected, and after encounters with young nationalists revealed the depths of Indonesian hostility to a Dutch return, a number of irregular armed groups were formed, consisting largely of former KNIL (*Koninklijk Nederlands-Indisch Leger*, Royal Netherlands Indies Army) soldiers, to protect the Dutch and to take the first steps towards restoring Dutch authority in the city. The largest and best organised of these groups was the so-called Battalion X, operating from the barracks of the pre-war 10th KNIL Battalion on Waterlooplein (now Lapangan Banteng). It consisted largely of Ambonese, with Dutch and Eurasian commanders, whose tolerance and restraint had been tested by their three and a half years of imprisonment. It probably received the blame for a greater number of acts of violence than it was directly responsible for, but it was undoubtedly the most prominent of several groups of such vigilantes, Dutch, Eurasian and Ambonese.[3]

The tide against the Republic began to run more strongly when the Allied representative in Jakarta, Rear-Admiral Patterson, aboard a British ship anchored in Jakarta Bay, repeated Mountbatten's instructions to the Japanese to restore law and order in the city. The instruction clearly meant that the Japanese were to prevent the Republic from coming to power. Until this time the Japanese, often sympathetic to the Republic and concerned that crushing it might lead to a full-scale rebellion against them, had avoided taking strong measures against it. With Patterson on the spot, however, this was no longer possible. The Japanese authorities in Jakarta increased patrols in the city and issued a decree banning public meetings and the carrying of arms.

In the minds of the Republic's leaders, this was no more than was to be expected. They freely acknowledged, indeed they were somewhat overawed by, the abject weakness of the Republic as a state. Expecting the Allies to land in force any day, they saw no hope of organising effective resistance and concentrated instead on positioning the Republic and themselves to benefit from the global acknowledgement of rights of self-determination foreshadowed in the Atlantic Charter. This strategy, however, met with blank incomprehension outside the immediate leading circles of the Republic. Whereas supporters of the Republic had at first passionately desired to be led by their new state and had simply placed themselves at its disposal, as time passed many were increasingly convinced that if they did not defend their Republic, then no-one would, their leaders included.

Agreeing on what should be done, however, was more difficult. As soon as the studied inactivity of the government became apparent, the nationalist youth divided over the strategy they should follow. One group, led by Khaerul Saleh and Sukarni and including many who had been active politically before the war and several who had been involved in the kidnapping of Sukarno and Hatta, advocated disregarding Sukarno and seizing power at once from the Japanese in Jakarta. A former medical student, Eri Sudewo, led those who favoured a more cautious policy of conserving the lives of the young elite for a protracted struggle. The latter group was dominated by former students of the NIAS (*Nederlands-Indische Artsenschool*, Netherlands Indies Doctors' School) in Surabaya, which had merged with the Batavia medical faculty (*Geneeskundige Hogeschool*) to become the *Ika Daigaku* in 1943. This medical school had been the first institution of higher education to re-open on Java during the Japanese occupation, and it attracted a high proportion of able youthful members of the Indonesian elite. During the occupation the medical students kept open lines of communication with Hatta and with the non-cooperating socialist leader Syahrir, and in 1943 organised a students' strike against restrictive Japanese regulations. The leaders of the strike were arrested and expelled from the school, but the students remained one of the centres of intellectual resistance to the Japanese. In Dutch times NIAS students in particular had been subject to a strict academic regime which left them little time for politics, and in 1945 leaders of this group were suspicious that the radical articulate leaders of the pre-war nationalist youth movement were seeking to manipulate the students for their own political purposes.[4]

Matters came to a head shortly after the declaration of independence. In an emotionally charged meeting on 25 August 1945 at Prapatan 10, formerly the principal dormitory of the medical students, Eri Sudewo and Khaerul Saleh put the case for their respective viewpoints. The meeting ended in victory for Eri Sudewo, and the radical leaders Khaerul Saleh, Adam Malik, Wikana and Sukarni were, in the words of one informant, 'thrown out' of the building.

The more cautious youth of Prapatan 10 then proceeded with their policy of preparing for a protracted struggle by forming a unit of the newly-established BKR (*Badan Keamanan Rakyat*, People's Security Organisation). The BKR had been created by Republican authorities on 20 August, apparently as the nucleus for a future army. Afraid, however, that a formally designated army would attract Japanese suppression, or if it did not would be tarred in the eyes of the Allies with the stigma of association with the Japanese, the Republican leaders concealed the nature of the BKR by tucking it away as a branch of a charitable organisation for war victims. At the same time, although they created a central headquarters for the BKR under the former battalion commander of the Jakarta PETA, Kasman Singo-dimejo, they formally handed responsibility for establishing and supervising local BKR units to local national committees (*Komite Nasional Indonesia*, KNI) throughout the country.

Although many observers have subsequently accused the Republi-can government of culpably neglecting to establish an army, it ap-pears that the BKR represented a compromise between the immediate need to avoid antagonising either the Japanese or the Allies, and the longer term need to prepare for a possible revolution-ary war. For those youth of the Prapatan 10 group who found the activism of Khaerul Saleh at best pointless and at worst dangerous, the BKR was an attractive alternative. The new unit, moreover, which drew its initial membership principally from the Prapatan 10 group, was all the more attractive because its leadership included a group of PETA officers who had been attached to the headquarters of the Japanese 16th Army in Jakarta. These officers included Kemal Idris and Daan Mogot, as well as two of the leaders of the medical students' strike, Daan Yahya and Utaryo, who joined the PETA after their expulsion from the medical school.[5]

The Prapatan 10 unit was only one of many local BKR units set up throughout Jakarta. The largest of these, soon to be recognised as the BKR Jakarta, was that set up in a former school in Jalan Cilacap in central Jakarta and headed by Mufreni Mu'min. This unit attracted many of the former members of the Jakarta PETA battalion. Muf-reni had not been a senior officer in this battalion but his superiors, Kasman Singodimejo and Latief Hendraningrat were involved in national politics and the organisation of the BKR headquarters and this left them little time for local affairs. Mufreni, moreover, had a considerable following outside the PETA, having supervised a num-ber of elementary training courses for the Barisan Pelopor and other youth groups. The BKR Jakarta stood formally under the local Jakarta KNI with its chairman Mohammad Rum, one of the promi-nent younger leaders of the pre-war nationalist movement, in charge of security matters. The committee, however, had little effective control over the unit, which undertook street patrols and sporadic, low-key attacks on Japanese posts on its own initiative.[6]

Expelled from Prapatan 10, the radicals established themselves a few days later in the hostel at Menteng 31, which had been the venue for the Japanese-sponsored youth political training course during the occupation. They were joined there by a small number of medical students, including Johar Nur, Bahar Rezak and Wahidin Nasution, and on 1 September together formed the API ('Angkatan Pemuda

Indonesia', Youth Generation of Indonesia) to organise and coordinate the many other youth groups in the city. The API attracted a wide following, particularly amongst less educated youth groups, and immediately issued a manifesto calling on the people of Indonesia to seize arms, offices and businesses from the Japanese. The call to action was also broadcast over a radio transmitter which the young nationalists shifted constantly to avoid a Japanese raid. API members went out into the city to encourage these activities and spearheaded the takeover of the railway and tram systems, the telephone exchange, and an increasingly larger number of private and public institutions. Buildings all over the city sprouted Republican flags, and the words *milik Republik Indonesia* (property of the Indonesian Republic) became a common sight.[7]

The Jakarta underworld, or at least the politically aware sections of it, was a natural part of the API constituency. Pre-war contacts and the Japanese-sponsored political training programme in which several API leaders had been involved had given them personal links with underworld leaders. While the API was an appropriate vehicle to which local bosses might hitch their personal and political ambitions, the API in turn coveted the local bosses' ready-made organisations and access to weapons. The API thus soon developed close ties with men such as Imam Syafe'i, also known as Sape'i or Bang Pi-ie, one of the most powerful bosses in the Senen market area, whose OPI *Oesaha* [i.e. 'Usaha'] *Pemuda Indonesia*, Endeavour of the Youth of Indonesia) guarded the major intersection at Senen. It was also effectively sponsor of the BARA in the countryside, the word *bara* ('the glowing of an ember') being chosen to complement *api* ('fire'). For all its accumulation of firepower and its calls to arms, however, the API remained largely non-violent in its first weeks, except for a few minor clashes with the Dutch vigilantes. It still hoped that the resources it had marshalled would be deployed by the Republic itself, not by the API alone.

The crucial test of the Republic's leaders' determination not to fight came only in mid-September, when, in an attempt to force the leaders into action, the API leaders announced a mass rally. This was to be held in the Koningsplein, then commonly called by its wartime name, Lapangan Ikada[8] on 19 September, in defiance of the Japanese regulations against public assembly. Despite a ring of Japanese tanks and armoured cars around the square, people attended the rally not only from Jakarta but from the surrounding countryside. Haji Darip sent a strong contingent of his followers from Bekasi, and the crowd reached an estimated 200,000. For Sukarno and his cabinet, meeting that morning for the first time, this was alarming news. The stage seemed set for a massive confrontation between the Japanese and the people of Jakarta, likely to end in hundreds, if not thousands, of deaths and to sweep away the Republic in the process. After several hours of discussion,[9] Sukarno decided to address the mass meeting and left with some ministers in a presidential cavalcade. On his arrival he made a brief speech repeating his commands concerning peace and order, and then instructed the crowd to disperse. To the surprise of many, the multitude did so and the crisis was averted.[10]

The Ikada rally demonstrated the power of Sukarno's rhetoric, while making it conclusively clear that the President of the Republic was not interested at this stage in rousing his people for violent revolution. Despite the arrest of leading youth by the Japanese after the rally, the API accordingly moved into gear for an armed struggle, along with dozens of other *badan perjuangan* or *strijdorganisaties* (struggle organisations: both terms were used) which now sprang up throughout the city.[11] By this time, late September, the API had transformed the original small armed unit established to guard the Menteng 31 building into a sizeable force commanded by Alizar Thaib. Thaib, a medical student in Jakarta before the war, had joined the *Tokubetsu Keisatsutai* (Special Police, a kind of militarised police), under the Japanese, and he brought to the API not only military training but also many of the weapons and members of the Special Police.[12]

There is little value in presenting even a partial catalogue of the struggle organisations which fought alongside the API. Their numbers ran into the hundreds and they ranged from the quasi-military BKR, moderately well-armed and dominated by former members of the Jakarta PETA, to small and evanescent clusters of young people of both sexes, armed, if at all, with bamboo spears. They formed, typically, around existing social nuclei—local bosses, religious leaders, ethnic associations, semi-skilled labour groups, school groups, neighbourhood associations and the many youth groups set up by the Japanese—and they drew on the increased organisational experience and political mobilisation which people had gained during the Japanese period. Only a few, however, had definite political affiliations beyond their nationalism. What they had in common was a fervent desire to share the state of mind that was the Republic. The idea of the Republic and the idea of independence were inextricably intertwined; to act as a free Indonesian was to embody the Republic and the way to demonstrate one's acceptance of the Republic was to act and to exult in the freedom to act. When the Republic came under threat from Dutch vigilantes and Japanese troops, the urge to act was given a focus and throughout the kampungs of Jakarta the badan perjuangan prepared with whatever weapons were at hand for an armed confrontation.

The battle for Jakarta was a protracted, sporadic affair, with bouts of intense local fighting interspersed with periods of relative calm. Most bands were based deep inside one or other of the kampungs where no Europeans cared or dared to enter and where they were assured of adequate warning if an Allied patrol approached. The months of October and November 1945 became known as the *bersiap* period, so called from the warning cry 'Bersiap!' ('Get ready!') used to summon young nationalists for battle with an approaching hostile force. Other badan perjuangan had sanctuaries outside the city and made periodic visitations on the capital. The British Indian troops who arrived in Jakarta at the end of September were able to avoid appearing to be a screen for a Dutch return by stressing that their tasks were no more than to accept the Japanese surrender and release the internees. The Indonesians of the city therefore reacted piecemeal to individual encroachments on the Republic's authority without ever escalating the conflict into a general offensive intended to drive the enemy from the city. Clashes typically began with an 'incident', the hauling down of a flag, a quarrel in the market place, unexplained shots or the search of a kampung for weapons. After a few days of heavy fighting hostilities would die down, only to spring up elsewhere soon afterwards.[13]

Equally a target, however, were those Indonesians who were willing to return to the pre-war condition of subordination by providing services once more to the Europeans. There were certainly many of these. Hundreds of Dutch old colonial hands tell of the warm greeting they received from their old *babu* (nursemaid) or *jonggos* (manservant) or *tukang kebun* (gardener) when they finally came home from the camps. The radical nationalist youth reserved a special contempt for those willing to serve or sell to the Dutch. Lurid hand-drawn posters surviving from the period display a barely credulous indignation that any Indonesian should stoop to do so: 'Dogs of the NICA [Netherlands Indies Civil Administration]', they would ask in fury, 'Why have you abandoned your own people?'.

At the same time, pressure was put on the British and the Dutch in other ways. Waterside workers in Tanjung Priok went on strike, forcing the British to use large numbers of Japanese prisoners of war to man the docks. Workers in other fields refused to serve Europeans, while in the markets young nationalists enforced a ban on the sale of food to Europeans. Servants of Europeans were interrogated if they were thought to be buying food for their employers and were followed about to make sure that they did not take food into the predominantly European area of Menteng. There were also reports of Chinese being killed for selling food to British Indian soldiers.[14]

For the Europeans, however, the most disconcerting aspect of this time was the terror. The last months of 1945 were a time of robbery, looting, kidnapping and random street murders, in which Europeans disappeared, even in the heart of the city, to be found a few days later floating in one of the canals. The number killed was not as terrifying as the randomness and unpredictability of the killings, and the fact that most Europeans could not distinguish assassins from the general Indonesian population.[15] The recourse of the badan perjuangan to terror was partly a consequence of the difficult strategic imperatives of Jakarta. There was no single logical target for revolutionary activity in the city, no citadel which permitted control or domination of the city. There were useful targets, to be sure, like the radio station, and symbolic ones, like the Koningsplein and the palace of the governors-general, which the Dutch Lieutenant Governor-General H. J. van Mook seized as soon as he arrived in the city, but Jakarta was so spread out and so complex socially, economically and politically that it was not possible to think of a manageable list of key buildings to be seized. A few weeks earlier, of course, the revolutionaries had tried to sidestep this problem by painting *milik Republik* on virtually every substantial building in the city, but this had worked to secure their control no more than Dutch property rights in Batavia had kept out the Japanese. Only gradually did it become clear that the key to Jakarta was not buildings at all but empty space. It was the roads, canals and railways which gave Jakarta its sustaining links with the hinterland and held together those dozens of supposedly key buildings up and down the city.

Like all modern cities, Jakarta was a complex organism with a developed regional division of labour within its boundaries. At perhaps the simplest level, this division was reflected in the structure of its markets. Scattered across the face of the city, the markets had each their own specialties, this one for cloth, that for fruit, another for stolen goods. Services were similarly scattered: whether one was European, Indonesian or Chinese, one would go here to deal with the local authorities, there for health care, somewhere else to have a pair of trousers made, and somewhere again to be buried. One might never need to traverse the entire length of the city in one's lifetime, but one could seldom avoid travelling regularly from one part of it to another. Travel was the lifeblood of the city and the idiom of urban warfare in Jakarta was the idiom of controlling travel, not to prevent travel altogether, for without it the city would die, but rather to reserve the right of travel to some groups and deny it to others.

Thus it was that the railways and tramways of the city were the first institutions to be seized by the API even before the unsatisfactory Ikada rally. Not only did carriages become mobile hoardings for nationalist slogans—'Merdeka!', 'Indonesians demand 100 per cent

Independence' and the like—but the right of the mass of the population to travel free of charge on public transport was quickly seized and became, somewhat to the chagrin of public transport officials, a symbol of the achievements of the revolution for the common people. On main roads out of the city and at entrances to the kampungs, barricades sprang up, staffed by the badan perjuangan, to weed out those whose loyalty to the Republic could not be demonstrated or relied upon.

These endeavours to control the roads, however, were not effective against the Japanese or the Allied occupation forces. Whether attacking or defending, the Allies and the Japanese possessed armies vastly superior in training, discipline, experience and equipment to the rag-tag collections of nationalists which had assembled in the badan perjuangan. It was apparent from early in the revolution, therefore, that the Japanese and the Allies could command the broadest of open spaces in Jakarta. One thinks of boulevards and squares as offering people a place to assemble for mass action but the truth is more often that they offer the authorities an unobstructed line of fire. The transparent danger of an open air massacre at the Ikada rally scored itself so deeply on the minds of those present that in the course of the revolution the square was never again used for mass rallies. There was little, too, that nationalists could do to stop well-armed British troops from speeding up and down the main thoroughfares in their American jeeps and trucks.

To keep Jakarta Republican, however, it was not really necessary to keep the Allies or the Japanese in their barracks; rather it was necessary to prevent the restoration of Dutch civil life. The main thrust of action by the badan perjuangan in Jakarta, therefore, was to deny the freedom of the city to the returning Dutch civilians. This was done by a campaign of terror against Europeans. Strolling Dutchmen were hauled off the street and strangled or hacked to pieces, their bodies being dumped in one or other of the canals. The Molenvliet, a long canal running south from the old city, was a favourite place for such ambushes; so was the main road from Senen to Jatinegara. The already colourful vocabulary of Indies Dutch acquired a new word, *getjintjangd*, meaning hacked to pieces. Family houses were also surrounded at night and their European inhabitants massacred, and every effort was made to terrify living Europeans by the painting up of threatening slogans or by unusual behaviour of young Indonesians near residences to suggest that they had been marked out for imminent doom.

For this kind of warfare Jakarta was well-suited. With the exception of Menteng, a relatively new and prosperous suburb south of the Koningsplein, there was no solidly European quarter which could be ringed with guards and barbed wire for the protection of its inhabitants. The kampungs which reached up to the back yards of houses and the back doors of offices and which had once provided the labour which had kept Batavia running, now took assassins within striking distance of their targets. Indonesians themselves could do even less to avoid the unwelcome attention of the nationalist youth. It was urban guerrilla warfare in which the attack was carried out and the attackers gone long before help could be summoned and in which the purpose of the action was far less its strategic value than its psychological impact.

The Allies learnt the lessons of urban guerrilla warfare later than the nationalists, but they learnt them nonetheless. Indonesians were subject to counter-terror, not at the hands of unseen assassins but from the highly visible soldiers of the Battalion X. Their activities were often not much more than brutal buffoonery; members would ride around in trucks singing Dutch songs and shooting wildly, and would happily beat up or shoot any Indonesian who publicly displayed Republican colours. Stories abound of Indonesians who were forced to swallow the Republican cockades many, wore pinned to their chests. When these were made of cloth, little harm was done beyond humiliation, but when little flag badges were painted on pieces of metal snipped from tin cans they did considerable damage to Republican alimentary tracts. Other victims were hauled off for 'interrogation' and some of these were never seen again. British Indian troops added to the threatening atmosphere with various cases of theft and arson.[16] But the importance of these activities was that they challenged the nationalists' freedom of the streets with the same kind of terror as that which the nationalists bands used to restrict the Dutch.

Some members of the Battalion X were subsequently absorbed into the *Depot Speciale Troepen* (Special Troops Depot, later Special Troops Korps) of R.P.P. Westerling, which employed counter-guerilla terror on a far greater scale in South Sulawesi. On the whole, however, the style of terror exercised by the Battalion X became less significant with the restoration of Dutch police forces in the city. With the help of a growing network of informants, the Dutch were able to replace the relatively indiscriminate violence of the Battalion X with the careful targeting of suspects.[17] Surveillance, though admittedly far from completely effective, enabled them to preserve the openness of the city, while denying access to those whose past activities had brought them to the attention of the Dutch. It was a return, in many respects, to the style of police control which had been in force before the Japanese occupation.

The Allies also began to make the most of the geography of

Jakarta. A consequence of the kampungs' proximity to most places of European residence and work was that the kampungs themselves were physically separate from each other. Divided by distance, by main roads and by the European buildings themselves, the kampungs were vulnerable to the piecemeal operations of the Allies to clear the city of badan perjuangan sector by sector. In a typical operation, the British would surround a kampung and carry out a thorough search for weapons, as well as picking up anyone they happened to recognise from their wanted list. Many kampungs had to be dealt with in this fashion on several occasions, but the overall effect was to make the operations of the badan perjuangan less and less effective, leaving growing areas of the city largely secure for Europeans. This neutralising of the kampungs had a more than cumulative effect, for the terror campaign could hope to be successful in preventing a re-establishment of Dutch civil life only if it made Europeans thoroughly insecure in every part of the city. When that became clearly impossible, the campaign itself died and the API leaders began to think of moving out of the city to re-group and re-think their strategies in the relative safety of the surrounding countryside.

1. Interviews: Mr E. O. Baron van Boetzelaer, The Hague, 24 November 1981; Dr R. W. van Diffelen, Ridgewell, Essex, 8 January 1981; confidential interviews. See also W. F. Wertheim, *Indonesië: van Vorstenrijk tot Neo-kolonie* (Amsterdam, 1978), 118–21
2. See, for example, J. H. W. Veenstra, *Diogenes in de Tropen* (Amsterdam, 1947), 82–3.
3. *Republik Indonesia Kotapradja Djakarta Raya* (Jakarta, 1953), 548. *Soeara Merdeka* (Bandung) 16 September 1945; *Berita Indonesia* 29 September 1945; *Merdeka* (Jakarta) 3 October 1945 and *passim*. Aneta berichten uit Batavia, *Alg.Sec.* I box I, file 2. Interviews: Mr Moedjaswardi, Jakarta, 12 January 1983.
4. T. Karimoeddin, 'Pendidikan dokter jaman pendudukan Jepang (Ika-Dai-Gaku)', in *125th Pendidikan Dokter di Indonesia 1851–1976* (Jakarta, 1976), 26–30. Interviews: Johar Nur, Jakarta, 11 October 1982; T. R. Tjoet Rachman, Jakarta, 5 October 1982; Abu Bakar Lubis, Jakarta, 13 January 1983; Eri Soedewo, Jakarta, 14 February 1983; Soejono Martosewojo, Jakarta 1 March 1983; Daan Jahja, Jakarta, 7 August 1982.
5. Interviews: Kemal Idris, Jakarta, 16 August 1982; Abu Bakar Lubis, Jakarta, 13 January 1883; Daan Jahja, Jakarta, 7, 10 August 1982.
6. Nasution, *SPKI* 1, 307–9. Interviews: Mr Moh. Roem, Jakarta, 28 October 1982, Saleh Tedjakusumah, Jakarta, 15 September 1982; confidential interviews.

7. On youth activity and ideology, see B. R. O'G. Anderson, *Java in a Time of Revolution: Occupation and Resistance, 1944–1946* (Ithaca, N.Y., 1972), 118–9 and *passim*; *Berita Indonesia* (Jakarta) 29 September 1945; E. Chaeruddin, *Proklamasi 17 Agustus dan Pemindahan Kekuasaan*. [Jakarta, 1973], 37–43; S. Z. Hadisutjipto, 'Bara dan Njala Revolusi Phisik di Djakarta' (Jakarta, 1971), 18–21, 45; H. Rosihan Anwar, *Kisah-kisah Jakarta setelah Proklamasi* (Jakarta, 1977), 23–4; B. M. Diah, 'Transition of power and responsibility: the young generation is not prepared', *Prisma: the Indonesian Indicator* 6 (June 1977), 44; Dinas Sejarah Militer Kodam V/Jaya [hereafter Semdam V/Jaya], *Sejarah Perjuangan Rakyat Jakarta, Tanggerang dan Bekasi dalam Menegakkan Kemerdekaan R. I.* [Jakarta, 1975], 54–6; *Kenangan Sekilas Perdjuangan Suratkabar: Sedjarah Pers Sebangsa* (Jakarta, 1958), 254–6. Kusnandar Partowisastro, 'Sekelumit ungkapan sejarah dan peranan Gedung Joang Menteng 31 Jakarta Raya' (Typescript, Jakarta, 1978). Interviews. The medical students who joined the API included Johar Nur, Bahar Rezak, Wahidin Nasution, Manaf Roni and Mohammad Darwis.
8. Not a Japanese name, but a contraction of *Ikatan Atletik Djakarta* (Jakarta Athletics Association), an officially sponsored organisation which trained in the square.
9. For an account recapturing some of the atmosphere of the cabinet meeting, see Margono Djojohadikusumo, *Herinneringen uit 3 Tijdperken: een Geschreven Familie-overlevering* (Amsterdam, 1970), 120–4.
10. On the Ikada rally, see Anderson, *op.cit.*, 119–24; Mohamad Roem, *Bunga Rampai dari Sedjarah* (Jakarta, 1972), 67–73; Nasution, *SPKI* I, 337; *Operations of the Army in the South-western Regions: the Defence of Malaya and the Dutch Indies* [official Japanese war history series vol. 92, typescript translation of ch. 7, section 7, 'Outline of the indonesian [sic] independence question and the demobilisation'], 11; Adam Malik, *Riwayat Proklamasi 17 Agustus 1945* (Jakarta, 1975), 93–7.
11. The *Public Peace Intelligence Bulletin* no. 9 (25 September 1945) of the Japanese army on Java reported, 'Of late, there is an increasing tendency among Indonesians to collect and carry revolvers', private archive of R. Abdulkadir Widjojoatmodjo.
12. Interviews: Alizar Thaib, Jakarta, 28 February 1983; Johar Nur, Jakarta, 11 October 1983.
13. Semdam V/Jaya, *op.cit.*, 33–42, 46–53; A. J. F. Doulton, *The Fighting Cock: being a History of the Twenty-Third Indian Division, 1942–1947* (Aldershot, 1951), 242; Paleisrapport RVD, 25 August 1947 [sic], ARA, Archief Procureur-Generaal bij het Hooggerechtshof van Nederlandsch-Indië [hereafter *Proc.Gen.*] 863. Interviews. The atmosphere in Jakarta as felt by an Indonesian serving in the KNIL is reconstructed in Y. B. Mangunwijaya's novel, *Burung-burung Manyar* (Jakarta, 1981).
14. Uittreksel uit inlichtingenrapport van C–23 Ind.Div., 10 November 1945, *MvD/CAD*, HKGS-NOI, Inv. nr. GG1, 1945, bundel 292, stuk 1173; Ch. O. van der Plas, 'Memorandum: recent violence, especially

against Chinese', 1 December 1945, *Alg.Sec. I* box XXII, file 12; Troepencommando, Kort verslag over November 1945, *MvD/CAD*, Ass. Adj. Gen. III A, doos 224, bundel IV, Geh.Ink.nr.17; Troepencommando, Inlichtingenrapport, 27 November 1945, *MvD/CAD*, HKGS-NOI, Inv.nr. GG 1, 1945, bundel 158, stuk 2017; Uittreksel uit inlichtingenrapport van C–23 Ind.Div., 27 October 1945, *MvD/CAD*, HKGS-NOI, Inv.nr. GG1, 1945, bundel 292, stuk 494; van der Plas, Memorandum, 11 December 1945, *Alg.Sec. I* box XXII, file 12; RVD, *Wekelijksche Kroniek* no. 2 (15 December 1945), 1–2, Archief voormalig Ministerie van Overzeese Gebiedsdelen, *Rapportage Indonesië* file AI. 'Soeara Merdeka' 13 November 1945. *Operations of the Army*, 15–16; Soeparno Soeriaatmadja, *Sedjarah Kepolisian dari Zaman Klasik sampai dengan Zaman Modern* (Jakarta, 1971), 107; Nasution, *SPKI* I, 251.,

15. Johan Fabricius, *Hoe Ik Indië Terug Vond* (The Hague, 1947), 24; L. G. M. Jacquet, *Aflossing van de Wacht: Bestuurlijke en Politieke Ervaringen in de Nadagen van Nederlandsch-Indië* (Rotterdam, 1978), 180–2. Uittreksel uit inlichtingenrapporten, October, November 1945, *MvD/CAD*, HKGS-NOI, Inv.nr. GG1, 1945, bundel 292, various numbers; War Diary of HQ 23 Indian Division, 'GS' Branch, Java, October 1945, *WO* 172/7021; Troepencommando, Kort verslag over November 1945, *loc.cit.*; 'Opgave van gekidnapte en/of vermoorde personen (Nederlandsche onderdanen)', May 1946?, *Proc.Gen.* 480; 'Alphabetische lijst van nog vermiste pers. t/m 28 Februari [1946]', *Proc.Gen.* 480. *Min Pao* (Jakarta), 7 November 1945.,

16. *Ra'jat* (Jakarta), *passim*; *Merdeka*, *passim*; *List of Material and Personal Outrages and Injuries Perpetrated Against Indonesians by Dutch Soldiery in the City of Jakarta October-December 1945'* (Jakarta, 1946); *Kotapradja Djakarta Raya*, 548–50; Semdam V/Jaya, *op.cit.*, 46–8.,

17. For an undoubtedly coloured account of Dutch police techniques in Jakarta in this period, see Mochtar Lubis, *A Road with no End* (London, 1968).

6

The Lasykar World of Karawang

The API had sprung into being on a platform of mobilising Indonesian patriotism for a quick victory. Indeed, its raison d'être was a conviction on the part of the young nationalists and their underworld allies that no concessions need be made to secure that victory. Accepting the notion of a strategic retreat from Jakarta was thus a bitter pill and the API allowed itself to be pushed in that direction only with the greatest reluctance. The transparent failure of the terror, however, was not the only impetus to this shift. Sheer military pressure on the API units in Jakarta presented them with an increasingly clear choice between retreat and extinction. The repeated kampung sweeps by British troops robbed the API of its bases, its weapons and its manpower. British detention centres in Jakarta itself and on the coral islands of Jakarta Bay swelled with increasing numbers of API troops, including the API military commander, Alizar Thaib, who spent six months incarcerated on the island of Onrust in the company, amongst others, of the later leader of the PKI, D. N. Aidit.

What enabled the API to change its strategy while retaining its self-respect, however, was an increasing realisation that its forces were needed in the ommelanden. Pressure on the ommelanden came partly from British armoured columns which began to strike east and west of Jakarta in order to discourage local badan perjuangan from venturing into the city. More seriously, it came from Dutch troops based to the south of Jakarta. The Dutch troops which had arrived in Jakarta in late September 1945 had been greeted with such suspicion and hostility in the streets of the city that the British commander had posted them to the airfield at Cililitan, away from the urban centres where conflict appeared more likely. Largely out of sight of the various authorities in Jakarta, Republican and Allied, and under the energetic command of Lieutenant-General W. Schilling, these troops had then begun to set up a zone of Dutch control on the semi-urban fringe of the city. Consisting at first of Ambonese KNIL troops which had fought with the Allies against the Japanese, these units were soon joined by re-mobilised Dutch prisoners of war. They also boosted their strength by recruiting local Chinese for active military service, the first time this had been done, at least in recent Indies history. And in direct defiance of British instructions, they had begun to expand their perimeters on 11 and 12 October 1945 with a success-ful attack on Kebayoran. By mid-November not only had they apparently stabilised control of a broad swathe of countryside across the southern flank of Jakarta, but they had begun to push at the edges of the fiefs of Haji Darip and Pa' Macem, east of the city.[1] With the battle for Jakarta looking more and more hopeless for the API, the task of guarding the gains of the revolution in the ommelanden thus appeared increasingly urgent.

The first step in the API's strategic reorientation was the creation of a joint command organisation, the *Lasykar Rakyat Jakarta Raya* (People's Militia of Greater Jakarta), or LRJR, formed in Salemba in central Jakarta on 22 November 1945. The term *lasykar* was a relatively new one. Derived from an Urdu word, *lashkar*, it could be translated variously as soldier, militia or army. During the Japanese occupation, *Lasykar Rakyat* had been used on Sumatra as the In-donesian translation of *Giyugun* (Volunteer Army), the local equiv-alent of the PETA.[2] From late 1945 the word *lasykar* was applied generally to the groups previously known as badan perjuangan and was taken to reflect the greater internal organisation of those groups. The new name and new organisation thus represented not just a convenient rubric for cooperation but an acknowledgement of the need to organise for a protracted struggle. The LRJR was headed by another former medical student, Bahar Rezak, better known as Sutan Akbar, and gathered under its wings, along with the API, several hitherto independent badan perjuangan, such as the OPI, Imam Syafe'i's band of patriotic toughs from Senen, though the number of armed units still active in Jakarta was steadily shrinking.[3]

This, of course, was precisely the kind of military planning which the more cautious youth of Prapatan 10 had advocated three months earlier, but it brought no reconciliation between the two groups. The main obstacle initially was growing institutional inflexibility: by the time of the foundation of the LRJR, the army had begun to take clear internal shape and there was now no possibility that the new captains, majors and colonels would offer positions of power or influence within the military hierarchy to newcomers, whatever their antecedents. The term lasykar therefore quickly came to denote those armed groups which excluded themselves, or were excluded, from the official armed forces of the Republic. Personal antagonisms survived, too, from the acrimonious discussions of August 1945, as did differences in style. The lasykar continued to place greater emphasis on the elan of nationalist fighters, while the army paid greater attention to formal strategy, though not until later did these differences crystallise into sharp strategic disagreements.

The formation of the LRJR was only the first step in the API's strategic reorientation. Determined not to let Jakarta go easily, the LRJR hung on for another five weeks of pummeling at the hands of British troops. Finally in late December, the British decided to take full military control of the city. After warning Republican officials and receiving their acquiescence, the British launched Operation 'Pounce' on 27 December, throwing a cordon around the city, occupying important public buildings, seizing all cars in civilian hands, arresting the Indonesian police force and other Indonesians they regarded as 'extremists', and finally beginning yet another series of intensive kampung searches intended to break the power and organisation of the badan perjuangan in Jakarta for once and for all. By the end of the year, 743 people were in detention and the city was firmly in Allied hands.[4]

Operation 'Pounce' left the LRJR with little alternative but to recognise the untenability of its position in Jakarta and it finally abandoned its battered city headquarters for the rural hinterland, withdrawing to Karawang in the ommelanden where it established a new headquarters. Imam Syafe'i, in a characteristically dramatic gesture, rode out of the city on a white horse at the head of his followers, promising to return. Leading youth figures such as Khaerul Saleh and Sukarni had already left for Central Java, where they joined their mentor, Muhammad Yamin, in the growing popular movement which opposed the government's diplomatic strategy and saw in the nationalist communist leader, Tan Malaka, the spokesman for a more radical national policy of *perjuangan* or struggle. Humiliating though the retreat from Jakarta was, it provided a final tempering of the bonds between the young radical nationalists of Jakarta and the city's underworld.

The retreat from Jakarta presented lasykar leaders, army and gangsters alike with the problem of re-formulating a strategy for the new situation. The immediate aim of that strategy was beyond debate: it was the swift recovery of Jakarta from its Allied occupiers. Broadly speaking, moreover, there was a loose consensus that the defeat in Jakarta had been brought about by lack of preparation and lack of unity. Many were disappointed as well with the policies of the government for conciliating the Allies, but most were realistic enough to recognise that their own weaknesses had forced them to go along with that policy in evacuating Jakarta. It was generally accepted, therefore, that unity and determined preparation were to be the order of the day during the period of enforced exile.

The various groups were further united by their commitment to confronting the Allies in Jakarta, though confrontation implied different things to different groups. To some, particularly those in the army, it was a technical manoeuvre, the laying down of an armoured front line which would confine the Allies to the city and prevent those flying raids across the Karawang plain. It could be extended even to the laying of an economic blockade around the city in order to strangle the Dutch in their enclave. To others, it was a more political gesture. The nationalist movement in Indonesia had long recognised that much of its struggle was to raise the nationalist consciousness of the Indonesian people, to destroy the mental and intellectual dimension of colonialism. For young nationalists such as Khaerul Saleh, for instance, the act of confrontation itself was important as an assertion of the self-confidence of the Indonesian people, an assertion which demanded the participation of the entire Indonesian people. For others still, confrontation was valued for its expected effect on the Dutch. Intimidation was a well-established tool of trade of the Jakarta underworld, and the terror campaign of late 1945 had probably been the single most effective obstacle placed by nationalists in Jakarta against the restoration of Dutch civil life in the city. The confrontation of an entire city was wholly appropriate to the expanded vision of the Jakarta underworld.

The corollary of confrontation, however, was stalemate. As the two sides eyed each other warily across the ricefields and swamps east of the city, the no-man's-land between them hardened into a demarcation line between two worlds. To the west was the occupied city, where well-spoken nationalist leaders negotiated, refused to negotiate, chatted and quarreled with the Dutch and British. To the east was a lasykar world where flux and turmoil, self-reliance and daring, crowding and mutual suspicion were the order of the day. The demarcation line was always clearer on Allied maps than on the ground. The Allies needed a legal distinction between enemy territory, where they might shoot freely, and occupied territory where there could not. The line made some effort to follow geographical features, but it was defined by the pattern of Allied patrols, not by barbed wire or notices. For all its lack of clear definition, however, the demarcation line not only dominated the thinking of the lasykar but shaped the region's political and economic order.

The town of Karawang, where the nationalist youth leaders and their underworld allies had gathered, was a kabupaten town lying on the eastern bank of the river Citarum, some eighty kilometres from the capital. The entire length of the railway line and accompanying main road, which ran from the demarcation line on the edge of Jakarta as far east as Purwakarta, was scattered with lasykar groups of varying degrees of internal organisation and varying kinds of ties with other groups along this axis. In spite of this, Karawang became the de facto revolutionary centre of the region as the headquarters of the LRJR. The LRJR stood out from most of the other lasykar in its sense of political direction. Although Sutan Akbar was leader, with R. F. Ma'riful as his deputy, the organisation's policy was directed by a political council (*dewan politik*) consisting of Khaerul Saleh, Armunanto, Johar Nur, Kusnandar and Akhmad Astrawinata, with later also Mohammad Darwis, Syamsuddin Can and Sidik Kertapati, all of them capable and experienced young politicians. This council held to a policy of unremitting and uncompromising resistance to the Dutch and, keeping in close contact with politics in Central Java through Khaerul Saleh and Armunanto, it urged this policy on the central government.

The LRJR used the *Radio Republik Indonesia* (RRI) transmitter in Purwakarta to broadcast programmes supporting its policies each evening, and for a time it published a newspaper, *Godam Djelata* (Hammer of the Poor). Responsible to the political council was the *Bagian Penggerak Masyarakat* (Social Mobilisation Section), headed by Syamsuddin Can, as a continuation of his work in the Barisan Rakyat. This section was in charge of political education, both for the armed units of the LRJR and for the community in general. It was intended to create positive commitment to the policies laid down by the council, and was inspired partly by political education courses given to youth leaders during the Japanese occupation, and partly by ideas of political education derived from the Soviet Union and China. Political education, however, often had to be preceded by basic education. The high level of illiteracy in the Jakarta region, which was a legacy of the pre-war private estates, made it necessary to conduct classes first in reading and writing. Political education also included the building up of a system of village defence (*pertahanan desa*) to support the armed lasykar units and release them for combat duty.[5]

The core of the LRJR consisted of seven units (*pasukan*) of varying strengths scattered around the town of Karawang, together with a unit left behind in Jakarta under the command of Akhmad Indin Natapraja which received some support from the Republican mayor of Jakarta, Suwiryo, who maintained a somewhat shaky Republican municipal administration in the otherwise Allied-occupied city. A military council headed by Sutan Akbar and including the pasukan leaders—Nurdin Pasaribu, Sidik Kertapati, Harun Umar, Wim Mangelep, Sujono, Panji and Mawardi Lubis—organised coordination between pasukans. There were also numerous affiliated units throughout the region from Cibarusa to Subang which sometimes participated in decision-making.[6] Closely associated with the LRJR in Karawang, but never actually a part of it, was the *Pesindo* (*Pemuda Sosialis Indonesia*, Indonesian Socialist Youth), led by Wahidin Nasution, who had fallen out with Manaf Roni in Cibarusa and established himself and a Pesindo lasykar unit in Karawang.[7]

The LRJR saw itself in the same mould as such organisations as Bung Tomo's BPRI (*Badan Pemberontakan Republik Indonesia*, Revolutionary Organisation of the Indonesian Republic) which had fought the British fiercely in the Battle of Surabaya in November 1945, and its immediate goal was the launching of attacks on Jakarta to drive the Dutch and the British back into the sea. The LRJR itself did not have enough men or arms for this task and it accordingly sought the help of other armed groups in the region. Building on their early contacts with Haji Darip and Pa' Macem, its leaders forged a broad alliance with those local bosses they regarded as sufficiently patriotic: Darip and Macem, together with Kyai Haji Nurali in the swamps north of Bekasi, Camat Nata in Bekasi itself, and others like them. Haji Darip was all the more attractive an ally for having received a consignment of weapons from the East Javanese revolutionary leader Dr Mustopo as a contribution to the struggle in Jakarta. The LRJR also cooperated with the KRIS (*Kebaktian Rakyat Indonesia Sulawesi*, Indonesian People's Loyalty Organisation of Sulawesi), a largely Menadonese organisation which traced its origins indirectly to a paramilitary force formed by the Japanese Navy Liaison Office in Jakarta during the occupation. Its military wing was commanded by J. Rapar, a former associate of Syafe'i in the Jakarta underworld. After retreating from Jakarta, it had re-established its headquarters in Rengasdengklok.[8] The LRJR also cooperated with the Barisan Srikandi, a female combat unit based at Pucung near Cikampek.[9]

The region was sprinkled, too, with organisations calling themselves *Barisan Banteng*, *Barisan Rakyat*, and *Hizbullah*. The numerous Barisan Banteng (Buffalo Brigades) tended to be successor organisations to the Barisan Pelopor of Japanese times. They had little but sentimental connection with Dr Muwardi's central Barisan Banteng Republik Indonesia. The Barisan Rakyat grew out of Syamsuddin Can's work in the countryside around Jakarta shortly after the Japanese surrender, but many of these, too, had virtually no connection with the LRJR. An organisation called Hizbullah (Army of

God) had been established by the Japanese in December 1944 as a kind of auxiliary to the PETA, and a group of five hundred cadets received training in organisation and some military technique in a camp in Cibarusa in early 1945, though the organisation never approached the size or skill of the PETA. After the declaration of independence, the 'official' Hizbullah was affiliated with the Muslim political party, Masyumi, but there were numerous other groups which also used the name. The Hizbullah of Haji Nawawi in Cibarusa probably drew on cadets from a second Hizbullah training course, which had not yet graduated when the war ended, but its connection with the central Hizbullah is unknown and it apparently dispersed after Nawawi himself was killed in a clash with the Dutch in 1946.[10] Along the north coast and in the swamps around the mouths of the Citarum delta was a largely Batak unit from Tanjung Priok led by Matmuin Hasibuan, calling itself the ALRI (*Angkatan Laut Republik Indonesia*, Navy of the Indonesian Republic). Although it cooperated with Nurali in Babelan, it had little contact with the Cikampek regiment and none at all with the naval headquarters in Yogyakarta.[11]

Most of these units, however, cooperated to form the East Jakarta Struggle Headquarters (*Markas Perjuangan Jakarta Timur*), a kind of council which attempted to bring some coordination into the struggle with the Allies. The headquarters operated principally as a forum for the exchange of ideas and plans and never became a directing body in its own right. Lack of cooperation with each other was very much a part of the lasykar style. Having grown from the social world of small-scale local bosses answerable to no-one, whose position was always at risk, both from the authorities and from each other, lasykar units tended to be distinctly suspicious of each other. Survival in the urban jungle of pre-war Batavia had depended on finding a favourable modus vivendi with these threats, but in order to establish that modus vivendi the bosses were dependent on their own resources and on holding their followers together with varying mixtures of charisma, reward and threat. The lasykar in Karawang inherited many of these characteristics and, although their common opposition to the Dutch could bring them into alliance, it was not capable of welding them into a coordinated machine.[12]

The tension amongst the lasykar was partly economic. The population of the Karawang area was swollen by refugees from Jakarta and the surrounding countryside, for each time the Allies pushed back the demarcation line, the lasykar encouraged and sometimes forced the local population to retreat with them, so that the countryside between Jakarta and the demarcation line became seriously depopulated.[13] The large number of armed units in the Karawang area placed an extra strain on the region's resources as groups competed for living space and access to resources and communications. The LRJR maintained a lasykar police unit under Ukon Effendi to help keep order, but it operated mainly around the town of Karawang and was never enthusiastic about, for instance, taking Camat Nata to task for his continuous theft of buffalo and his kidnapping of women for his harem. Lack of weapons was a major problem and it was always tempting for units to try to increase their supply of weapons by disarming other units. Although a wide range of weapons was in use—field guns, bren guns, machine guns, mortars, rifles, pistols and grenades—only a few small units in the area came near to having a weapon for each of their soldiers. Many fighters were forced to continue using *bambu runcing* (bamboo spears). The Pesindo in Karawang owed its prominence partly to its possession of a grenade factory set up late in 1945.[14]

Weapons and ammunitions also formed a major element in the trade between Jakarta and Karawang. For all its apparent military impermeability, the demarcation line was highly porous when it came to trade. Here the pre-war underworld connections of the LRJR were particularly important, for weapons were obtained by theft, through smuggling from Singapore, and with the help of prostitutes in Senen who obtained them from Indian soldiers. Other Indian soldiers sympathetic to the Republic supplied weapons directly to the army and lasykar. The Indonesian Civil Police in Jakarta, who were licenced by the Allies to carry weapons, formed another useful link in the weapons trade. The underworld connections were also necessary to get the weapons out of Jakarta, for military equipment was a contraband item in the occupied city and the Allies gave a great deal of attention to attempting to stop the flow to Karawang. Equally contraband was the medical trade across the demarcation line, with wounded lasykar being treated secretly in Jakarta by doctors of the general hospital and medicines being smuggled out to Karawang to help the ill and wounded there. The clandestine trade extended into numerous fields, encompassing the sale of stolen goods in Senen, Glodok and the so-called *Pasar Atoom* (Atomic Market) in Harmonie, the plundering of Dutch warehouses, illicit trade in opium, and of course the rice trade between Karawang and Jakarta.[15]

One of the first measures which the lasykar took on their arrival in Karawang was to establish a blockade around the city to prevent the export of rice to Jakarta. The lasykar invoked the Japanese regulations which had banned people from carrying more than five kilograms of rice across residency boundaries, five kilos being considered a reasonable amount for personal use. All who crossed the demarcation line, whether by rail, by road or on foot, were searched to ensure that they did not exceed this amount. Since the entire population of Jakarta then numbered around 600,000, at least 90% of them Indonesians, it was clearly impossible for everyone to go out to Karawang to collect their own rice. There is not much evidence that the lasykar thought carefully before introducing this measure. A rice blockade was a singularly ineffective way to hurt the Dutch directly, since many Europeans preferred not to eat rice and those that did could generally afford to pay for rice imported from elsewhere in Southeast Asia. The lasykar loathed and despised Indonesians who were working for the Dutch, but it was those Indonesians who also had access to imported rice. The blockade was most likely to harm those Indonesians who were attempting to survive in the city without collaborating. These people were not identified as the target of the blockade, though the fact that they were its victims put pressure on the Allies as the prospect of starvation in Jakarta raised the spectre of food riots.

In the interests of ensuring that the ordinary people of Jakarta did not suffer, so it was said, the LRJR sponsored a trading organisation called the *Badan Ekonomi Rakyat Indonesia* (BERI, Economic Organisation of the Indonesian People), founded in Karawang on about 19 January 1946. BERI delivered rice to local people's cooperatives which had been formed originally during the Japanese occupation, and claimed that none of its shipments came into the hands of the Dutch or the Chinese. As the number of lasykar-sponsored trading organisations expanded, however, the flow of rice into Jakarta increased and the possibility of keeping it all in the right hands—always remote given the underworld traditions of the lasykar—diminished. The rice trade became an enterprise half-concealed at best, with all participants nodding at the blockade while seeking economic advantage for themselves.

The smuggling trade heightened mutual suspicion amongst the lasykar. The gangster leaders brought with them a tradition of distrust which had been prudent in the pre-war underworld but which severely hampered cooperation between nationalist groups in the area. Any group which traded across the border was automatically suspected by its colleagues of dealing secretly with the Dutch, whether or not it traded with Republican institutions such as the municipal rice purchase agency. The fact, of course, that the large number of traders crossing the demarcation line each day provided excellent cover for intelligence-gathering and other clandestine activities by all sides only exacerbated suspicions. Every organisation in the region had its own intelligence unit or units which not only infiltrated into occupied Jakarta but placed agents in other organisations in the region.

The Dutch, of course, were heavily present in the intelligence field. During the war, they had formed the NEFIS (Netherlands Forces Intelligence Service) as part of the Dutch military contribution to the Allied war effort. The NEFIS was also intended to take over political and criminal intelligence responsibilities in the newly-occupied areas of Indonesia prior to the re-establishment of normal civil government. In the disturbed political climate of the revolution, it was maintained as an organisation far longer than had been expected and after its commander, Colonel S. H. Spoor, was promoted to become commander of the KNIL in early 1946, it remained the foremost intelligence-gathering operation on the Dutch side.[16] In the Jakarta region it was under the command of a Eurasian, Colonel H. Agerbeek, who had reportedly worked with political intelligence in Banten during the 1926 uprising, had later fought in Aceh against a local rebellion, and had a reputation for highly efficient intelligence operations. Agerbeek exploited the constant flow of traffic across the demarcation line, and there was consequently a pervasive fear of spies amongst Republicans on the Karawang side. All travellers passing through the region were under suspicion. Although it was the Chinese who suffered most, even Indonesians found carrying something as trivial as a match box printed in the Dutch colours of red, white and blue could be imprisoned or killed for it.[17] When the Dutch issued their new post-war Indies currency in March 1946, the new notes quickly became potentially fatal *tanda NICA* (signs of the NICA) for those carrying them.

The search for tanda NICA in red, white and blue, however, was not simply an attention to trivia, an attempt to extirpate the presence of the Dutch even to the point of removing their juxtaposition of colours from Indonesian wardrobes and design palettes. Rather it was an aspect of the lasykar style which grew directly from the underworld culture of the Jakarta gangs. In the first place it was a search for the jimat, or charms, of Dutch agents. Most of the lasykar carried charms of one sort or another to give them invulnerability or extra strength in the struggle. Haji Darip gave his followers little bamboo spears imbued with magic power. The lasykar widely and correctly assumed that Dutch intelligence was operating in the area, and it seemed improbable to them that agents would venture across the demarcation line without some such spiritual protection. The searching of travellers was thus, from the lasykar point of view, an important part of maintaining local security. The humiliation and fear visited on suspects was also a simple way of carrying on that style of terror which had generally worked so effectively in Jakarta during the bersiap period. Conversely, when Republican currency or ORI (*Oeang* i.e. *Uang Republik Indonesia*, Indonesian Republican money) was issued in November, lasykar patrols attempted to ensure that everyone carried this *tanda Republik*. When the Republic issued its currency, it demonetised the Japanese occupation currency which had been circulating until that point. Then, in order to start circulation of the new currency, officials distributed a single paper rupiah to each of its citizens. In many parts of the Jakarta plain, the distribution of the new currency was turned into a nationalist ceremony and possession of one of the new notes thus took on much more significance than the mere buying power it represented.[18]

This attitude to charms was by no means exceptional. A sense of the supernatural pervaded the lives of many of the rank and file lasykar. The ghosts of the Japanese naval guards killed at Bekasi returned to haunt the spot, marching in formation across the bridge with their heads tucked neatly beneath their arms. Haji Darip put mercury into the veins of favoured followers as a guarantee of invulnerability. There was said to be a trade in human flesh: according to Dutch reports, Chinese youths and girls were kidnapped in Jakarta, often drugged with chloroform as they travelled by becak, and delivered for five hundred to a thousand guilders to one or other haji who gave their hearts to young lasykar to eat to increase their strength, and sold the remains as meat in the Pasar Atoom, Jakarta's principal market for goods of suspect origin.[19] The story sounds at first like black propaganda from the Dutch or Chinese, but even sources sympathetic to the Republic report similar cases of cannibalism for the sake of absorbing an enemy's spiritual strength.[20]

Even without the supernatural element, the atmosphere was tense. The young nationalists who kidnapped Sukarno and Hatta at the outset of the revolution to force them to declare independence in August 1945 had set a precedent, and for much of the revolution kidnapping one's political opponents was a common, though seldom effective, technique for attempting to change their minds. The various lasykar units of the Karawang plain regularly kidnapped each others members, sometimes for presumed economic or political misdeeds, sometimes merely to disarm them, and each kidnapping commonly led to a prolonged bout of counter-kidnapping and reprisal. Overshadowing the region, too, was the constant threat of an attack by the Allies—Bekasi had been devastated on 28 November 1945 in reprisal for the murder of the British Indian crew of an Allied plane downed near the town—and the Republic's own army, as we shall see, was an increasing threat. On one occasion, several hundred people attending the regular market in Rengasdengklok suddenly scattered in panic after someone began running through the crowd to catch up with the small gauge train which was just pulling out of the town station.[21]

On the other hand, the charged atmosphere of Karawang spawned a surprising literary outburst. There were of course the predictably banal campaign songs:

Ka Djakarta, ka Djakarta
Kita menjerboe!
Ka Djakarta, ka Djakarta
Kita menggempoer moesoeh!

To Jakarta, to Jakarta
We attack!
To Jakarta, to Jakarta
We strike the enemy![22]

But alongside these were the writings of the poet Khairil Anwar and the novelist Pramudya Ananta Tur. Both took a somewhat jaundiced view of the revolution, Tur contrasting the squalor and tedium of daily life behind the lines with the swagger of the troops at the front,[23] Anwar constructing terse sharp verses such as his well known 'Krawang-Bekasi':

We who now lie between Karawang and Bekasi
Can no longer cry 'Freedom' or bear arms.

But is there anyone who cannot hear our cries
Cannot glimpse us proudly advancing?

We speak clearly to you on lonely nights
When your breast feels empty and the clock on the wall is ticking.

We died young. All that remains is bones wrapped in dust.
Remember, remember us.

We did what we could
But our work is not yet finished, not yet anything.

We have already given our souls
Our work is not yet finished, four or five thousand deaths still have no meaning

We are just scattered bones,
But they belong to you.
It is you who will decide what value these scattered bones should have,
You will let our souls fly towards independence, victory and hope
Or towards nothing at all.

We do not know, we cannot say anything any longer
You are the ones who must say.

But we speak to you on lonely nights

When your breast feels empty and the clock on the wall is
ticking

Remember, remember us
Carry on, carry on our spirits
Guard Bung Karno
Guard Bung Hatta
Guard Bung Syahrir

We are now corpses
Give us meaning
Safeguard the borders between reality and dreams.

Remember, remember us
who are bones wrapped in dust
There are thousands of us lying between Karawang and
Bekasi.[24]

The lasykar had economic relations with regions to the east, into
Republican territory, as well as with Jakarta. Early in the revolution,
the LRJR received considerable amounts of Japanese currency from
Gatot Tarunamiharja, who had been attorney-general in the first
Republican cabinet and who had obtained a large amount of money
for the Republic, and later for various groups within it, from the safes
of Japanese banks in Jakarta. Even after this support dried up, they
continued to obtain a regular flow of donations from sympathetic
organisations and individuals in the interior. Thanks, moreover, to
the effective rail link via Cirebon and Purwokerto to Yogyakarta and
East Java, trade with other regions was possible. Most lasykar units
soon set up trading organisations to exchange the agricultural produce of the Karawang region, together with surplus goods from the
trade with Jakarta, for produce from the rest of island and imported
goods entering the country through ports such as Cirebon. From the
Jakarta region went rice, rubber, teak and cassava (*singkong*),
together with tyres, medicines and cloth from the occupied city, and
in return came cattle (for meat), sugar, weapons, and even tankers of
crude oil from the oil fields at Cepu, which was distributed to the
population as fuel. In addition to taking direct part in the trade itself,
the LRJR made a handy profit out of taxing all imports from the town
of Karawang at ten to twenty percent.[25]

If the Jakarta underworld had hoped to use the revolution to break
into positions of power, influence and authority in the Jakarta region,
they must have been fairly satisfied with what they had achieved by
mid-1946. Their followings were greatly expanded, they had moved
into government offices throughout the region and they had expanded the scope of their business operations to encompass a new
range of legitimate and semi-legitimate activities. These signs of

strength, however, were deceptive. The lasykar world of Karawang was in too many respects a product of the demarcation line. That line provided the focus which kept—only just—the antagonisms of the lasykar focussed outwards rather than on each other. It added nationalism to the range of forces which a local boss could use to recruit and retain his followers. And it opened up new economic opportunities which enabled the bosses to sustain their swollen followings. Without the demarcation line, little of this would have been imaginable. For all its rough, tumble and bravado, therefore, the lasykar world was fragile, a frontier society based on a border which could not be expected to last. The local bosses' prospects of preserving their newly-won pre-eminence after the revolution were slim.

1. Netherlands, Staten-Generaal, Enquêtecommissie Regeringsbeleid 1940–1945, *Verslag houdende de Uitkomsten van het Onderzoek: deel 8A en B, Militair Beleid 1940–45: Terugkeer naar Nederlandsch-Indië (Punt P van het Enquêtebesluit): Verslag en Bijlagen* [hereafter *Militair Beleid*] (The Hague, 1956), 606–7, 611; HQ SACSEA [Supreme Allied Commander in South East Asia], Director of Intelligence, 'Situation in Netherlands East Indies: paper no. 2', 27 October 1945, *WO* 208/1699; AFNEI to WO, 14 December 1945, *WO* 209/1699; Patterson to CiC-NEI, 1 November 1945, *FO* 371/53779. Troepencommando, Kort verslag over November 1945, *loc.cit.*; Troepencommando, Analyse van den militairen toestand op 26 October 1945, 29 October 1945, *MvD/CAD*, HKGS-NOI, Inv.nr. GG 1, 1945, bundel 158, bundel ZL 28/1/13; Territoriaal tevens Troepencommando, Inlichtingendienst, Verslag over Januari 1946, 8 February 1946, *MvD/CAD*, HKGS-NOI inv.nr. GG 8, 1946, ongen., maandverslagen inlichtingendienst, stuk 533 M; van der Plas to CiC-AFNEI, 27 November 1945, *Alg. Sec. I* box XXII, file 12. Sewaka *Tjorat-tjaret dari Djaman ke Djaman* (Bandung, [1955]), 84–5. Gani, 'Kebayoran Lama - tahun 1945', *Perpustakaan 45* no. 848/XLIII. Interview: H.Moh. Damsjik, Bekasi, 18 January 1983.
2. George Sanford Kanahele, 'The Japanese Occupation of Indonesia: Prelude to Independence' (Ph.D. dissertation, Cornell University, 1967), 128.
3. S. L. J. van Waardenburg, 'Lasjkar Rakjat van Java en Madoera', NEFIS Publicatie no. 15, 22 July 1946, *Proc.Gen.* 123. 'Dokumentasi ikhtisar singkat sejarah perjuangan rakyat pemuda Senen Shiku Jakarta-Raya dalam mempertahankan Proklamasi Kemerdekaan Republik Indonesia 17–8–45' (typescript, Dewan Harian 'Angkatan 45' Ranting Kecamatan Senen, 1982). Interviews: Johar Nur, Jakarta, 4, 7, 11 October 1982; Soepardi Shimbat and Batjo Marsad, Jakarta, 18 November 1982; Sidik Kardi, Jakarta, 15 February 1983; Kusnandar Partowisastro, Bogor, 20 January 1983.

4. Mountbatten to Cabinet Offices, 31 December 1945, *FO* 371/53769; Noel Buckley [British correspondent in Jakarta], 'British control Batavia', *WO* 208/1699; AFNEI to ALFSEA 30, 31 December 1945, *ibid.*; Troepencommando, Kort verslag over December 1945, personal archive of R. Abdulkadir Widjojoatmodjo; B. W. A. Plunket and C. M. Anderson [Foreign Office officials], 'Summary of events in Java since August 1945', *FO* 371/53775.
5. Interviews: Kusnandar Partowisastro, Bogor, 20 January, 3, 21 February 1983; Johar Nur, Jakarta, 11 October 1982, 13 April 1983; R. F. Ma'riful, Jakarta, 23 August 1982.
6. Interviews: Abdul Karim Abbas, Jakarta, 30 October 1982; Johar Nur, Jakarta, 11 October 1982; Kusnandar Partowisastro, Bogor, 20 January, 3, 21 February 1983; Hasjim K. Notokoesoemo, Jakarta, 11 November 1982; Sidik Samsi, Jakarta, 2, 17 November 1981. Lt.Kol. Z. Loebis, Overzicht situatie (van 19–12–48 tot 31–5–49), 7 June 1949, *MvD/CAD*, HKGS-NOI, Inv.nr. GG55, 1949, bundel 6323, C.M.I. Doc. No. 5434, 9. Johar Nur left the Jakarta region in late 1946 for medical treatment in Central Java and remained there in hiding until 1948.,
7. Syarif Alwahidin Nasution, 'Titik-titik (Saat-saat) perjuangan bersama Syarif Alwahidin Nasution dengan Idris P. Siregar sejak zaman mahasiswa Ika Daigaku sampai kepada tahun 1950' (Typescript, Jakarta, n.d.). Interviews: Johar Nur, Jakarta, 11 October 1982; R. F. Ma'riful, Jakarta, 6 October 1982.
8. B. R. O'G. Anderson, *Java in a Time of Revolution: Occupation and Resistance, 1944–1946* (Ithaca, N.Y., 1972), 261; Warsa Djajakusumah, 'Api '45 dari masa kemasa', in *Aku Akan Teruskan* (Jakarta, 1976), 103–5. Interviews.,
9. *Biografi Prof. dr. Moestopo* (n.p, 1980), 5; Titik Pamudjo, 'Nyimah Srikandhi "Patok Besi" yang buta huruf', *Perpustakaan 45* no. 701/XXXVI. Interview: K. H. Nurali, Babelan, Bekasi, 17 January 1983.
10. Sutrisno Kutoyo and Surachman, *Riwayat Hidup dan Perjuangan Mohammad Ramdhan* (Jakarta, 1977), 5; C. van Dijk, *Rebellion under the Banner of Islam: the Darul Islam in Indonesia* (The Hague, 1981), 72–6. Interviews: K. H. Nurali, Babelan, Bekasi, 17 January 1983; Abdul Muis, Cileungsi, 9 February 1983; Noer Achmad, Cileungsi, 12 February 1983.
11. Interviews: Moh. Husein Kamaly, Bekasi, 17 January 1983; K. H. Nurali, Babelan, Bekasi, 17 January 1983. Dinas Sejarah Militer Kodam V/Jaya, *Sejarah Perjuangan Rakyat Jakarta, Tanggerang dan Bekasi dalam Menegakkan Kemerdekaan R. I.* [Jakarta, 1975], 28, 73, 76, 136; W. I. Panji Indra et al., *Perjuangan Phisik Rakyat Jakarta Mempertahankan Proklamasi 17 Agustus 1945* (Jakarta, 1982), 13, 16; S. Z. Hadisutjipto, *Bara dan Njala Revolusi Phisik di Djakarta* (Jakarta, 1971), 51–66.
12. M. H. Kamaly, *Rakyat Bekasi Berjuang* (Bekasi, 1973), 6; Panji Indra et al., *op.cit.*, 16. Interviews: Sidik Samsi, Jakarta, 17 November 1982;

K. H. Hasboelah, Klender, 19 October 1982; K. H. Nurali, Babelan, Bekasi, 17 January 1983.

13. R. M. Soleh Suriaamijaya, 'Pasar Minggu waktu subuh', *Perpustakaan 45* no. 166/IX. Indonesian pamphlet, undated, ca 1946, *Proc.Gen.* 544. Pramoedya Ananta Toer, 'Revenge', translated by Ben Anderson, *Indonesia* 26 (October 1978), 49. Interviews: Abdul Muis, Cileungsi, 9 February 1983; H. Moh. Damsjik, Bekasi, 18 January 1983; K. H. Hasboelah, Klender, 19 October 1982; Suhendro, Bekasi, 19, 22 January 1983.,

14. Rachyadi, 'Kisah perjuangan antara tahun 1945 s/d 1950', *Perpustakaan 45* no. 165/IX; Sanusi W. S., 'Perjuangan 45 untuk pembangunan bangsa', *Perpustakaan 45* no. 823/XLII; Soemaatmadja, *op.cit.*, Didi Tanuwidjaja, 'Setitik ujung-pena pengorbanan bagi perjuangan bangsaku periode 1945–1950', *Perpustakaan 45* no. 289/XV. Van Waardenburg, 'Lasjkar Rakjat van Java en Madoera', *loc.cit.*. Interviews: Sidik Samsi, Jakarta, 1, 17 November 1982; Abu Bakar Lubis, Jakarta, 13 January 1983; Kusnandar Partowisastro, Bogor, 20 January, 3 February 1983; R. F. Ma'riful, Jakarta, 6 October 1982; Abdul Muis, Cileungsi, 9 February 1983; Noer Achmad, Cileungsi, 12 February 1983.

15. Trisnojuwono, *Peristiwa 2 Ibukota Pendudukan* (Jakarta, 1970), 5–6; M. Lubis, *A Road with No End* (London, 1968), 79–88; H. Rosihan Anwar, *Kisah-kisah Jakarta Menjelang Clash ke-I* (Jakarta, 1979), 38; *Sejarah Kesehatan Nasional Indonesia* (Jakarta, 1978) I, 105–7, 162–3. Territoriaal Commando, Contact Br.Ind. met T. R. I., 4 August 1946, *MvD/CAD*, HKGS-NOI, Inv.nr., GG1a, 1946, bundel 49, stuk 75; Hoofdcommissariaat van Politie, Batavia, P. I. D. [Politieke Inlichtingen Dienst], report, 11 November 1946, *Proc.Gen.* 3. Interviews: Kusnandar Partowisastro, Bogor, 20 January 1983; Abdul Karim Abbas, Jakarta, 30 October, 2 November 1982; Eri Soedewo, Jakarta, 14 February 1983; Moh. Husein Kamaly, Bekasi, 18 January 1983; M. Kooistra, The Hague, 22 November 1981; Jos Masdani, Jakarta, 30 July 1982; Sidik Samsi, Jakarta, 1 November 1982; Sofjan Tandjoeng, Jakarta, 13 September 1982.

16. L. G. M. Jaquet, *Aflossing van de Wacht: Bestuurlijke en Politieke Ervaringen in de Nadagen van Nederlandsch-Indië* (Rotterdam, 1978), 184; Spoor, Memorandum inzake de organisatie van de NEFIS bij de herbezetting van Nederlandsch Indië, 15 August 1945, *Alg.Sec.II* 672; Agerbeek to Koets, 16 June 1949, *Alg.Sec.II* 299; D. J. Ball, 'Allied Intelligence Cooperation involving Australia during World War II', *Australian Outlook* 32, 3 (1978), 301.

17. Toer, *op.cit.*, 50–53; Pramoedya Ananta Toer, *Ditepi Kali Bekasi* (Jakarta, 1957), 169; Lubis, *op.cit.*, 96; *Perang Kolonial Belanda di Aceh: the Dutch Colonial War in Aceh* (Banda Aceh, 1977), 224. Rachyadi, *op.cit.*; Dja'man, *op.cit.*; Wakrim Wahyudi, 'Kisah nyata perjoangan kemerdekaan Republik Indonesia, periode 1945–1950', *Perpustakaan 45* no. 504/XXVI. Dagelijks Overzicht Belangrijkste Inlichtingen (hereafter DOBIN) 8 April 1946, *Alg.Sec.I* box I, file 21, no. 4;

NEFIS, Rapporten van speciale agenten van Afdeeling IV, 28 April 1946, *Alg.Sec.I* box I, file 21, no. 5. *Berdjoeang* (Malang), 21 February 1946. Interviews: Abdul Karim Abbas, Jakarta, 30 October 1982; Suhendro, Bekasi, 22 January 1983; Hasjim K. Notokoesoemo, Jakarta, 11 November 1982; Ong Eng Die, Rijswijk, 12 December 1980; Abdulkadir Widjojoatmodjo, Rijswijk, 25 November 1981; M. Kooistra, The Hague, 22 November 1981. For a parody of the Indonesian spy mania, see *De Ronde Tafel* 1, 2 (31 August 1946).

18. R. Cribb, 'Political Dimensions of the Currency Question, 1945–1947', *Indonesia* 31 (1981), 124–5. Inlichtingendienst AMACAB, Inlichtingen Nr 10/Tj, 26 November 1946, *Alg.Sec.I*, box XXII, file 12.

19. DOBIN, 12, 15 April 1946, *Alg.Sec.I* I–21–4. Confidential interviews.

20. A. Hanifah, *Tales of a Revolution* (Sydney, 1972), 179; Anderson, *op.cit.*, 155.

21. Confidential sources.

22. DOBIN, 3 June 1946, *Alg.Sec.I*, I–21–4.

23. Toer, *Ditepi Kali Bekasi*.

24. Translated from the Indonesian original in H. B. Jassin, *Chairil Anwar: Pelopor Angkatan 45* (Jakarta, 1956), 66.

25. Suwarsih Djojopoespito, 'Yang tak dapat kulupakan', *Perpustakaan 45*, no. 317/XVI; Titik Pamudjo, *op.cit.*; A. H. Nasution, *Memenuhi Panggilan Tugas, jilid I: Kenangan Masa Muda* (Jakarta, 1982), 78. Interviews: Didi Kartasasmita, Jakarta, 18 June 1982; K. H. Hasboelah, Klender, 19 October 1982; Djilis Tahir, Jakarta, 30 November 1982; Saleh Tedjakusumah, Jakarta, 15 September 1982; Sidik Samsi, Jakarta, 1 November 1982; Mr Sumarno, Jakarta, 21 March 1983; Hasan Gayo, Jakarta, 1 March 1983; Johar Nur, Jakarta, 7, 11 October, 12 November, 3 December 1982; R. F. Ma'riful, Jakarta, 6 October 1982; Kusnandar Partowisastro, Bogor, 20 January, 3 February 1983.

III
WORLDS IN COLLISION

7

Lasykar and the Republican State

The failure of the lasykar to create a political and economic base secure against the changing fortunes of the war of independence was matched by their failure to win a place in the Republican state. For all their commitment to independence and their success in seizing power in the Karawang region, the lasykar never made themselves more than marginally useful to the Republican state. Rather, the Republic rapidly accumulated a list of reasons why it should wish to be rid of them sooner or later. At the top of this list was the Republic's attitude to law and legality.

In seizing government in the ommelanden and replacing local officials, the Jakarta underworld had followed an old path towards incorporation in the state. In pre-colonial times, the central authorities would have had little hesitation in acknowledging new realities of local power and accepting the newcomers into the loose hierarchy of officialdom. The bureaucracy and the structure of government, however, had changed enormously during colonial rule, becoming both more aristocratic and more expert.[1] By the end of the colonial period, there was a clear, self-conscious and powerful bureaucratic elite which held together the colonial state. Entry into and promotion within this elite depended no longer on brute military prowess of the kind the local bosses could show, but on family connections and administrative competence.

As an agent of Dutch and Japanese rule, as we have seen, this elite had become thoroughly unpopular in many parts of the country, and this unpopularity helped the local bosses in Karawang and elsewhere to spearhead social revolutions against them. In the chaotic weeks which followed the declaration of independence, it seemed that the pre-colonial path to political power was at least partially re-opened.

The Resident of Jakarta, Mas Sewaka, who had established his headquarters in Subang in the offices of the P. & T. Lands, attempted initially to establish his authority by officially appointing successful local bosses to the positions in local government which they had in effect seized. Bantir of Bekasi, for example, became a *mantri* (local police official), Nata and others like him became *camat* (sub-district heads), and in Karawang even Pa' Bubar was able to get some sort of recognition for his claim to be bupati. In Cibarusa, meanwhile, the redoubtable Pa' Macem was installed as chief of the local police by none other than Sukarno who passed through the region campaigning for the Republic in late 1945.[2]

The Republic, however, quickly came to realise its dependence on the old bureaucracy. Although the Republic unquestionably had the support of the vast mass of the people, the nationalist movement itself was badly disorganised as a result of internal division, Dutch repression and the peculiar combination of suppression and channelled institutionalisation introduced by the Japanese. Unlike the communist parties in China and Vietnam or the Congress in India, Indonesian nationalists lacked the autonomous political organisation which might have enabled them to create their own state apparatus or merely to take charge of the state and begin moulding it in their own image. Without the bureaucracy in 1945, the Republic would have been barely perceptible as an entity. The price of bureaucratic support, however, was the protection of bureaucratic privilege and practices and an end not just to the violence of the social revolutions but to the subversion of bureaucratic procedure by ad hoc appointments at the local level.[3] This did not mean, of course, that the Republic could move everywhere to re-establish the old order, but it placed the Republic firmly on the side of the bureaucracy and gave notice that whatever power the local bosses might exercise in Karawang and elsewhere was temporary and on sufferance.

It was not long in fact before the Republic moved to rid itself of some of those uncongenial new officials it had recruited. Early in 1946, the army launched an operation in Cibarusa to crush Pa' Macem, who had shown himself to be one of the more rapacious of the local bosses. Macem himself managed to escape what was apparently a fairly heavy-handed operation, but Macem's political adviser from the old API, Manaf Roni, was killed in the fighting. Pa' Bubar in Karawang, too, was removed. Units of the army's Purwakarta regiment descended on the town and surrounded Bubar in the kabupaten office. Bubar was apparently told at first that this was just a routine army exercise, but soon realised something was afoot. When, however, according to army accounts of the incident, he and his lieutenants attempted to leave the building under the cover of magically-assumed invisibility, the military proved too clear-sighted and he was gunned down as soon as he emerged.[4]

The Republic's incipient hostility to the underworld was compounded by its emerging strategic vision. From the start, the Republic endeavoured to present itself as the legal successor state to the Netherlands Indies. One of its first acts was to acknowledge the validity of all Netherlands Indies laws and regulations, except as far as they were changed by new decree. And subsequently the new state made only piecemeal adjustment to these inherited laws, leaving a wholesale revision of the colonial legal order until well after the formal transfer of sovereignty from the Dutch in 1949. Internationally, too, the Republic's spokesmen presented a careful legalistic argument that the failure of the Netherlands to defend the Indies adequately against the Japanese in 1942 had forfeited Dutch sovereignty, making the 1945 declaration of independence a legal act in international law. The full range of colonial-era sanctions against criminals thus remained in force, at least in principle.

The Republican leaders remained convinced, moreover, that the Republic could never secure its independence in the face of international hostility and they accordingly modified their nationalist programme so that it was acceptable to great power interests. Perhaps the most striking demonstration of this flexibility was the accession of Sutan Syahrir as prime minister on 14 November 1945. The Republic's constitution adopted three months earlier had envisaged a presidential style of government, the office of the president largely inheriting the prerogatives of the colonial governor-general, with some more democratic influences from the United States model. Sukarno, however, who had been elected president on 18 August, was deeply distrusted by the Allies for his apparent collaboration with the Japanese during the occupation, and it became clear that his position as chief executive was a diplomatic liability for the Republic. Syahrir, by contrast, was an eminent nationalist and had not worked for the Japanese. His political following, however, was limited to a small urban elite, while Sukarno's popularity with the mass of the Indonesian people made it inconceivable that he could simply be removed from office. The prime ministerial system, therefore, was introduced without precedent or constitutional justification as a measure to preserve Sukarno's presidency while giving executive authority, and the power to deal with the Dutch, to Syahrir and his associates.

The demands of international opinion, of course, were not satisfied by the mere accession of Syahrir. The new prime minister realised from the start that the Republic would have to guarantee the relative freedom of international capital to operate in Indonesia.[5] Bitter controversy still exists over just how much freedom Syahrir was prepared to concede in practice. On the one hand, it can be argued that he was simply using a ploy to extract formal international recognition of the Republic's sovereignty and that once secure he intended to carry out a radical nationalist restructuring of the economic order. On the other hand, it can be argued that Syahrir's minimum programme was all he had to offer, that he proposed leaving the county in international capitalist hands—perhaps American rather than Dutch, in recognition of changes in the global economic order—in exchange for a nominal independence which would be of benefit only to the educated apparatchiks of his own Socialist Party who might expect to hold senior government positions in the new state.

Whatever the reality of Syahrir's long-term intentions, however, the Republic made considerable play of its commitment to preserving and protecting foreign assets within its territory. This had both specific and general implications for the Republic's relations with the Jakarta lasykar. In the first place, it meant that the lasykars' potentially lucrative control of the former private estates of the Karawang plain was at risk. The Republic had inherited formal ownership of the private estates from the Japanese, along with a host of other enterprises seized during the occupation. While it was unlikely that the Republic would find any strategic need to restore the smaller, formerly Chinese-owned estates to their former owners,[6] larger agribusinesses such as the British-owned P. & T. Lands in Subang and the Dutch-owned Michiels-Arnold-Landen in Cibarusa were prime candidates for restoration.

More generally, too, the preservation of foreign capital had to be accompanied by a restoration of law and order in the countryside. The estates and plantations of rural Java were vulnerable institutions, dependent on tractable, poorly-paid labour and on secure means of transporting produce to depots. As the lasykar were to show in the later guerrilla campaigns of 1948 and 1949, estates and plantations could not operate in conditions of lawlessness and social disorder. Whatever the attitude of the lasykar to the Republican state, therefore, the state itself had good reason to be distinctly unenthusiastic about them.

What tended to protect the lasykar in the face of these reasons for the Republic's hostility, of course, was the fact that the Dutch were also distinctly unenthusiastic about them. For all that the Republic asserted its international respectability and its continuity with Dutch rule and practice, it clearly needed to argue more than that it could do as well as the Dutch. And the argument which it could present was that it could rule without generating the antagonisms and consequent social and political tensions which the Dutch presence clearly engendered. The Republic's leaders gained useful political capital with the British on the various occasions in late 1945 when they were able to appeal successfully for order. While the topmost levels of the Republic presented a conciliatory face to the world, it suited them that gangs of toughs in the ommelanden and elsewhere should be making it clear that they would tolerate no-one but the Republican government as their masters. Indeed, the main disincentive for a Dutch attack across the demarcation line to Karawang was not the resistance that the lasykar were likely to offer on the front line but the daunting task of trying to police the area once it was conquered. And in Dutch business circles, there was said to be a small but growing feeling in favour of acknowledging Indonesian independence quickly on generous terms simply in order to ensure a minimum of destruction of Dutch plant and property on the ground. By 1946, thus, the Karawang lasykar had largely failed in their attempt to break into legality as local rulers in the new political order and they found themselves uncomfortably cast as spoilers in local government, manoeuvred into a position where their usefulness to the Republic was largely a function of their expendability.

Nor was the Republic really interested in the lasykar as a part of its armed forces. The creation of an army had been strikingly low on the agenda of the new Republican government. As we have seen, the government was convinced that the way to survive was to trim its sails to the rising wind of Allied power, and it refrained from establishing an army which might have suggested hostile intent, forming instead the decentralised and ambiguously-named BKR. Even when it became clear that the Republic needed more to protect itself than a conciliatory international profile, and the BKR was officially transformed into an army, the TKR (*Tentara Keamanan Rakyat*, People's Security Army) on 5 October 1945, the government paid relatively little attention to establishing it as an effective military arm of the Republic. Sukarno's first minister of defence, appointed only on 7 October, was a former PETA officer, Supriyadi, who had led an uprising of PETA soldiers in Blitar in early 1945. His appointment was a clear gesture of distancing the Republic from the Japanese, but since Supriyadi had not been seen since the uprising and was probably dead, his appointment was more symbolic than practical.[7]

With the accession of Syahrir, the government did begin to pay serious attention to military development. Syahrir appointed as minister of defence his deputy, Amir Syarifuddin. Together with Sukarno and Hatta, Syarifuddin formally shifted to Yogyakarta a few days after Operation Pounce on 4 January 1946, but he had effectively based himself in Central Java since Syahrir took office. Syahrir, in his capacity as prime minister and foreign minister, stayed in Jakarta together with a few officers closely associated with the diplomatic process, while Syarifuddin took charge of the defence effort in the interior. Syarifuddin was one of the most fascinating and ambiguous figures to emerge during the revolution. A Batak from North Sumatra, he was raised as a Muslim but converted later to Christianity while in Dutch imprisonment for his nationalist activities. He received his secondary education in the Netherlands and later graduated from the Law School in Batavia. Even before he graduated, he was active in the nationalist movement, joining the Partindo and gaining a reputation for powerful mass oratory. Alarmed by the prospect of a Japanese invasion, he cooperated with the Dutch colonial government in the department of economic affairs shortly before the Second World War. He was fond of Western music and art and was highly regarded in liberal Dutch circles as a genial and capable intellectual of the kind to whom the Dutch could safely hand over power in Indonesia. It was he whom Idenburg chose to head an underground resistance movement during the Japanese occupation, set up with funds from the Dutch shortly before the Japanese arrived. For this he was imprisoned and condemned to death by the Japanese; only the personal intercession of Sukarno saved him. Sukarno appointed him minister of information in his first cabinet while he was still in prison in Malang and it was reportedly a Dutch request to the Japanese which had him released from detention and brought back to Jakarta. On his release, he founded the *Parsi* (*Partai Sosialis Indonesia*, Indonesian Socialist Party), which soon fused with Syahrir's (*Partai Rakyat Sosialis*, Socialist People's Party) to form the *Partai Sosialis*. He remained on good terms with his pre-war Dutch colleagues and strongly reinforced the international acceptability of the Syahrir cabinet. Since the 1930s, however, Syarifuddin had been under Dutch police surveillance as a suspected member of the illegal PKI, which had been banned since the risings of 1926–27. He himself subsequently confirmed his membership in 1948, a few months before he was killed for his part in the Madiun uprising.[8]

Amir Syarifuddin's task was to make the army an effective and responsive tool of government policy. This meant an army which was capable of holding the Dutch at bay in order to keep them interested in negotiations. Few on the Republican side had any illusions that the Dutch would be negotiating if the Republic's military strength were not forcing them to do so. The army also had to be sufficiently disciplined and skilled to carry out the tasks assigned to it by the government, for this was an important part of the government's effort to show the world that the Republic was a responsible and effective state. On 19 November, only days after he took office, Syahrir ordered all Indonesian armed forces, regular and irregular, out of the city to reduce the likelihood of further clashes. Given Jakarta's tradition as a channel for contact with the outside world, it was logical that international negotiation over Indonesia's future should take place there. Jakarta in fact became known during the revolution as *kota diplomasi*, the city of diplomacy. The price of diplomacy, however, which was the price for keeping the British well-disposed and the Dutch willing to negotiate, was the Republic's acquiescence in increasing Allied control of the city in the name of law and order. Syahrir's intention was to put an end to the street-fighting which was casting Republican forces in the role of enemies of the Allies, to create a peaceful atmosphere for the conduct of negotiations and to demonstrate his own political authority. Within the city, then, a Joint Contact Committee of British officers and Indonesian municipal leaders, including the new Republican mayor Suwiryo, and Mohammad Rum, was established to coordinate cooperation between the Indonesian police and the British.[9] Army units in the city accepted the instruction, half grudgingly, half relieved to have responsibility for abandoning the city taken out of their hands, but the API/LRJR forces refused out of hand, withdrawing only much later, when they faced military defeat in the city. For Syahrir and his colleagues, the incident showed that the lasykar were neither obedient nor capable, and added to the reasons for planning their eventual destruction.

The inability of the lasykar to make themselves militarily essential to the Republic is perhaps not surprising. The army itself, despite all its weaknesses and deficiencies, was developing an expertise in that area which quickly overtook that of the lasykar. Perhaps a well thought-out theory of guerrilla warfare would have salvaged the lasykar from strategic irrelevance, but the lasykar themselves were too wedded to the notions of confrontation and frontal warfare for such ideas to take hold. The failure of the gangs to capitalise on their illegality, however, is more puzzling. If one examines the role of gangsters in the Vietnamese and Chinese revolutions, one finds that their successes, spectacular in some cases, arose not from their mobilisation of pre-revolutionary power bases for military action but from finding new opportunities for lucrative criminality in the revolutionary environment. The Binh Xuyen of Saigon, for instance, whose career otherwise parallels that of the Jakarta lasykar in many respects, grew wealthy on a massive opium, gambling and prostitution empire in Saigon and Cholon.[10] The substantial military power of the Binh Xuyen was financed by these new enterprises and, more important, the organisation became an essential part of the political order through the substantial sums of money it channeled to political power holders. In China, similarly, gangs in control of the opium trade virtually bankrolled the Nationalist government in the 1930s, making it impossible for the government to attempt to suppress them.[11]

The Jakarta lasykar, by contrast, found relatively little scope for diversifying their economic base. There seem to have been two reasons for this. First, the wealth to be plundered from the Karawang landlords was clearly limited and was soon seized, while the takings to be had from plundering traffic on the roads and railways out of Jakarta were probably not much more than before the war. Desperate for funds to support their increased following, the lasykar leaders eagerly took part in trade across the demarcation line. Profitable though this trade could be, however, there was little scope for monopolisation. Rice, the main commodity flowing into Jakarta, was too readily available from other sources and too abundant locally to be controlled tightly. Indeed, this applied to much criminal activity in general. Although the Republic insisted on legality, it was so unable to enforce its laws that criminality of many kinds—smuggling, extortion and so on—became commonplace. Without a powerful state to keep amateur criminals out of business, the scope for organised crime was more limited. The proceeds of the Karawang trade, thus, were invariably swallowed up by the day-to-day needs of the lasykar themselves. There was no question of the lasykar channeling funds back to Central Java to win favour and influence there.

Part of the problem for the lasykar, thus, seems to have been the lack of a lucrative commodity for trade. Gangster empires everywhere appear to flourish best when trading in illegal drugs, whether alcohol, marijuana, cocaine or opium. The lasykar could make use of none of these. Alcohol and marijuana, both long established in the archipelago, were legal drugs not traditionally supplied from the Karawang region. Cocaine might have been harvested from the naturalised coca bushes which grew wild in parts of West Java, but the lasykar totally lacked the technology to develop this resource. There is no evidence even that they were aware of the existence of the raw material, and in any case no significant market existed for the product at this stage. As for opium, that was in the hands of the Republican government itself and there was no prospect at all of the lasykar prising it away from them. From the Dutch and Japanese official opium monopolies, the Republic had inherited about twenty-two tonnes of raw opium and three tonnes refined, as well as the staff and equipment from the opium factory in Jakarta.[12] Although opium sales were limited at first to established addicts, served through the existing distribution network of opium shops and related opium dens, the Republic's straitened financial conditions soon led it to begin trading opium outside its own territory to Jakarta and Singapore. For the most part, however, those actually involved in this clandestine trade were either government officials or members of the Chinese business community. There was no thought of allowing indigenous criminals to take charge of the trade.

Probably a greater difference between the Jakarta underworld and its more successful counterparts in Vietnam and China lay in their respective social structures. Whereas the Vietnamese and Chinese gangs possessed a sense of corporate identity, an abstract notion of the organisation to which they belonged, the Jakarta gangs seem to have remained creatures of their founders and leaders. The frequent changes of name which the gangs underwent reinforces this sense of organisational flux. The *bapak* of each gang might, or more commonly might not, accept some degree of collegiality in decision-making, but the major decisions were his alone and the gang had no existence independent of him. Delegation under such circumstances was difficult, for handing responsibility to another amounted to shedding authority, which was fatal in the long term. The Jakarta underworld therefore had little scope to develop even the glimmerings of a corporate structure in which a range of complex operations might be coordinated for a common purpose.

The structural reasons for government hostility to the lasykar were reinforced by political antagonisms. Although their primary focus was the Jakarta front line, the lasykar of the LRJR took a lively interest in Republican politics in central Java, where debate over the desirable extent of concessions to the Dutch had emerged as the dominant political issue. Not until March 1946 did Syahrir make definite proposals to the Dutch, but by the beginning of the year all could see that his strategy involved trading off a watering-down of nationalist ideals for the preservation of the Republican state. Within the Republic, opposition to the government quickly grew. A rallying point for this opposition was provided by the veteran nationalist communist leader Tan Malaka who had returned to Indonesia from exile in 1942 but had only revealed his presence to the public after the declaration of independence. Tan Malaka argued that international recognition was irrelevant, that there was therefore no reason to make concessions to the Dutch to obtain it, and that Indonesia could defend itself if only Indonesians were united in uncompromising opposition to the enemy. He argued further that they could only be united behind a programme of basic nationalist demands which included no diminution of the Republic's sovereignty and an elimination of foreign economic power from Indonesia.

Tan Malaka avoided creating a formal party organisation of his own, aiming instead to provide an alternative national leadership. His principal backing, however, came from a small group of

nationalist politicians associated with the Japanese occupation, notably Akhmad Subarjo and Mohammad Yamin, who had been
pushed aside in the rise to power of Syahrir and Syarifuddin. Tan
Malaka was also actively supported by many of the API members
who had retreated from Jakarta to Central Java in late 1945, including Khaerul Saleh, Sukarni and Armunanto. Khaerul Saleh and
Armunanto, in particular, also kept in close contact with the LRJR in
Karawang, which was one of the 133 organisations to send delegates
to a popular front congress held at Solo on 15 and 16 January 1946 at
which the Persatuan Perjuangan (Struggle Union), or PP, was
formed as a coalition of all those opposed to the government's
diplomatic activities.[13]

Karawang was too far from Yogyakarta to affect the balance of
power between the government and the opposition, but the lasykar
also conducted a vigorous campaign against the negotiations in the
area they controlled. They sponsored a drama group which toured
the countryside presenting the perjuangan message and carrying a
large poster showing Syahrir as a dog wearing a crown, symbolic of
Dutch sovereignty, and eating human faeces. Other lasykar maintained that the letters of Syahrir's name stood for *Saya yang akan
hancurkan Republik Indonesia Raya* ('I am the one who will destroy
the great Indonesian Republic').[14]

Occasionally, too, the lasykar were able to obstruct the government's plans directly. In January 1946, for example, the TKR had
agreed with the British to take responsibility for evacuating Allied
prisoners of war and internees, generally referred to at the time by
the acronym APWI, from the interior to Jakarta. It was an important
agreement, amounting to de facto recognition of the TKR by the
British, and demonstrating to the world that the Republic had a
humanitarian concern for the victims of Japanese internment, but the
army was unable to evacuate more than a few hundred of the
thousands of prisoners involved, partly because of political pressure
in Central Java, but partly also because it could not guarantee the
safety of the internees at the hands of the Lasykar Rakyat during the
passage through the Karawang area.[15]

Whereas Tan Malaka's thought, however, foreshadowed a radical
transformation of Indonesian society, the LRJR's ideology remained
a pure and rather simple nationalism and it tried to make something
of a virtue of being unaffiliated with any political party. This was due
partly to the lack of education amongst LRJR rank and file. Many
lasykar were unable to read and certainly could not understand Tan
Malaka's complex thought. Even relatively well-educated lasykar
who visited Central Java to attend PP rallies described Tan Malaka's
lengthy lectures as boring. But there was also a basic difference in

Khaerul Saleh (*Album Perjuangan*)

A.H. Nasution (*Album Perjuangan*)

Amir Syarifuddin (*Album Perjuangan*)

Dr Mustopo (*Album Perjuangan*)

Guarding a bridge on the east Jakarta front, 1946 (*Album Perjuangan*)

Destruction at Bekasi after an Allied attack, 19 December 1945 (Ipphos)

Members of the central Biro Perjuangan, from left to right Commodore S. Suryadarma, Lt-Gen. Urip Sumoharjo, Maj.-Gen. Sutomo (Bung Tomo), General Sudirman, Maj.-Gen. Sakirman, Rear-Admiral Nazir, Maj.-Gen. Jokosuyono. (*Album Perjuangan*)

Haji Darip in 1978 (Titiek W.S.)

Members of the KRIS (Ipphos)

Imam Syafe'i, gang leader from Senen and
later Minister of State for People's Security

The surrender of Panji's gang (the late Lt-Col. K. Bavinck)

Lasykar armed with bamboo spears

orientation between the two, reflected partly in the fact that Tan Malaka apparently never visited the Jakarta front to encourage the LRJR or to see the fighting at first hand. Tan Malaka's plans were focussed on winning control of the Republican state, reversing the policies of Syahrir and using the government to lead the Indonesian people against the Dutch and towards a new society. The LRJR, although vitally interested in changing government policy, had no real interest in central state power and simply focussed on direct action to drive out the Dutch. Their propaganda made occasional reference to egalitarian slogans such as *sama rata sama rasa* (on the same level, feeling the same) but these, like their infrequent appeals for a more ascetic, puritan approach to matters such as gambling and prostitution, were peripheral to the political orientation of the Jakarta lasykar and indeed fell largely on deaf ears.[16]

Although the PP won the support of a wide range of individuals and organisations in the Republic, and succeeded in forcing Syahrir's resignation on 28 February 1946, its success was short-lived. It was a coalition held together only by a broad general opposition to the extent of Syahrir's concessions, and many of its members distrusted the political ideas and ambitions of Tan Malaka and his supporters. It was also outmanoeuvred politically at the last minute, for Syahrir was sworn in again as prime minister with the slightly more broadly based cabinet, which he used to break up the unity of the PP. Then, once the immediate challenge had been repelled, he moved swiftly to arrest Tan Malaka and his closest associates, Khaerul Saleh, Sukarni and Gatot Tarunamiharja, whose store of Japanese currency had helped to finance both the PP and the LRJR.[17] Armunanto, Haji Usman Debot and a few lesser figures were able to make their way to Karawang to join the LRJR, strengthening the government's hostile view of the lasykar.

Although the lasykar hold on Karawang continued to grow stronger in the course of 1946, therefore, their future appeared increasingly bleak as the niches open to them in an independent Indonesia progressively closed. Nonetheless, their intervention in central politics, unproductive though it was in this instance, later provided a life-line. Though Republican forces assembled to destroy the LRJR, this external connection, as we shall see in chapter twelve, gave it an extended lease of life.

1. H. Sutherland, *The Making of a Bureaucratic Elite: the Colonial Transformation of the Javanese* **Priyayi** (Singapore, 1979).

2. Soeparno Soeriaatmadja, *Sedjarah Kepolisian dari Zaman Klasik sampai dengan Zaman Modern* (Jakarta, 1971), 108; Nasution, *SPKI* II, 527; Sewaka, *Tjorat-tjaret dari Djaman ke Djaman* (Bandung, [1955]), 88–89. Interviews: H. Moh. Damsjik, Bekasi, 18 January 1983; Abdul Muis, Cileungsi, 9 February 1983; Moh. Husein Kamaly, Bekasi, 17 January 1983; Camat Nata, Cibitung, Bekasi, 26 January 1983; Noer Achmad, Cileungsi, 12 February 1983.

3. On the Republic's efforts to woo the bureaucracy, see B. R. O'G. Anderson, *Java in a Time of Revolution: Occupation and Resistance, 1944–1946* (Ithaca, N.Y., 1972), 113–115.

4. Interviews: Alizar Thaib, Jakarta, 28 February 1983; Abdul Karim Abbas, Jakarta, 30 October 1982; Moh. Husein Kamaly, Bekasi, 18 January 1983; K. H. Nurali, Babelan, Bekasi, 17 January 1983; Didi Kartasasmita, Jakarta, 18 June, 30 August 1982; Sumarna W. S., Bluburlimbangan, Garut, 6 September 1982; Ngadam Suradji, Karawang, 1 November 1982; Sidik Samsi, Jakarta, 17 November 1982; H. Moh. Damsjik, Bekasi, 18 January 1983; confidential interview.

5. See S. Sjahrir, *Our Struggle* (Ithaca, 1968).

6. On this question, see Twang Peck Yang, 'Indonesian Chinese Business Communities in Transformation, 1940–50' (Ph.D. dissertation, Australian National University, 1988), chapter 4.

7. On the establishment of the TKR, see U. Sundhaussen, *The Road to Power: Indonesian Military Politics 1945–1967* (Kuala Lumpur, 1982), 5–9.

8. J. Ingleson, *Road to Exile: the Indonesian Nationalist Movement 1927–1934* (Singapore, 1979), 174, 185, 212, 214; Wolf, *op.cit.*, 96–7; Anderson, *op.cit.*, 37, 413–4; P. J. A. Idenburg, 'Het Nederlandse Antwoord op het Indonesisch Nationalisme', in H. Baudet and I. J. Brugmans, eds, *Balans van Beleid: Terugblik op de Laatste Halve Eeuw van Nederlandsch-Indië* (Assen, 1961), 130–1; T. B. Simatupang, *Report from Banaran: Experiences During the People's War* (Ithaca, N.Y., 1972), 78–83; A. E. Lucas, 'The Bamboo Spear Pierces the Payung: the Revolution against the Bureaucratic Elite in North Central Java in 1945', (Ph.D. dissertation, Australian National University, 1981), 308–9; J. Leclerc, 'Underground Activities and their Double: Amir Syarifuddin's Relationship with Communism in Indonesia', *Kabar Seberang* 17 (June 1986), 72–98. Interviews: Dr P. J. Koets, Ellemeet, Zeeland, 24 November 1980; Dr R. W. van Diffelen, Ridgewell, Essex, 8 January 1981.

9. *Mohamad Roem 70 Tahun: Pejuang-Perunding* (Jakarta, 1978), 50; The, *op.cit.*, 115.

10. A. W. McCoy, *The Politics of Heroin in Southeast Asia* (New York, 1972), 109–126.

11. J. Marshall, 'Opium and the Politics of Gangsterism in Nationalist China, 1927–1945', *Bulletin of Concerned Asian Scholars* 8, 3 (1976), 19–48.

12. For details of Republic's opium transactions, see R. Cribb, 'Opium and

the Indonesian Revolution', *Modern Asian Studies* 28, 4 (1988), 701–722.

13. Interviews: Johar Nur, Jakarta, 11 October 1982; R. F. Ma'riful, Jakarta, 6 October 1983. On Tan Malaka and the Persatuan Perjuangan, see B. R. O'G. Anderson, *Java in a Time of Revolution: Occupation and Resistance 1944–1946* (Ithaca, N.Y., 1972), 269–95.

14. DOBIN, 5 February 1947, *Alg.Sec.I* I–21–4. Interviews: Sidik Samsi, Jakarta, 17 November 1982; Johar Nur, Jakarta, 9 March, 10 April 1983.

15. See minutes of a meeting held at Headquarters Allied Forces, Batavia, 9 January 1946, S. L. van der Wal, ed. *Officiële Bescheiden Betreffende de Nederlands-Indonesische Betrekkingen 1945–1950* (The Hague, 1971–1989) [hereafter 'OBB'] III, 163–5; Verslag van het bezoek aan Djokjakarta van Major West op 3 maart 1946, *ibid.*, 513; van Mook to Clark Kerr, 7 March 1946, *ibid.*, 517. *Antara* (Yogyakarta), 7, 15 February 1946.

16. S. L. J. van Waardenburg, 'Lasjkar Rakjat van Java en Madoera', NEFIS Publicatie no. 15 (22 July 1946), p. 10, *Proc.Gen.* 123; Hoofdcommissariat van Politie, Batavia, P.I.D., Mededeeling van gegevens no. 43, 12 December 1946, *Proc.Gen.* 3; HQ 23 Ind.Div., Weekly Intelligence Summary no. 9 (9 January 1946), *Proc.Gen.* 549. H. Rosihan Anwar, *Kisah-kisah Jakarta Menjelang Clash ke-I* (Jakarta, 1979), 26. *Repoeblik* (Cirebon), 17 December 1946. Interview: R. F. Ma'riful, Jakarta, 6 October 1982.

17. Anderson, *op.cit.*, 310–19. Interview: Johar Nur, Jakarta, 11 October 1982.

8

New Rivals: The Rise of the Army

Not only did the lasykar attract the general hostility of the Indonesian state, they quickly found institutional rivals in the form of the Indonesian army. Many lasykar had chosen deliberately not to join the army, and tension quickly rose between the two, for each challenged in many ways the other's legitimacy. The lasykar, with their deep roots in the local societies from which they had sprung and their impeccable revolutionary credentials, tended to regard a professional army as mercenary and too close in spirit to the colonial armies of the Dutch and Japanese. Army leaders on the other hand, with their professional military training and official status, tended to look on the lasykar as undisciplined and troublesome amateurs, whose insistence on their own autonomy wasted men and equipment and prevented effective military planning. Disorganised and ineffective though it was in its early days, the army soon became influential enough first to exclude the Jakarta lasykar from full official recognition and powerful enough eventually to crush them.

As we have seen, the Republican government paid relatively little attention to its armed forces in the first weeks of the revolution, and much of the practical construction of the army was left therefore in the hands of military officers themselves, within first the BKR and then the TKR. The creation of an army high command was largely the work of a retired major from the KNIL, Urip Sumoharjo, and a group of younger officers who had received military training for the so-called CORO (*Corps Reserve Officieren*, Reserve Officers Corps) at the Bandung Military Academy established after the fall of the Netherlands in 1940. These officers had absorbed not only Dutch strategic thinking but also conventional Western views of the army as a professional military organisation whose place should not be usurped by civilians. While they were gratified by the general appreciation of the importance of military struggle, they were disturbed by the chaotic nature of military organisation and the vast number of armed organisations outside the formal institutions of the armed forces. They focussed their energies, therefore, on the task of turning the loose allegiance of a multitude of TKR units into an effective military hierarchy.

It was not an easy task. Mufreni's Jakarta BKR, like other units throughout the country, had duly become a part of the TKR on 5 October 1945. At the time it was still fighting in the streets of Jakarta, but like the API found itself under increasing pressure from the British. When Syahrir ordered Indonesian armed forces out of the city on 19 November, therefore, Mufreni recognised a convenient opportunity to cut his losses and to consolidate out of reach of the superior Allied forces. He took his troops through Karawang to the town of Cikampek, lying at the junction of the railway lines from Jakarta, Bandung and Cirebon and established a new headquarters there.

Cikampek had originally fallen within the responsibilities of the TKR's Purwakarta unit, commanded by Sumarna. This unit had originally taken over responsibility for the Karawang area from the Purwakarta battalion of the PETA and it was units of this battalion which had seized power in Rengasdengklok on 16 August before the declaration of independence. The battalion, however, had been unable to capitalise on this early success. The PETA units had allowed themselves to be disarmed by the Japanese soon after, and had retreated to the hill country around Purwakarta, leaving a power vacuum on the coastal plain which was quickly filled by the local bosses. Thereafter, the unit concentrated on the Bandung front not far to the south, and intervened only sporadically on the plains below.[1]

Mufreni's unit continued active recruiting in Jakarta for some time after its retreat. Recruits were taken by train to Cikampek and were given a brief training at headquarters before being formed into sub-units and assigned to one or other of Mufreni's deputies. Some recruits from Jakarta, aware only that they had signed up to join 'the struggle' (*perjuangan*), were apparently surprised, though not disconcerted, to discover that it was the army that they had joined. The regiment was also reinforced by a unit of volunteers from East Java which arrived in early 1946 under the command of Banu Mahdi, and by regular temporary tours of duty of Central Javanese units, including one reportedly under the command of Suharto, later president of the Republic.[2]

Like the lasykar, Mufreni concluded from the experience of the fighting in Jakarta that the most pressing need in the independence struggle was for unity. From the start, therefore, he set out to establish good relations with the lasykar. He had none of the formal military training of the CORO officers, but instead cultivated an image of bravado and self-assurance which was a much swifter and more effective way to win and keep his followers' obedience than relying on formal qualifications or rank. He was known, for example, to direct military operations sitting in a chair in the middle of the main road. With the help of able and popular deputy commanders such as Sadikin and Sambas Atmadinata, Mufreni held his forces together in much the same way as other lasykar leaders and had no particular need to assert over the lasykar the military authority he would not have liked to see asserted over himself. Thus, without unduly antagonising the lasykar, he was able to establish posts in their territory: an operational headquarters under Sadikin across the river Citarum west of Karawang at Lemahabang, five battalions stationed at various points along or near the railway line from the demarcation line to Cikampek, and a police and intelligence unit headed by Adel Sofyan which penetrated occupied Jakarta. Adel Sofyan had worked in the propaganda department (*Sendenbu*) under the Japanese and later became chief of staff of the Cikampek regiment.[3] Mufreni was even able to persuade the lasykar for a time to accept the authority of Sadikin as front commander to coordinate all units, army and lasykar, actually on the front line. Although his troops took part in a major lasykar attack on Dutch positions in Cililitan on the night of 31 December 1945, he was in a position to discourage the lasykar from carrying out further, premature attacks.[4]

Under Mufreni's general supervision, the east Jakarta front turned from a demarcation line defined solely by Allied patrols to something more closely approaching a front line. The KNIL troops of Major-General Schilling, after gaining control of Pasar Minggu, Cililitan and Kebayoran had followed the tried and effective techniques they had learnt in numerous 'pacification' campaigns before the war. Dutch commanders avoided posting their men to static guard duty but rather kept them mobile, seeking out Republican troops wherever they could be found with patrols deep into Republican territory, to destroy troop concentrations and throw the Republican forces off balance. By early 1946, however, the Republicans had strung their forces along a front line, making use of natural barriers such as rivers and thereby creating a kind of military tripwire which made Dutch penetration of Republican lines a more difficult operation. There was also some coordinated rotation of troops and lasykar on the front line, to make the most of the forces available.[5]

Mufreni was fortunate that his Allied counterparts were also interested in a more or less stable front east of Jakarta. With only limited troops at their disposal, the Allies were concentrating on completing what was called the 'minimum-plan' for West Java, which meant control of the road corridor running from Jakarta through Bogor to Bandung. Thus although there was often heavy fighting on both the east and west Jakarta fronts, the Indonesian forces there did not suffer the fate of the TKR unit in Bogor, which was pushed further and further back, ending finally far to the south beyond Sukabumi.[6]

The High Command's first step in attempting to bring Mufreni under their effective authority was to allocate him a place in the military hierarchy. This was done in late November 1945, when Daan Yahya returned from Yogyakarta with a mandate from the new Chief of Staff, General Urip Sumoharjo, to form regiments in Tanggerang, Bogor and Cikampek.[7] At a stroke, thus, Mufreni became a colonel, his deputies majors and so on. His unit became the 5th Regiment of the TKR's Division II Sunan Gunungjati and acquired an order of battle as follows:

Battalion	I	Cikampek, commanded by	Banu Mahdi
	II	Cikarang,	Sadikin
	III	Bekasi,	Sambas Atmadinata
	IV	Telukjambe,	Rulyamin
	V	Cibungur,	Priyatna

Although the new hierarchy placed Mufreni formally under the authority of the Sunan Gunungjati Division in Cirebon, this had little meaning to begin with and Mufreni had virtually no contact with divisional headquarters. The Jakarta regiment was thus at first unaffected when, in January 1946, all three West Javanese divisions of the army (Banten, Cirebon and Priangan) were grouped into a single West Java Command, headed by General Didi Kartasasmita, another former KNIL officer who had played a key role in establishing the army High Command. Didi was instructed not only to improve the lines of communication and level of training in the army in West Java, but to coordinate the activities of the army with the diplomatic activities of Syahrir in Jakarta. He chose for his headquarters first Tasikmalaya and then Purwakarta and his presence on the fringe of the 5th Regiment's domain enabled him to begin nibbling at the edges of Mufreni's autonomy.

Didi brought with him to Purwakarta a considerable sum of money from the Republican treasury to back his reorganisation plans, but he wisely preferred to distribute this to units he judged to be disciplined already, rather than attempting to buy obedience from independent-minded officers like Mufreni. Like the lasykar, of course, Mufreni was quick to develop his own independent sources of finance, trading through the regiment's own *badan ekonomi* with selected organis-ations in Jakarta. Like virtually all units on Java, the regiment suffered from a critical shortage of weapons and was forced to resort to home-made alternatives such as bamboo spears and mortars made out of metal electricity poles. They also enjoyed the occasional bonus contribution. Mufreni had no particular respect for Syahrir's policy of cooperating with the British, and he had no qualms therefore about stopping and confiscating a supply train sent by the British in Decem-ber 1945 for their beleaguered troops in Bandung after convoys heading south by way of Bogor had been severely mauled by Repub-lican forces along the way.

Realising the futility of simply issuing commands to Mufreni, Didi sought to bring him under slightly more control by asserting his authority over the hierarchy within the regiment. When, for instance, the Cibarusa battalion of Katamsi was separated from the rest of the Bogor regiment by the southward thrust of the Allies, Didi attached it to the 5th Regiment. He was also able to have Suroto Kunto, one of the former medical students associated with Prapatan 10, ap-pointed as Chief of Staff to Mufreni in place of Adel Sofyan. These were small steps, but they began to install within the regiment individuals and units dependent on, and therefore more likely to be loyal to, the army hierarchy.

While Mufreni's relations with Didi were cautious at best, on the other side of the city the Tanggerang regiment quickly emerged as a favourite. This regiment had grown out of the BKR unit formed in Jakarta in August 1945 by former medical students and PETA officers attached to the Japanese army headquarters. It was different from most Indonesian regiments in not being based on a former PETA battalion, although its commander, Singgih, had been a junior officer in the Jakarta battalion. The former medical students who dominated the regiment's officer corps, many of whom had been in contact with Hatta and Syahrir during the occupation, tended to share those leaders' rather Westernised internationalist view of In-donesia's position in the world. Within the regiment great stress was laid on the development of formal military skills and discipline, and it was the first important armed unit to withdraw permanently from the city in late 1945. The regiment retreated to Tanggerang, east of the city, where it sponsored the Republic's first Military Academy, under the command of Daan Mogot, with the intention of training the officer corps of the future Indonesian army. Despite Didi's support and encouragement, however, the Tanggerang regiment had its problems. It was armed largely with pre-war Italian rifles taken from

Jakarta police, weapons reportedly captured by Australian forces in the North Africa campaigns of World War II and brought to Java shortly before the Japanese invasion. Whatever ammunition had once been with the weapons was long gone and bullets of a different make and calibre had to be wrapped individually with cotton cloth to fit the bore of the rifles. Misfires and explosions were frequent. Like most other units, the Tanggerang regiment followed a policy of keeping its weapons at the front line and rotating the groups which used them. The Tanggerang regiment suffered a severe setback when thirty-eight of its members, many of them cadets of the Tanggerang Military Academy, were killed in an attempt to seize weapons from a Japanese post at Lengkong south of Tanggerang in January 1946.[8]

The officers commanding the Tanggerang regiment and instructing the cadets at the academy laid considerable emphasis on obedience to the civilian authorities and the regiment therefore became an important tool in the hands of Syahrir in his dealings both with the Allies and with other army units.[9] After Mufreni, for instance, had seized the Bandung supply train, Syahrir offered to provide an armed guard for future consignments. This guard was drawn from the Tanggerang Regiment, and Mufreni was persuaded to let the trains past by his chief of staff, Suroto Kunto. Altogether three supply trains were sent under army guard, and all arrived safely. The trains ceased when the Allies finally succeeded in carrying out their minimum plan for West Java and opening up the road corridor through Bogor.[10]

With its commitment to military discipline, the Tanggerang regiment was less restrained than Mufreni in dealing with local lasykar. It eyed Haji Akhmad Khaerun warily across the Cisedane river for about two months after leaving Jakarta while it built up its strength and organisation. Then on 7 January 1946 it moved, occupying key positions in the town and arresting two of the four original members of Khaerun's Central Directorate. Singgih, along with other army representatives and Mas Sewaka, as Republican Resident of Jakarta, then met Khaerun and his followers to discuss ways of ending the dispute without further fighting. Khaerun, according to accounts available, agreed to accept the army as the sole body responsible for internal and external security, and in return he was appointed Republican bupati of Tanggerang. Syekh Abdullah and other local strong men were involved in an advisory committee on security with Daan Yahya as army representative. The compromise, however, collapsed soon afterwards and in early March 1946 the army arrested Khaerun, Abdullah and others and exiled them to prison far away in Sukabumi. The administration was reorganised, a new bupati installed and Republican authority was more or less re-established. Lasykar groups from Banten continued to be active in the area, but

the Tanggerang Regiment benefited from the fact that the area
produced less rice than it consumed, and hence lacked the economic
base to support a large local lasykar movement.[11]

Aside from assisting the civilian bureaucracy to recover its pre-war
prerogatives, Didi also worked to discipline particularly recalcitrant
sections of the army. Amongst the groups dispersed on his orders was
the PMK (*Penyelidik Militer Khusus*, Special Military Intelligence),
which had been based near Purwakarta. This shadowy organisation
was established in late 1945 by Zulkifli Lubis, a former PETA officer
who had received intelligence training from the Japanese during the
occupation. He had been involved in Japanese plans to build up
underworld groups in various parts of Java as a guerrilla force to fight
the Allies if they landed on the island. After the declaration of
independence, Lubis was involved in seeking the allegiance for the
Republic of these same local underworld leaders. He was active in
Cibarusa, and he also reportedly recruited criminals from the prison
island of Nusa Kambangan off the south coast of Java for his
organisation.[12] He was distrusted by the API in Jakarta and was
arrested by them at one stage but later released. The PMK was said
to be directly responsible for Sukarno, though in the confused situation this would have meant that it was directly responsible to no-one,
and its task included both intelligence operations on Java and the
sending of armed units to other parts of the archipelago to further the
nationalist struggle there. It recruited a sizeable unit of lasykar from
Sulawesi under the command of Kahar Muzakkar which was later
sent on underground missions to Sulawesi. The Purwakarta branch of
the PMK apparently provoked the army's violent reaction in April
1946 by what seemed to be arbitrary arrests and seizures of goods,
and by the fact that it stood wholly outside the military hierarchy
which officers like Didi were attempting to establish. Similar objections from other regions led to the abolition of the PMK by the army
general headquarters on 3 May 1945 but, although dispersed, the
organisation survived and soon re-emerged in the Purwakarta area in
different form.[13]

Didi's efforts were backed by the Defence Minister, Amir Syarifuddin. Although few former KNIL officers shared Syarifuddin's
political ideas, they had many other things in common in the context
of 1946, notably Western education and an interest in discipline,
hierarchy and effective military organisation. This community of
interest resulted in an informal alliance between the defence ministry
and the former KNIL officers. One of the first tangible results of this
cooperation at the centre was the formation of a committee to review
the organisation and structure of the ministry of defence and the
armed forces. The formation of this committee was announced at the

same time as the TKR was renamed TRI (*Tentara Republik Indonesia*, Army of the Republic of Indonesia) as a sign of its official subordination to the Republican state rather than to the Indonesian people.[14] The reorganisation committee, headed by Didi Kartasasmita (still head of the West Java Command),[15] was dominated by former KNIL officers, and its report, published on 25 May 1946, formally subordinated the army headquarters to the ministry of defence, instead of to the President, as had previously been the case. The army general headquarters under General Sudirman was reduced to the planning and carrying out of military operations, while the ministry of defence was expanded and former KNIL officers were placed in key positions.[16]

In Central and East Java, these moves were effective in limiting the army's freedom of political movement, but Syarifuddin was able to do little to alter the predominance of former PETA officers in field commands. In West Java, by contrast, former KNIL officers, particularly from the CORO, were on the ascendant. The CORO drew on younger members of the Western-educated, non-aristocratic elite who tended to share the general outlook of the civilian nationalist leadership. Their rise helped to turn the army in West Java from one of the weakest components of the TRI to one of its strongest, a powerful ally of the government as long as the two saw eye to eye, and set it on a course that was to lead to a bitter clash with the Jakarta lasykar.[17]

This process had begun with the appointment of Didi Kartasasmita to the West Java Command in January 1946. During the following months, however, Didi was increasingly eclipsed by his chief of staff, a young Batak officer trained for the CORO, named A. H. Nasution. Nasution had joined the BKR in Bandung on its formation, though only as an adviser, but he quickly emerged as one of the most able military leaders in the region. In the fighting in Bandung in November 1945 he attracted the attention of Syarifuddin and was appointed by him to replace the older and less capable Aruji Kartawinata as commander of the TKR's Priangan Division.[18] When Didi's reorganisation committee subsequently recommended the fusion of the three West Javanese divisions into a single division, the Siliwangi, Nasution was elected by other officers of the division to become its commander.[19]

In Bandung, Nasution's dominance within the TKR enabled him to proceed with incorporating irregular units into the army, and his command soon included a cluster of 'Special units' which had originally been independent lasykar. Other lasykar, including the Bandung API, were simply disarmed and dispersed. With the forces under his control, Nasution carried out a sustained programme of rationalisation, seeking to reduce the number of soldiers to match the weapons available and reorganising them where possible into effective units.[20] Outside Bandung this task was less easy, since there were still many army units dominated by officers in the PETA mould such as Mufreni, who had reached their own local accommodation with the lasykar. In the Jakarta area, however, the defence ministry pulled off a coup by organising the defection of three units from the LRJR to the army in April 1946. The units involved were those originally from Senen, including the redoubtable Imam Syafe'i, and their defection was the result of both Syafe'i's increasing unease with the radical stance of LRJR, and an offer of legitimacy and training from the army, reportedly approved by Amir Syarifuddin himself. The units were transferred to the Cirebon area, leaving the LRJR more sharply divided from the army and government.[21] The LRJR was further weakened when the Hizbullah unit of Kyai Haji Nurali in Babelan pulled out of the East Jakarta Struggle Headquarters in protest against what he saw as its drift to the left.[22]

There were no KNIL officers serving in any of the three Jakarta area regiments. In spirit, however, the officers of the Tanggerang regiment, who had sponsored the Tanggerang Military Academy, were close to the former CORO officers, and, with the approval of Didi Kartasasmita and later Nasution, they gradually gained ascendancy in the Jakarta regiments. The Tanggerang regiment was always the army unit on which Syahrir could rely most, but its allegiance to the government was confirmed by the removal of its commander, Singgih, in a bloodless coup in late April 1946 organised by other officers of the regiment, notably Kemal Idris and Daan Yahya. As a former officer in the Jakarta PETA and a participant in the kidnapping of Sukarno and Hatta in August 1945, Singgih was sympathetic to the ideas of the PP and the style of the lasykar. His successor, Daan Yahya, on the other hand, was an intellectual closely associated with the Socialist Party. Suroto Kunto, who had been installed as chief of staff of the Cikampek regiment, was a close friend of Daan Yahya and, like him, expelled from the medical school for leading the student's strike.[23]

The experience of the Tanggerang regiment, however, was no advertisement for the advantages of cooperation with the government and the Allies. In early April, at the request of the British, the regiment agreed to open negotiations to adjust the demarcation line at Pesing, a few kilometres west of Jakarta, in favour of the British. According to Daan Yahya, the British were willing to supply arms to the Tanggerang regiment in return for its acting as a peacekeeping force along the demarcation line, presumably protecting Jakarta from the more militant lasykar of Banten, and in return for the border adjustments. At preliminary talks, the Indonesians agreed to evacuate the town if they could get exemption from Sudirman's standing orders that the army was not to retreat by a single step. The matter was being taken up with the army command in Yogyakarta when the nearby village of Pesing was suddenly attacked and occupied by Dutch troops on 15 April. This attack was in direct contravention of British orders to the Dutch, and when challenged officially the Dutch commander, Colonel S. de Waal, merely stated that he could not accept that kind of order. Pesing was never returned to Republican hands.[24]

Six weeks later the regiment suffered a further humiliation when the Dutch occupied the town of Tanggerang with little resistance. The TRI did no more than destroy a few buildings in the town before retreating across the Cisedane in the face of a larger Dutch force. These incidents destroyed the authority the regiment had won in the region by its crushing of Haji Akhmad Khaerun, and lasykar from Banten quickly moved in to defend the frontier from further attacks. It was apparently these lasykar who carried out numerous killings of Chinese in the area on the strength of rumours that the Chinese were amongst the Dutch troops attacking Tanggerang. Both Chinese houses and Indonesian kampungs were destroyed and a large stretch of country north-west of Tanggerang was burnt out.[25]

Having retreated from Tanggerang, the Tanggerang regiment now found its relations with the army command in Banten increasingly strained. The two had little in common: the army in Banten was dominated by fiery local Islamic leaders with little regard for technical military proficiency and less for young intellectuals who had retreated in the face of a Dutch attack. Tension was only relieved after a visit to the area by Nasution, as army commander in West Java. He authorised the regiment to retreat through the hills to Sukabumi, leaving the Banten units in charge of the west Jakarta front.[26]

Although some members of the Tanggerang regiment circled around Jakarta to join Mufreni's regiment in Cikampek and others left for Cirebon to rejoin their former commander, Singgih, most made their way to Sukabumi, where Nasution instructed them to merge with the Sukabumi and Bogor regiments, both also based in that area. The Bogor commander, A. E. Kawilarang, was appointed to command this new regiment, while Daan Yahya was detached, first to assist Didi's army reorganisation committee and then to become commander of the 3rd Brigade (later called Kiansantang) in Purwakarta. The establishment of brigades in mid-1946 was another of Nasution's measures to bring about greater coordination and control in the Siliwangi Division. There were five brigades, covering Banten, Bogor-Sukabumi, Jakarta-Purwakarta, Priangan and later

Cirebon, and each brigade included two to three regiments. The practical authority of brigade commanders was limited, but they did encroach increasingly on the old autonomy of the regimental commanders. Daan Yahya, for instance, played an important role in the removal of Mufreni from his command in mid-1946. Mufreni seems by this time to have lost some of the energy and drive which had made him the obvious leader of the Jakarta BKR in 1945. He was blamed, moreover, for a serious military defeat at the hands of the Allies in June 1946 in which a number of cannon were lost and the town of Bekasi fell into Allied hands.[27] As his replacement, the regiment chose Sadikin, an able and popular battalion commander who had served in both the KNIL and the Heiho as a non-commissioned officer. Daan Yahya, however, with the backing of Nasution, overruled this election and appointed instead his old colleague Suroto Kunto, Mufreni's chief of staff, as regimental commander.[28]

Daan Yahya's brigade included the regiments based at Cikampek under Suroto Kunto and at Purwakarta under Umar Bahsan, who had led the PETA revolt at Rengasdengklok in August 1945, together with a number of smaller units, notably that of Dr Mustopo in Subang. Mustopo, a dentist by training, had been a PETA officer in East Java under the Japanese and had become one of the leaders of the Indonesian forces in the Battle of Surabaya of November 1945. He was an eccentric but imaginative officer. During the Japanese occupation he had attempted to relieve unemployment in Surabaya by setting up workshops to produce soap and toothbrushes and, in the absence of a living Republican minister of defence, had briefly appointed himself to the position in October 1945. He had the idea of smearing horse manure on the points of the sharpened bamboo stakes which many units used as weapons in order to infect the enemy with tetanus and he encouraged his troops to eat cats, so that they could see in the dark. It is said that he honoured the contribution of the cats to the struggle by establishing a heroes' cemetery for the feline leftovers. In February 1946 he joined the army's political education staff in Yogyakarta, though by no means sharing Amir Syarifuddin's political ideas, and he also taught for a time at the Military Academy there. In mid-1946 he was appointed political education officer for Subang and arrived there with an unusual armed unit called the Pasukan Terate; *terate* means 'lotus', but the name was also an acronym for *Tentara Rahasia Tertinggi*, Supreme Secret Army. This unit consisted partly of students from the Yogyakarta Military Academy receiving field training, and partly of prostitutes and pickpockets from Surabaya and Yogyakarta whom he sent across Dutch lines into the Bandung area to steal weapons, clothes and other materials and generally to sow alarm and confusion amongst the Dutch troops. Mustopo later became Jakarta regional head of the *Biro Perjuangan* (Struggle Bureau), a government-controlled coordinating body for lasykar throughout Java.[29]

Under Suroto Kunto, relations between the Cikampek regiment and the LRJR deteriorated. Suroto Kunto was less careful in his relations with the lasykar than Mufreni had been, and was inclined to demand rather than request their assistance. By assembling armed force, he was able to impose on the lasykar government policies which they deeply distrusted. In April 1946, for instance, the government resumed the evacuation of Japanese troops and Allied prisoners of war and internees from the interior. Soon after his accession to power, Syahrir had announced his intention to hand over European prisoners of war stranded in Republican territory at the outbreak of the revolution. This gesture of surrendering potential hostages was meant to show the Republic's civilised character and general good will, but the evacuation had been stalled since January 1946 because of suspicion on the part of lasykar and other groups in the Republic. The evacuation was placed in the hands of an organisation called POPDA (*Panitia Oentoek* [i.e. *Untuk*] *Pengembalian Bangsa Jepang dan Asing*, Committee for the return of Japanese and other foreigners), headed by yet another former KNIL officer, Major-General Sudibio. The resumption was particularly attractive for the army since it was arranged that the British should lend the TRI trucks, fuel, weapons and ammunition to transport and guard the evacuees, and these of course could be used surreptitiously for many other purposes. In West Java, the evacuation was in the hands of Didi Kartasasmita, and the first evacuees from Purwakarta and Cirebon arrived safely in Jakarta in early May.[30]

The LRJR was also alarmed by Nasution's campaigns to disarm the lasykar in the Priangan. Their greatest criticism, however, was that the army was following a policy of retreat. It seemed to the lasykar that their vigorous resistance on the east Jakarta front had kept the Allies in check, while weak and defeatist attitudes in the army had allowed the Dutch and British to force a corridor through to Bandung. High level coordination meetings were held between the LRJR and representatives of the Army High Command and the First and Second Divisions covering Jakarta and Cirebon, but the two groups were becoming increasingly impatient with each other.[31]

In their assessment of army weakness, however, the lasykar were increasingly mistaken. For all its problems, by the middle of 1946 the army in the Jakarta area had come considerably closer to Amir Syarifuddin's goal of an obedient and professional military force.[32] It would not be long before that military force was turned against the lasykar.

1. Ngadam Suradji, 'Riwayat Singkat Peristiwa "Rengasdengklok"' (Type-script, Karawang, 1976), 15–17. Interviews: Sumarna W. S., Blubur-limbangan, Garut, 6 September 1982; Ngadam Suradji, Karawang, 1 November 1982; Saleh Tedjakusumah, Jakarta, 15 September 1982
2. Mohamad Dja'man, 'Naskah revolosi perjuangan kemerdekaan: Negara Republik Indonesia (Pengalaman selama tahun 1945 s/d 1949)', *Per-pustakaan 45* no. 206/XI; Mohd Soiz, 'Jalan-jalan yang kususuri', *Perpustakaan 45* no. 832/XLII. NEFIS, Rapporten van speciale agen-ten van Afdeeling IV, 9 April 1946, *Alg.Sec.I* box I, file 21, no. 5; Dienst der Algemene Recherche, Report on factors that may be considered to threaten order and peace at Batavia, 16 July 1946, *Proc.Gen.* 13; HQ 23 Ind.Div. Bandung, Weekly Intelligence Sum-mary, no. 16 part 2 (6 March 1946), pp. 4–6, *Proc.Gen.* 549. Inter-views: Saleh Tedjakusumah, Jakarta, 15 September 1982; Sadikin, Jakarta, 23 March 1983; Eri Soedewo, Jakarta, 14 February 1983
3. Interviews: Saleh Tedjakusumah, Jakarta, 15 September 1982, 23 March 1983; A. E. Kawilarang, Jakarta, 16 August 1982; Daan Jahja, Ja-karta, 2 December 1982; Sadikin, Jakarta, 23 March 1983. Dinas Sejarah Militer Kodam V/Jaya [hereafter Semdam V/Jaya], *Sejarah Perjuangan Rakyat, Jakarta, Tanggerang dan Bekasi dalam Mene-gakkan Kemerdekaan R. I.* (Jakarta, 1975), 68–69, 136, 141. Terri-toriaal Commando, Infiltratie en verhoogde activiteit van laskar en contra spionnage, 9 September 1946, *MvD/CAD*, HKGS-NOI, Inv.nr. GG la, 1946, bundel 49, stuk 174; Territoriaal Commando, Nadere berichten over ondergrondsche actie, 2 August 1946, *MvD/CAD*, HKGS-NOI, Inv.nr. GG la, 1946, bundel 49, stuk 72
4. Dja'man, M. Sani, 'Yatim dan perjuangan bangsa', *Perpustakaan 45* no. 10/I. Nasution, *SPKI* III, 197. Interviews: Eri Soedewo, Jakarta, 14 February 1983; Djilis Tahir, Jakarta, 30 November 1982; Suhendro, Bekasi, 22 January 1983; Sadikin, Jakarta, 23 March 1983; Sidik Samsi, Jakarta, 17 November 1982; Daan Jahja, Jakarta, 16 August 1982
5. KNIL, Nota operaties Java, 28 March 1946, *Alg.Sec.I* box I, file 4. Interview: Sadikin, Jakarta, 28 March 1983. See also Pramoedya Ananta Toer, 'Revenge', *Indonesia* 26 (1978), 43–62
6. KNIL, Nota operaties Java, *loc.cit.* Interview: A. E. Kawilarang, Jakarta, 16 August 1982. For details of Dutch military operations, see KNIL/KL, Operatieve rapporten, 8 February 1946–25 July 1946, *Alg. Sec.I* box I, file 5, no. 2
7. Interviews: Daan Jahja, Jakarta, 2 December 1982; Saleh Tedjakusumah, Jakarta, 15 September 1982. See also Sanusi W. S., 'Perjuangan 45 untuk pembangunan bangsa', Perpustakaan 45 no. 823/XLII. Accord-ing to Sedjarah Militer Kodam VI Siliwangi, *Siliwangi dari Masa Kemasa* (Jakarta, 1968), 60, initiative for the formation of regiments came not from Yogyakarta but from the West Java Command of General Didi Kartasasmita. Didi, however, was not appointed until January 1946, shortly after formation of the regiments in Jakarta.
8. Rachyadi, 'Kisah perjuangan antara tahun 1945 s/d 1950', *Perpustakaan*

45 no. 165/IX; Sanusi W. S., 'Perjuangan 45 untuk pembangunan bangsa', *Perpustakaan 45* no. 823/XLII; M. S. Soemaatmadja, 'Kisah nyata suka-duka pengalaman pada masa revolusi physic tahun 1945', *Perpustakaan 45* no. 832/XLII; Didi Tanuwidjaja, 'Setitik ujung-pena pengorbanan bagi perjuangan bangsaku periode 1945–1950', *Perpustakaan 45* no. 289/XV. Nasution, *SPKI* III, 105–12; *Sejarah Pertumbuhan dan Perkembangan Kodam VI/Jaya: Pengawal-Penyelamat Ibukota Republik Indonesia* (Jakarta, 1974), 139–41. S. L. J. van Waardenburg, 'Lasjkar Rakjat van Java en Madoera', NEFIS Publicatie no. 15, 22 July 1946, *Proc.Gen.* 123. Interviews: Daan Jahja, Jakarta, 1 September 1982; Kemal Idris, Jakarta, 16 August 1982; Sidik Samsi, Jakarta, 1, 17 November 1982; Abu Bakar Lubis, Jakarta, 13 January 1983; Kusnandar Partowisastro, Bogor, 20 January, 3 February 1983; R. F. Ma'riful, Jakarta, 6 October 1982; Abdul Muis, Cileungsi, 9 February 1983; Noer Achmad, Cileungsi, 12 February 1983; Suhendro, Bekasi, 19, 22 January 1983; Sumarna W. S., Bluburlimbangan, Garut, 6 September 1982.

9. Interviews: Kemal Idris and Daan Jahja, Jakarta, 16 August 1982. Singgih, who had played a minor role in the kidnapping of Sukarno and Hatta on 16 August 1945, was not the son of the nationalist leader Mr Singgih, as reported in Benedict R. O'G. Anderson, *Java in a Time of Revolution: Occupation and Resistance, 1944–1946* (Ithaca, N.Y., 1972), 25, but in fact his son-in-law.

10. Rachyadi, *op.cit.*; M. Siradz, 'Pertempuran', *Perpustakaan 45* no. 764/XXXIX. J. R. W. Smail, *Bandung in the Early Revolution, 1945–1946: a Study in the Social History of the Indonesian Revolution* (Ithaca, N.Y., 1964), 102, 112, 137. Interviews: Kemal Idris and Daan Jahja, Jakarta, 16 August 1982; Djilis Tahir, Jakarta, 30 November 1982; Saleh Tedjakusumah, Jakarta, 15 September 1982; Daan Jahja, Jakarta, 1 September 1982.

11. *Ra'jat*, 7 March 1946. Sewaka, *Tjorat-tjaret dari Djaman ke Djaman* (Bandung, [1955]), 88–9; *Republik Indonesia Propinsi Djawa Barat* (Jakarta, 1952), 153–4. Interviews: Daan Jahja, Jakarta, 7, 10 August 1982; Kemal Idris, Jakarta, 16 August 1982.

12. 'Aanknoopingspunten m.b.t. het ontstaan van de P. M. C.', NEFIS Publicatie no. 17, 24 July 1946, *MvD/CAD*, HKGS-NOI, Inv. nr. GG 16, 1946/47, bundel 1519; DOBIN, 3 April 1946, *Alg.Sec.I*, I–21–4. Interviews: R. F. Ma'riful, Jakarta, 6 October 1982; Abu Bakar Lubis, Jakarta, 13 January 1983.

13. 'Aanknoopingspunten', *loc.cit.*; NEFIS, Afdeling Militaire Intelligence, Bulletin no. 23, Field Preparation, 24 July 1947, *Proc.Gen.* 202; NEFIS, Rapporten van speciale agenten van Afdeeling IV, 29 April 1946, *Alg.Sec.I* box I, file 21, no. 5. Nasution, *SPKI* III, 6, 474. Interviews: R. F. Ma'riful, Jakarta, 6 October 1982; Didi Kartasasmita, Jakarta, 18 June 1982; Abu Bakar Lubis, Jakarta, 13 January 1983; Sidik Samsi, Jakarta, 17 November 1982; Sidik Brotoatmodjo, Bandung, 16 March 1983; Hasjim K. Notokoesoemo, Jakarta, 11 November 1982.

14. Nasution, *TNI* I, 246–9.,
15. Interview: Didi Kartasasmita, Jakarta, 18 June 1982. NEFIS, Rapporten van speciale agenten van Afdeling IV, 5 April 1946, *Alg.Sec.I* box I, file 21, no. 5.
16. Nasution, *SPKI* III, 6, 124–34
17. See A. H. Nasution, *Memenuhi Panggilan Tugas, jilid l: Kenangan Masa Muda* (Jakarta, 1982), 43–8; G.McT. Kahin, *Nationalism and Revolution in Indonesia* (Ithaca, N.Y., 1952), 184–5. Kahin probably overstates, though, the extent to which the Siliwangi Division was the creation of Syarifuddin and the Ministry of Defence.
18. Nasution, *TNI* I, 252; Anderson, *op.cit.*, 373–4.
19. Smail, *op.cit.*, 130.
20. *Ibid.*, 133–5; Nasution, *SPKI* III, 150–56, 446.
21. *Merdeka*, 21 May 1946. Nasution, *SPKI* III, 196. Interviews: Sidik Kardi, Jakarta, 15 February 1983; Kusnandar Partowisastro, Bogor, 20 January, 3 February 1983; Moh. Supardi Shimbat, Jakarta, 15 November 1982; Hasjim K. Notokoesoemo, Jakarta, 11 November 1982.
22. Interviews: K. H. Nurali, Babelan, Bekasi, 17 January 1983; H.Moh. Damsjik, Bekasi, 17 January 1983. See also S. Z. Hadisutjipto, *Bara dan Njala Revolusi Phisik di Djakarta* (Jakarta, 1971), 88.
23. NEFIS, Rapporten van speciale agenten van Afdeling IV, 26 April, 2 May 1946, *Alg.Sec.I* box I, file 21, no. 5. Nasution, *SPKI* II, 321. Interviews: Didi Kartasasmita, Jakarta, 18 June 1982; Daan Jahja, Jakarta, 7 August 1982; Kemal Idris, Jakarta, 16 August 1982; Saleh Tedjakusumah, Jakarta, 28 March 1983.
24. NEFIS, Rapporten van speciale agenten van Afdeling IV, 14 April 1946, *Alg.Sec.I* box I, file 21, no. 5; SACSEA to Cabinet Offices, 21 April 1946, FO 371/53793. J. H. W. Veenstra, *Diogenes in de Tropen* (Amsterdam, 1947), 131; H. J. Ansems, *Een Jaar 'W'-Brigade: Gedenkboek uitg. ter Gelegenheid van het Eenjarige Bestaan der 'W'-Brigade* (Cianjur, 1947), 38–40. Interview: Daan Jahja, Jakarta, 7 August, 1 September 1982. Dutch troops were accused of various atrocities in their occupation of Pesing. See Veenstra, *op.cit.*, 132–3; *Nota Betreffende het Archievenonderzoek naar Gegevens Omtrent Excessen in Indonesië Begaan door Nederlandse Militairen in de Periode 1945–1950* (The Hague, 1969), bijlage V, 4
25. *Netherlands News* (London), 6, 7 June 1946. Mackereth [British consul-general in Batavia] to Special Commissioner for South-East Asia [Clark Kerr], 6 June 1946, *FO* 371/53796; Pol.Int., 'The Tangerang incident', 13 June 1946, *FO* 371/53801. H. Rosihan Anwar, *Kisah-kisah Zaman Revolusi: Kenang-kenangan Seorang Wartawan* (Jakarta, 1975), 39–45; Nasution, *SPKI* III, 384–6. Interview: Daan Jahja, Jakarta, 7 August 1982. There were reports of murders on a lesser scale of Chinese in the Karawang area at about this time; see DOBIN 9 April 1946, *Alg.Sec.I* box I, file 21, no. 5. *Het Dagblad* (Jakarta), 29 July 1947.
26. Nasution, *Memenuhi Panggilan* I, 145–6; Nasution, *SPKI* III, 390. Interviews: Daan Jahja, Jakarta, 7 August 1982; Sukanda Bratamanggala, Bandung, 5 September 1982.

27. The Allied attack on Bekasi took place after the British had been unable to get TRI agreement to an evacuation of Bekasi along the line of the suggested evacuation of Pesing. Nasution, *SPKI* III, 403–7. *Negara Baroe* (Yogyakarta), 22 June 1946. Interviews: Sadikin, Jakarta, 28 March 1983; Suhendro, Bekasi, 22 January 1983.
28. *Ra'jat*, 6 July 1946. Nasution, *Memenuhi Panggilan* I, 138; Nasution, *SPKI* III, 389–408. Interviews: Daan Jahja, Jakarta, 7, 10 August, 1 September, 2 December 1982; Kemal Idris, Jakarta, 16 August 1982; Djilis Tahir, Jakarta, 30 November 1982; H. J. Syamsuddin Penyalai, Jakarta, 18 November 1982; Sadikin, Jakarta, 23 March 1983; Kusnandar Partowisastro, Bogor, 3 February 1983.
    Cirebon and Tasikmalaya were assigned to Division II of the TRI in the reorganisation of May 1946, but the transfer to Cirebon of Mufreni and Singgih, like that of Imam Syafe'i and the lasykar from Senen, indicates the relative flexibility of divisional boundaries at this stage. Both regions were later reassigned to the Siliwangi Division. KNIL/ KL, Operatief rapport, 7–6–'46 t/m 13–6–'46, *Alg.Sec.I* box I, file 5, no. 2. Suroto Kunto was one of the fifteen officers from West Java present in Yogyakarta in May 1946 to elect the commander of the new Siliwangi Division. Nasution, *Memenuhi Panggilan* I, 136–7.
29. Moestopo, *Memori Pengalaman* (Jakarta, 1977), 2–7; *Biografi Prof. dr. Moestopo* (n.p., 1980), 1–10; Nasution, *Memenuhi Panggilan* I, 143. NEFIS, 'Enige figuren uit de Republiek Indonesia' [1948?], *Alg.Sec.I* box XXI, file 9, no. 2; NEFIS, Terate-Signalement, 25 August 1947, *MvD/CAD*, HKGS-NOI, Inv.nr. GG 16, 1947, bundel 1519. Interviews: Daan Jahja, Jakarta, 7 August 1982: Sukanda Bratamanggala, Bandung, 5 September 1982; Kosasih Purwanegara, Jakarta, 30 August 1982.
30. NEFIS, Rapporten van speciale agenten van Afdeeling IV, 12, 15, 16, 18, 25 April 1946, *Alg.Sec.I* box I, file 21, no. 5; 'Rapport betreffende de bewapening van de T. R. I. door de Engelschen in verband met de evacuatie van geïnterneerden en Japansche krijgsgevangenen op Java', 1 June 1946, Minog verbaal no. Z 26, 4 June 1946; HK-CMI [Centrale Militaire Inlichtingendienst] Batavia, Vervolg Interrogatierapport inzake Didi Kartasasmita, 8 November 1948, *Proc.Gen.* 290; SACSEA to Cabinet Offices, 7 May 1946, *FO* 371/53792. Interview: Didi Kartasasmita, Jakarta, 30 August 1982.
31. Interviews: Johar Nur, Jakarta, 13 February 1983; R. F. Ma'riful, Jakarta, 6 October 1982; Hasjim K. Notokoesoemo, Jakarta, 11 November 1982; Saleh Tedjakusumah, Jakarta, 15 September 1982. Nasution, in *TNI* II, 16–17 and *SPKI* III, 151–3, 430, 455, describes these meetings in somewhat different terms, but his accounts point clearly to a deterioration of relations between the army and the LRJR.
32. In their negotiations with the Allies for the resumption of APWI evacuation in April 1946, Republican representatives reportedly stated that about 25 per cent of the armed troops on Java were 'reliable'. See 'Rapport betreffende de bewapening', *loc.cit.*,

9

Lasykar in the Republic's Defence Structure

By mid-1946, thus, the LRJR had accumulated an impressive list of enemies, from the Dutch to Syahrir and Nasution. Beyond the province of West Java, however, they managed to retain a slender niche in the Indonesian state by cultivating an alliance with political forces in central Java. Although this alliance did not save them from partial destruction at the hands of the army in April 1947, it laid the basis for an unexpected come-back by the lasykar only a few months later.

The position of the lasykar in the Republic's defence structure was the subject of debate as soon as the army was formally established in October 1945. Even at this early stage there were far too many separate armed units for the army even to consider claiming a full monopoly of armed force, especially since many of these units were associated with powerful political forces in the Republic. The Sultan of Yogyakarta, for instance, had his own armed unit, which he named *Lasykar Rakyat* (People's Militia) as early as 26 October 1945. On 30 October 1945, thus, in an effort to assert the army's pre-eminence in national defence, army headquarters in Yogyakarta issued a statement announcing the formation of their own Lasykar Rakyat which, it was stated, was to be used both to fight alongside the TKR and to perform support tasks such as the guarding of supplies which would relieve the TKR for battle duties. The Lasykar Rakyat was thus to be a locally based territorial army, with the TKR acting as a mobile battle force. The announcement was an attempt, like so many others in the period, to produce a formula accommodating the wide disparity between hopes and the reality of power, and nothing came of this organisation, though the term was soon appropriated both by the LRJR and by another armed group in Central Java led by Ir Sakirman and Sayuti Melok.[1]

Most groups in the Republic soon found it useful to support the existence of lasykar groups as a bulwark against the concentration of armed force in a single organisation. In early 1946, Tan Malaka clearly drew some of his most important support from lasykar groups gathered in Central and East Java. Even the defence minister Amir Syarifuddin, otherwise a strong supporter of central military authority, found it prudent to support sympathetic lasykar groups alongside the army. Syarifuddin's suspicion of sections of the army stemmed partly from events shortly after he took office. Army regimental and division commanders had met in Yogyakarta on 12 November 1945, apparently unaware that Syahrir was in the process of forming his first cabinet, and proceeded to elect not only an army commander, General Sudirman, but also a minister of defence, the Sultan of Yogyakarta, Hamengku Buwono IX, then a lieutenant-general in the TKR. The new government, not surprisingly, refused to accept this action, insisting on Amir Syarifuddin as minister, and appointing General Urip Sumoharjo as army commander. Although the election had not been meant as a direct challenge to the government, the army resisted the government's appointments. For six weeks the two sides were deadlocked. The dispute finally ended with Syarifuddin and Sudirman recognising each other's position with ill grace.[2] The atmosphere was further soured during this dispute by remarks Syarifuddin made attacking the KNIL and PETA for their supposed mercenary and fascist attitudes respectively, which were taken personally by officers who had served in either army.[3]

Syarifuddin soon mended his fences with the former KNIL officers, who found his views on military discipline congenial, but he continued to face serious resistance from the former PETA officers who dominated command positions in central and east Java. Partly as a result of their Japanese training, which emphasised the importance of fighting spirit over technical skill, partly because of their experience as young men in a time of revolution, these officers tended to be highly sympathetic towards the ideas of uncompromising struggle articulated by Tan Malaka and the PP. Even the army commander, General Sudirman, gave a good deal of moral support to the PP and provided military guards for some of its meetings. Although he stopped short of coming to Tan Malaka's rescue after the arrests of March 1946, he issued a public statement disassociating himself and the army from the move.[4]

Syarifuddin at first tried in a fairly clumsy way to get his ideas accepted within the army by means of a political education staff (*Staf Pendidikan Politik* or *Pepolit*), formed in mid-February 1946 as part of the ministry of defence. Syarifuddin was perhaps influenced by the model of the Red Army, which he saw as being composed of politically motivated fighters inspired not only by nationalism but by socialist ideology, and unshakably loyal and obedient to the ruling party. The Pepolit, therefore, was intended to erase 'the evil influences introduced by the colonialists—the imperialist Dutch and the fascist Japanese' and to turn each soldier into a willing instrument of the state.[5] In April 1946 the system was further expanded with plans to attach Pepolit officers to each divisional command, after the manner of political commissars in the Red Army. The former API leader, A. M. Hanafi, was reportedly sent as Pepolit officer to Purwakarta, while Dr Mustopo was appointed Pepolit officer in Subang.[6] Both the general staff and Siliwangi officers, however, were strongly suspicious of the Pepolit officers attached to their units. Pepolit staff were largely Pesindo cadre and tended to propagate not just support for government policies towards the Dutch, but socialist ideology in general. The social background of the general staff and Siliwangi officers tended to be more privileged than in the rest of the army,[7] so they were not naturally receptive to socialism. Professionally, moreover, they had strong reservations about the influence of ideology on military discipline. Many of the Pepolit officers posted to army units, therefore, were never permitted to operate.

Syarifuddin began also to cultivate those lasykar he considered to be more sympathetic to his point of view. Even before he became defence minister he was one of the backers of a youth congress on 10 and 11 November organised to create a 'fusion of Indonesian youth on the basis of socialist principles for the establishment of an Indonesian republic founded on genuine popular sovereignty'.[8] The meeting was attended by twenty-eight major armed youth organisations, and Syarifuddin apparently had hopes of forming these into a single organisation. In the event, only seven of the lasykar did so, forming the *Pesindo* (*Pemuda Sosialis Indonesia*, Indonesian Socialist Youth) on the first day of the congress. Most prominent of these was the Jakarta API, enroled on the authority of Wikana, with the support of Khaerul Saleh and Sukarni but apparently without reference to the organisation's members in Jakarta.[9]

Although stopping short of complete fusion, the congress agreed to establish struggle councils (*Dewan Perjuangan*) at each administrative level in the regions to coordinate the activities of all non-army units. Wikana himself subsequently departed for Karawang, where he encouraged Wahidin Nasution to establish a local Pesindo unit and himself set up a *Dewan Perjuangan Jawa Barat* (West Java Struggle Council) or DPJB. Wikana, however, underestimated the annoyance of the Jakarta API at having been merged into Pesindo without consultation, and the growing distrust of the fighters on the frontline in Jakarta of the negotiating policies of the Syahrir government, represented by such things as the order to evacuate Jakarta. When it arrived in Karawang after its final retreat from Jakarta, therefore, the LRJR made no move to join the Pesindo and paid little attention to Wikana's DPJB, though its leaders apparently retained good personal relations with Wahidin. After Wikana's departure for Yogyakarta, the DPJB fell under control of the LRJR and became a body coordinating its activities with those of the Lasykar Rakyat units in Cirebon led by Abdul Khamdi, Sastrosuwiryo and Mohammad Tirwan.[10]

Although the Pesindo in Central and East Java was also independent minded for a time—it joined the PP briefly at the urging of Khaerul Saleh and Sukarni—it soon became clearly and closely associated with Syarifuddin, and took part in the arrests of Tan Malaka and his associates in March 1946. Unlike the Pesindo in Karawang, moreover, it soon became a major military force, and was widely believed to receive weapons and funds directly from the ministry of defence, although it had no official standing at first.[11] It also provided much of the cadre for the *Biro Perjuangan* (Struggle Bureaux) set up by Syarifuddin in late July 1946 to replace the Dewan Perjuangan as coordinating bodies for the various lasykar. A senior adviser to the Pesindo, Major-General Jokosuyono, headed the central Biro Perjuangan. Regional bureaux were established throughout Java—Wahidin Nasution headed the bureau in Karawang—and these provided a channel for funds and instructions with which the ministry of defence attempted to draw the various lasykar closer to it, with varying degrees of success.[12]

Towards the end of 1946, Syarifuddin took a further step in establishing a separate lasykar hierarchy alongside the army. On 4 October 1946, the Republic's State Defence Council (*Dewan Pertahanan Negara*, DPN) issued an ordinance laying down a number of changes in the formal defence organisation of the Republic. It created a *Dewan Kelasykaran Pusat* (Central Lasykar Council), established on 12 November, consisting of the leaders of the nine major lasykar in Central and East Java. The lasykar organisations represented in the Dewan Kelasykaran Pusat were Hizbullah, Sabilillah, BPRI, Barisan Banteng, Pesindo, Lasykar Buruh (Labour Militia), Lasykar Tani (Peasant Militia), Lasykar Merah (Red Militia) and the Lasykar Rakyat of Sakirman. A separate *Dewan Kelasykaran Seberang* (Outer Regions Lasykar Council) was formed directly under the DPN and consisted of leaders of lasykar units from the occupied territories of Kalimantan and eastern Indonesia. Under this central body were regional councils (*Dewan Kelasykaran Daerah*), coordinated by the local Biro Perjuangan, consisting of locally important lasykar leaders. On each front the army and lasykar

were to form a battle headquarters (*markas pertempuran*), headed by
the senior local army officer with the head of the Biro Perjuangan as
his deputy, and a joint staff of army officers and lasykar leaders. The
ordinance provided that the lasykar would for the first time receive
payment from the government but that their numbers would be
reduced in a rationalisation similar to that under way in the army.[13]
This was followed in the course of 1947 by the series of announce-
ments mentioned in chapter eight which led to the creation of the
TNI in June. The new organisation not only left lasykar autonomy
untouched and gave the lasykar full formal military status but created
a six-man central leadership council of which three members were
lasykar leaders of whom two, Sakirman and Jokosuyono, were
closely associated with the government. The lasykar were thus being
given a position alongside, not beneath, the army hierarchy, without
any prospect of further integration or subordination.[14]

In West Java the army had sought to control the lasykar by
disarming them or incorporating them into itself, and it had seen
Syarifuddin's Dewan Perjuangan and later the Biro Perjuangan as
steps in the gradual bringing of the lasykar under army authority. The
former KNIL officers in the general staff shared the view that the
ultimate fate of the lasykar was either demobilisation or simple
incorporation in and subordination to the army.[15] In the eyes of the
Siliwangi and general staff officers the Dewan Kelasykaran raised the
prospect of a second, ideologically motivated army in the Republic,
politically favoured by the government at the expense of the older
professional armed forces. Not only was their own position threatened
but they saw in the idea of a second army an attack on the principle of
military hierarchy which they had been struggling to impose. The
alliance of the Siliwangi Division and general staff, dominated by
former KNIL officers, with Syarifuddin's ministry of defence thus
began to fray. The two had been natural allies in 1945 and 1946 as
they sought to create a disciplined, Western-style army in the face of
the Javanese and Japanese populist style represented by Sudirman.
By 1947, however, the two allies were sufficiently strong for interests
to begin to collide. There was no sudden break but the alliance
became more clearly one of convenience rather than conviction and
the basis was laid for a later realignment of political-military forces in
the Republic.

Not only Amir Syarifuddin but the embattled army commander,
General Sudirman, saw value in preserving a lasykar presence in the
Republic. From early in the revolution Sudirman had found himself
opposed to the government over a wide variety of government
policies flowing from the negotiations, such as the evacuation of
prisoners of war and internees, the supply of rice to the occupied

territories and successive truces and cease-fires. Recognising the difficulty of opposing the government on matters of general policy, he had sought allies amongst other groups opposed to the negotiations, notably the PP, giving them words of encouragement and occasional armed guards, though he refrained from defending them by force when Syarifuddin's Pesindo troops marched in. Syarifuddin's plans for military organisation were also unpalatable for Sudirman. The army commander's style laid heavy emphasis on military mystique, drawing on imagery of the Javanese warrior knights (*ksatriya*) portrayed in the legends of old Java. It was a style which called forth deep and sonorous echoes from Javanese society, but it nonetheless set the army apart. In a tradition which can be traced back to Hindu ideas of *dharma* (duty) expressed in the Mahabharata, Sudirman's soldier did his noble duty to society, pure in heart, asking nothing and demanding nothing, and with a belief that death in battle was the noblest death of all, but without expecting the rest of society to do the same. Syarifuddin's plans for an ideological army assaulted this style by making military virtues secondary to political ones.[16]

Under heavy pressure from both Syarifuddin's ministry of defence and the former KNIL officers of the general staff, Sudirman turned to lasykar groups who shared some of his views. On 20 April, after the PP was crushed by the government, he created an advisory council (*Dewan Penasehat*), on which opposition figures such as Sutomo of the BPRI and Muhammad Tirwan of the Dewan Perjuangan Jawa Barat in Cirebon had a prominent position.[17] The alliance was strengthened by the arrival of Sutan Akbar in Yogyakarta as LRJR representative to the central Biro Perjuangan, and of Alizar Thaib, the former military commander of the API in Jakarta, who had finally been released by the British from prison on Onrust.[18] Outnumbered by Syarifuddin's supporters on the Biro Perjuangan, these two figures drifted into Sudirman's orbit, creating a loose coalition between Sudirman and the LRJR group. Sudirman in turn showed his sympathy by sending his special representative, Anwar Cokroaminoto, to a major Lasykar Rakyat conference in November 1946. Cokroaminoto told the assembled lasykar that the army would have to do its duty but that it had no objection to the radical demands of the West Java LR.[19]

An important, though by no means entirely clear, role was played in this rapprochement by the intelligence organisation of Zulkifli Lubis. The KNIL-PETA division in the army at large appears to have been repeated within the army's intelligence organisations. One section of army intelligence, allied to Syarifuddin and the Pesindo, was headed by Abdul Rakhman, who had reportedly served with the NEFIS in Australia during the war. Opposed to him had been Lubis'

PMK and the *Penyelidik Militer Umum* (PMU, General Military Intelligence) of Dr Sucipto. Sucipto had been medical officer in the Purwakarta battalion of the PETA, and had played a significant role in the kidnapping of Sukarno and Hatta on 16 August 1945. He had then been in close contact with the API pemuda in Jakarta and he maintained these contacts after his appointment by Sudirman as head of army intelligence. His was one of the few sections left directly under Sudirman's command in Didi Kartasasmita's re-organisation of the army of May 1946. It was Didi's committee which ordered the abolition of Zulkifli Lubis' PMK throughout Java in the same month. Sucipto was arrested in July 1946 as part of a general crack-down on civilian and military supporters of Tan Malaka, but Lubis survived and re-grouped his PMK into the so-called Field Preparation (FP), with branches in many parts of Java and special units for infiltration to Kalimantan and eastern Indonesia. In the Jakarta area he re-cruited a number of lasykar leaders, both as local agents and as cadre for his central organisation. Most notable of these was Ma'riful, deputy leader of the LRJR, who became for a time Lubis' deputy in the FP organisation.[20] Since Lubis, too, was opposed to the rising tide of former KNIL officers' influence in the army, his FP provided another link in the Sudirman-LRJR alliance.

1. S. L. J. van Waardenburg, 'Lasjkar Rakyat van Java en Madoera', *NEFIS Publicatie* 15 (22 July 1946), *Proc.Gen.* 123; Territoriaal tevens Troepencommando, Inlichtingendienst, Verslag over Januari 1946, 'loc.cit.'; A. H. Nasution, *Tentara Nasional Indonesia* [hereafter TNI] I (Bandung, 2nd ed., 1963), 146–8; U. Sundhaussen, *The Road to Power: Indonesian Military Politics 1945–1967* (Kuala Lumpur, 1982), 85–7; B. R. O'G. Anderson, *Java in a Time of Revolution: Occupation and Resistance, 1944–1946* (Ithaca, N.Y., 1972), 268; Nasution, *TNI* I, 139–41.
2. See Anderson, *op.cit.*, 244–7; Sundhaussen, *op.cit.*, 20–23; A. H. Nasution, *Memenuhi Panggilan Tugas, jilid I: Kenangan Masa Muda* (Jakarta, 1982), 81–2; S. Said, 'The Genesis of Power: Civil-Military Relations in Indonesia during the Revolution for Independence, 1945–1949' (Ph.D. dissertation, Ohio State University, 1985), 80–84.
3. Anderson, *op.cit.*, 247–50. See also Mohammad Hatta, *Memoirs* (Singapore, 1981), 250–51.
4. Anderson, *op.cit.*, 328; Said, *op.cit.*, 119–120, 126–141, argues that Sudirman withdrew his support from Tan Malaka as early as January 1946 and that his concern thereafter was simply to avoid being exploited politically by either government or opposition.

5. *Antara*, 26 January, 19 February 1946. A. H. Nasution, *TNI* I, 253, 260; Nasution, *SPKI* III, 6; Said, *op.cit.*, 108–110.
6. *Antara*, 8 April 1946, cited in Anderson, *op.cit.*, 371. Interview: Daan Jahja, Jakarta, 10 August 1982.
7. U. Sundhaussen, 'The Political Orientations and Political Involvement of the Indonesian Officer Corps 1945–1966: the Siliwangi Division and the army headquarters' (Ph.D. dissertation, Monash University, 1971), 57–8, 65–7. Interview: Didi Kartasasmita, Jakarta, 18 June 1982.
8. *Berita Indonesia*, 5 November 1945, cited *ibid.*, 254.
9. Interview: Johar Nur, Jakarta, 23 August 1982. Anderson, *op. cit.*, 254–256.
10. Interviews: Sidik Samsi, Jakarta, 17 November 1982; Djilis Tahir, Jakarta, 30 November 1982; Kusnandar Partowisastro, Bogor, 20 January, 3 February 1982; Hasjim K. Notokoesoemo, Jakarta, 11 November 1982; Johar Nur, Jakarta, 7, 11 October 1982, 9 March 1983. Nasution, *SPKI* III, 455; Anderson, *op.cit.*, 371 n3; G. W. Overdijkink, *Het Indonesische Probleem: Nieuwe Feiten* (Amsterdam, 1948), 95. *Antara*, 26 January, 15 February 1946. Recomba voor West-Java, Rapport inzake de communistische beweging te Cheribon, 8 April 1948, *Proc.Gen.* 779 no. 1
11. Anderson, *op.cit.*, 259.
12. Overdijkink, *op.cit.*, 34; Nasution, *SPKI* III, 135, 137; Angkatan 45 Jakarta, 'Riwayat hidup Sjarif Wahidin Nasution' (Typescript, Jakarta, n.d.). On Jokosuyono, see T. B. Simatupang, *Pelopor dalam Perang, Pelopor dalam Damai* (Jakarta, 1981), 78. Interview: Kusnandar Partowisastro, Bogor, 20 January 1983. Anderson, *op.cit.*, 371, apparently places the formation of the Biro Perjuangan in about April 1946, while Nasution, *SPKI* III, 131, gives May 1946, but the actual establishment of the Bureau seems to have been later than either of these accounts suggest. This confusion over dates is perhaps political in background. The rapport between Syarifuddin and the Western-oriented army officers was later to break down over Syarifuddin's shift to the left, his attempts to impose his ideology on the army, and his buildup of various lasykar in Central and East Java as a separate army, the TNI Masyarakat (People's National Army of Indonesia). The split between the two became total when Syarifuddin took part in the Madiun rebellion of 1948, and there is a tendency for officers to recall their misgivings about and hostility towards Syarifuddin earlier in the revolution than was probably the case. Thus Nasution (*TNI* I, 267, 298) gives the impression that the TNI Masyarakat was established in 1946 soon after the Biro Perjuangan, when in fact it was not formed until after the Dutch Military Action of July 1947 and was first of all a response to the official army's apparent collapse in the face of Dutch attacks. See G.McT. Kahin, *Nationalism and Revolution in Indonesia*, (Ithaca, N.Y., 1952), 261.
13. Nasution, *SPKI* III, 457, *TNI* II, 30–33; Overdijkink, *op.cit.*, 34–7. *Star Weekly* 20 October 1946.

14. Nasution, *SPKI* IV, 65–8, 440–9, *TNI* II, 28–9.
15. See, for instance, Simatupang, *op.cit.*, 88–9. The relationship of lasykar to the army is assessed in these terms in Sundhaussen, *op.cit.*, 84–92, 109.
16. On the military thought of Sudirman, see Anderson, *op.cit.*, 250–1, 375–8.
17. Anderson, *op.cit.*, 292–3, 310–11, 370–2; Overdijkink, *op.cit.*, 85–7; Nasution, *TNI* II, 15. *Merdeka* 31 May 1946.
18. Interviews: Alizar Thaib, Jakarta, 28 February 1983; Johar Nur, Jakarta, 13 February 1983; Kusnandar Partowisastro, Bogor, 3 February 1983; Muhidin Nasution, Ciluer, 14 October 1982. See also Nasution, *SPKI* III, 454.
19. Interviews: Kusnandar Partowisastro, Bogor, 20 January, 3 February 1983; Sidik Samsi, Jakarta, 17 November 1982; Hasan Gayo, Jakarta, 1 March 1983; Johar Nur, Jakarta, 11 October 1982; R. F. Ma'riful, Jakarta, 23 August 1982. See also 'Vergadering van de Lasjkar Rakjat op 22, 23 en 24 November 1946 te Krawang', *Proc.Gen.* 890. *Merdeka* 28 November 1946.
20. Nasution, *SPKI* III, 6; Anderson, *op.cit.*, 74–5, 372, 387, 405; H. Agustaman, *5 Tahun Melawan SAC Subandrio Aidit Chaerul* (Bandung, 1966), 32. Algemene Politie Soerabaia, Afd. Inlichtingen Dienst, Interrogatie-rapport: Fatkoer, 28, 29 April 1949, *Proc.Gen.* 652; NEFIS, Nota naar inleiding van het uittreksel uit de 'Mededeeling van gegevens' no. 31 van de inlichtingendienst van de stadspolitie van Batavia, 12 September 1946, *Proc.Gen.* 13; Korpsleiding Algemene Politie te Zuid-Borneo, Door Kapitein Moeljono, Hoofd van de 'Field Preparation, afdeeling Kalimantan' gestrekte gegevens, 30 September 1948, *Proc. Gen.* 793; NEFIS, Afdeling Militaire Intelligence, Bulletin no. 23, Field Preparation, 24 July 1947, *Proc.Gen.* 202. Bezwaarschrift, Idham Rasjid and sixty others to President Sukarno, 25 January 1948, C. M. I. Document no. 5683, *MvD/CAD*, HKGS-NOI, Inv.nr. GG 58, 1949, bundel 6323H. Interviews: R. F. Ma'riful, Jakarta, 23 August, 6 October 1982; Kusnandar Partowisastro, Bogor, 21 February 1983.

10

The Karawang Affair

The Republic's continued negotiations with the Dutch finally precipitated armed conflict between the army and the lasykar in April 1947. After many delays and false starts in the course of 1946, senior Republican and Dutch officials met in Jakarta in early October to begin hammering out the terms of a settlement to the conflict. The lasykar watched this progress towards an agreement with increasing hostility. On 26 September 1946, during the ceasefire discussions which preceded the formal negotiations, the LRJR launched a major attack on a Dutch barracks at Tanah Tinggi on the east of Jakarta, well inside the demarcation line. When the talks shifted for their final phase to the hill resort of Linggajati south of Cirebon, the Lasykar Rakyat in Cirebon sought to disrupt the negotiations themselves.[1] Then on 22–24 November 1946, a week after the Linggajati agreement was initialled, the LRJR sponsored a congress at Karawang of Lasykar Rakyat organisations in western Java which bitterly condemned the agreement and announced the formation of a *Lasykar Rakyat Jawa Barat* (West Java People's Militia) as a federation of LR units in Karawang, Cirebon, Sukabumi, Banten, Bogor, Purwokerto and Tegal. Sidik Kertapati was chosen as head of the organisation, with Akhmad Astrawinata, a former leader of the Bandung API, as his deputy. Maulana, another pemuda originally from Bandung, was secretary, while Armunanto headed the *Bagian Politik* (Political Section).[2] Sutan Akbar, meanwhile, was succeeded as military commander of the LRJR by Nurdin Pasaribu, a Muslim Batak and former leader of the API in Sawah Besar in Jakarta.[3]

The new federation established its headquarters in Cirebon and had its greatest success in bringing closer co-operation between the dominant Karawang and Cirebon units. The West Java Lasykar

Rakyat were enthusiastic supporters of the Benteng Republik and they participated in a defence council (*Dewan Pembelaan*) of the coalition which announced plans for a new 17 August Division of the lasykar to oppose the Dutch 7 December Division.[4] The Benteng Republik appeared to have sufficient numbers to defeat the Linggajati agreement in the KNIP, and it was only after Sukarno more than doubled the number of KNIP members that the agreement was finally ratified in early March 1947.[5]

The beginning of 1947 thus saw the LR in West Java at the peak of their power. They were the dominant military force on the northern coastal plain and were backed by Syamsuddin Can's village defence system which gave them deep roots in the local countryside. They also had a central secretariat which was beginning to act effectively to formulate policy, and which published its own newspaper, *Genderang* (Drum).[6] They remained unable, however, to overcome the fundamental weaknesses outlined in chapter 7 and their prominence merely made the army and the government more determined that the lasykar should not be allowed to survive indefinitely.

The ceasefire discussions which preceded the Linggajati negotiations resulted in an agreement, reached on 14 October 1946, which required local Indonesian and Dutch commanders on each front to meet and agree on just where the demarcation line had run on that date. On the east Jakarta front it was Suroto Kunto who was due to meet his Dutch counterpart, Major-General H. J. J. W. Dürst Britt, but it was not until the end of November that a meeting could be arranged. On 27 November, then, two days before the arranged meeting, Suroto Kunto and his chief of staff Adel Sofyan, disappeared while travelling between Karawang and Cikampek. No trace of the men was ever found except for their abandoned car and a boot belonging to Adel Sofyan, but it is assumed that they were kidnapped and killed.

The disappearance of Suroto Kunto, like the earlier kidnapping of Oto Iskandardinata in Bandung, is one of the mysteries of the revolution. It was logical at the time to attribute it to the Karawang lasykar. Kidnapping was an important element in the political style of the lasykar and as antagonisms grew more bitter it became increasingly a tool for removing enemies altogether, rather than simply for admonishing them. As commander of the Cikampek regiment Suroto had not been sympathetic to the LRJR, and at the time of his death he was attempting to impose on the lasykar a ceasefire to which they had deep strategic and ideological objections. On the other hand, Suroto had no particular hostility towards the LRJR, and was implementing a policy not of his own making. Sadikin, attending the lasykar conference a few days earlier on 24 November, had re-

portedly told the lasykar that the army was as unhappy with Linggajati as they were. The LRJR had very little to gain from Suroto's
death, unless it were publicised widely as a measure of the strength of
lasykar opposition to the ceasefire. Yet they did not do this, and
LRJR leaders denied, and have continued to deny, any knowledge of
the disappearance. While LRJR involvement is certainly possible,
the disappearance may have been the work of lasykar units outside
their control, or of Dutch intelligence agents operating in the area.
Rumours circulated at the time that Adel Sofyan, an intelligence
officer, had defected to the NEFIS, though this is probably best seen
simply as a reflection of the prevailing atmosphere of suspicion and
insecurity in Karawang. It is also by no means impossible that Suroto
was kidnapped and killed by or at the instigation of members of his
own regiment, dissatisfied with his appointment over the heads of
more experienced officers such as Sadikin.[7] After hasty consultations
with Nasution as division commander, Sadikin was appointed to
replace Suroto, with the regimental medical officer, Dr Eri Sudewo,
as his chief of staff. Eri attended the meeting with Dürst Britt in
Bekasi on 29 November, but the two sides came to no agreement at
all on where the demarcation line had run on 14 October and the
meeting broke up without any decision.[8]

Assuming—reasonably under the circumstances—that the LRJR
was responsible for Suroto Kunto's disappearance, Daan Yahya,
Suroto's immediate superior, moved quickly, arresting Muhammad
Darwis of the LRJR in order to get information on Suroto's where-
abouts and, presumably, to have a hostage to exchange for him if he
were still being detained. Daan Yahya and others were keen to strike
down the LRJR for once and for all, but they were overruled by
Nasution, on the grounds that LRJR guilt was not proven. The
strength of the LRJR was certainly an unspoken consideration in
Nasution's decision to avoid conflict for the time being; according to
his estimates, the LRJR had about half as many weapons again as the
army. He also took the precaution of replacing Daan Yahya with
another CORO officer, Sidik Brotoatmojo, as commander of the
Purwakarta brigade.[9]

Relations between the army and the lasykar continued to be
strained. Tension was exacerbated by Sukarno's announcement on 18
March 1947 that all tactical armed forces, including the lasykar,
would be incorporated into the army under General Sudirman. The
announcement was made with the idea of giving the lasykar formal
military status—and therefore a securer position within the Republic
and in dealings with the Dutch—rather than bringing them under
army control.[10] For the LRJR, however, the idea of being placed
even formally under Nasution was chilling. Aside from Nasution's

reputation as a *tukang lucuti* (disarmer), the ministry of defence had established a second reorganisation committee (*Panitya Pertimbangan Pucuk Pimpinan Tentara*) on 15 February, again headed by Didi Kartasasmita. This committee began the process of demobilising excess soldiers of the TRI with the goal of creating a smaller, more efficient army. One of the first concrete steps in this direction was the establishment of a re-education institute in Subang where reportedly several thousand former soldiers were retrained as farmers, to be settled later in the areas north of Bandung and south of Cianjur. The hand of the indefatigable Dr Mustopo is probably to be seen in these arrangements.[11] There can have been no doubt in lasykar minds where they would end up if Nasution had his way.

Relations were made worse by Republican attempts to halt the LRJR's lucrative trade with Jakarta. All the armed groups in the Karawang region had trade links with occupied Jakarta and, in the absence of financial support from Yogyakarta, depended on those links for their survival. Many of them tried, and perhaps a few succeeded, to ensure that the goods they traded kept out of the hands of the Dutch and Chinese, but in practice most of the cross-border trade was controlled on the Jakarta side by representatives of the old colonial order. One of the most common accusations flung between groups in the area was that their trade helped the enemy. The boundary between legitimate trade and smuggling was open to interpretation, and the lasykar had been enthusiastic confiscators of army trade from early in the revolution. In early April 1947, however, customs posts were established both at Cikampek and at Tambun on the demarcation line to police the official but ineffective monopoly of the Republican Government Purchase Office in Jakarta. Army patrols along the border were also stepped up. As a result there were a number of small incidents between army and lasykar which gave the army an opportunity to intervene forcefully against smaller units and set up an atmosphere of impending crisis.[12]

Whether Nasution decided on military action against the LRJR at the time of Suroto Kunto's disappearance is not clear.[13] Soon afterwards, however, extra units were brought into the region, including regular troops from Central and East Java, and a mortar unit called the *Beruang Merah* (Red Bears) from Tasikmalaya. This largely Batak unit had been one of the first lasykar units absorbed under Nasution's command in Bandung in 1945, and was considered close to Amir Syarifuddin. An artillery unit was also introduced.[14] A propaganda war against the LRJR was launched, with accusations flying that the LRJR was collaborating with the Dutch, and that TRI patrols had found Dutch flags in lasykar camps. The lasykar responded with accusations that the army was trying to deprive the poor of their livelihood and they accused the army of stealing cloth-ing which should have been distributed to the public.[15]

On 5 April, a meeting of army leaders in Purwakarta completed a plan of action. The TRI commander in Purwakarta, Sidik Brotoato-mojo, sent a telegram to his Dutch counterparts, Dürst Britt in Jakarta and Colonel A. A. J. J. Thomson in Bogor: 'I am planning to clean up my area. I would appreciate gentlemanly behaviour on your part.' On receiving a favourable reply, he began to move.[16] The army first rounded up the small LR unit in Purwakarta and then disarmed the KRIS at Rengasdengklok. This enabled them to surround Kara-wang and on 17 April, after Harun Umar's troops unwisely provided a pretext by lobbing a mortar in the direction of the TRI, the artillery and mortar units began to bombard LRJR positions in Karawang. The lasykar possessed only a few artillery pieces and mortars to return the attack, and under heavy bombardment their morale col-lapsed, though not before they had inflicted heavy casualties on the Beruang Merah and killed its commander. One by one they sought to break through the TRI perimeter and most of the actual fighting took place between lasykar units in disorganised retreat and pursuing army units. On the evening of 19 April the army entered a Karawang virtually empty of lasykar and all fighting was over by the 26th. Of the leaders only Wahidin Nasution remained. He was arrested and placed in prison in Purwakarta.[17]

The operation in Karawang was accompanied by a less violent razzia in Cirebon, where it coincided with a conference of the West Java LR which had recently passed motions cutting all links with Sakirman's LR in Central Java and urging the abolition of the Biro Perjuangan.[18] Sidik Kertapati, Akhmad Astrawinata and Hasan Gayo were arrested and imprisoned in Tasikmalaya. Armunanto, Hasnan Cinan and Kusnandar escaped by train to Central Java, where they went underground. Other leaders dispersed into the countryside. An important role in neutralising the local lasykar was played by the former lasykar of Imam Syafe'i, then stationed near Cirebon as a 'Special Unit' of the local TRI. They persuaded some units to accept simple incorporation into the new TNI (*Tentara Nasional Indonesia*, Indonesian National Army) formed on 3 June 1947 to incorporate the TRI and lasykar as forecast by Sukarno in March. A new battalion was formed, composed largely of Sidik Kertapati's old unit, together with that of the Lasykar Rakyat from Kosambi and Walahar and commanded by another former lasykar, Major Rivai. This battalion, Syafe'i's Special Unit, and a part of Sukanda Bratamanggala's old north Bandung regiment were then merged to form a *Resimen Perjuangan* (Struggle Regiment) based in Subang under the command of Major Rambe, a veteran of the battle

of Surabaya and former political education officer. Mustopo, meanwhile, continued as head of the Jakarta Biro Perjuangan, but with all
lasykar who would cooperate with the army now incorporated in it,
his role was unimportant and after being wounded in a clash with the
Dutch he was transferred to East Java in May 1947.[19]

In the Karawang area, this incorporation took place on a lesser
scale, with small units under Haji Darip and Supardi Mangkuyuwono
joining the Cikampek regiment. Nurali's Hizbullah merged with the
ALRI along the north coast, though neither force had been involved
in the April clashes. Other lasykar units simply dispersed. Ukon
Effendi reportedly fled to Singapore. Nurdin Pasaribu turned up in
Jakarta and took a job with the Nederlandsche Handel Maatschappij, the firm whose far from honourable appearance in Multatuli's
Max Havelaar had made it a symbol of Dutch colonial oppression.[20]

The fall of Karawang irrevocably destroyed the LRJR hegemony
on the Karawang plain. The organisation's command structure was
too fragile, its economic base too weak, and its reputation too badly
damaged for it to reassemble. Not all of its component parts disappeared or accepted merger into the army. Weakened and demoral-
ised, scattered units fled into the remoter parts of the region to
continue the struggle. Mangelep, for instance, returned with his
troops to Lamaran and the country northeast of Karawang, where he
formed the Pasukan Macan Citarum (Tiger of Citarum Unit). Some
joined remnants of the Cirebon LR under Sastrosuwiryo in a retreat
to the mountainous area south of Cirebon around the town of
Ciwaru. A few fled to Central Java to join Sutan Akbar. Many made
their way to the slopes of Mt Sanggabuana south of Karawang.[21]
Several groups, however, decided to cross over the demarcation line
into occupied Jakarta. It had always been the intention of the LRJR
to carry the struggle back into Jakarta. As early perhaps as January
1947, Panji and Fakhruddin, who now commanded most of Haji
Darip's old unit, moved back into the Klender area, which was then
somewhat depopulated by the flight of refugees to Jakarta and
Karawang. Syamsuddin Can began to set up an underground organisation in the city, drawing on LRJR contacts from before the clash and
cooperating with other Republican undergrounds, notably the Pos
Kelelawar (Bat Post) of Mustapha Dullah which was a part of Zulkifli
Lubis' Field Preparation network.[22]

With the passing of the LRJR, however, not just advantages of
scale were lost, but focus and status. Without the LRJR, its sense of
purpose and its pretensions to national significance, the armed units
of the Karawang plain were almost indistinguishable from the bandit
gangs that had originally spawned them. In the wake of the Karawang affair, therefore, the lasykar felt an urgent need to find a larger

framework within which they could gain recognition. Ironically, it was their erstwhile opponents, the Dutch and the Republic, who were to provide these opportunities.

1. H. Rosihan Anwar, *Kisah-kisah Jakarta Menjelang Clash ke-I* (Jakarta, 1979), 88–9. Interview: Hasan Gayo, Jakarta, 1 March 1983.
2. Interviews: Kusnandar Partowisastro, Bogor, 20 January, 3 February 1983; Sidik Samsi, Jakarta, 17 November 1982; Hasan Gayo, Jakarta, 1 March 1983; Johar Nur, Jakarta, 11 October 1982; R. F. Ma'riful, Jakarta, 23 August 1982. See also 'Vergadering van de Lasjkar Rakjat op 22, 23 en 24 November 1946 te Krawang', *Proc.Gen.* 890. *Merdeka* 28 November 1946. Delegates to the conference included Kusnandar (LRJR), A. M. Khamdi (LR Cirebon), Waluyo (LR Sukabumi), Sumo (LR Banten), Umar Laudin (LR Banyumas/Purwokerto) and Zubir (LR Tegal). The formation of the LRJB was apparently not approved by LR leaders in all the regions mentioned. Zubir in Tegal, for instance, came originally from Karawang and was a shadowy figure well outside the mainstream of the local revolutionary movement. LR leaders from Banten, Priangan, Banyumas and Pekalongan issued a special joint statement in April 1947 that they were not to be considered part of the LRJB. See Nasution, *SPKI* IV, 441–2. Anton Lucas, personal communication. The formation of the LRJB may have been in part a response to the fusion of all other LR organisations on Java into a single Lasykar Rakyat led by Sakirman at a LR conference in Central Java on 15 November 1946. See G. W. Overdijkink, *Het Indonesische Probleem: de Feiten* (The Hague, 1946), 35.
3. Interviews: Kusnandar Partowisastro, Bogor, 20 January, 3 February 1983; Sidik Samsi, Jakarta, 17 November 1982.
4. DOBIN no. 217, 20 December 1946, *Proc.Gen.* 19. Nasution, *SPKI* IV, 202, 235–236; Anwar, *op.cit.*, 119. *Ra'jat* 30 December 1946, 3 January 1947. *Kedaulatan Rakjat* 4 January 1947. Sutomo had raised the idea of a 17 August Division as early as October 1946. See NEFIS, Wekelijksch Militair Overzicht, 7 October 1946, *Alg.Sec. I* box 1, file 10.
5. G. McT. Kahin, *Nationalism and revolution in Indonesia* (Ithaca, N.Y., 1952), 199–206; P. Harahap, *Saat bersedjarah* (Jakarta, 1947). Interview: Moh. Hasan Gayo, Jakarta, 1 March 1983. The LRJB subsequently accused the Benteng Republik of inconsistency and weakness over its handling of the Malang session and withdrew from the opposition coalition. See *Repoeblik* 12 March 1947, *Soeara Oemoem* 18 March 1947 and Nasution *SPKI* IV, 442.
6. Interviews: Sidik Samsi, Jakarta, 17 November 1982; Moh. Hasan Gayo, Jakarta, 1 March 1983.
7. Confidential interviews. 'Suroto Kunto hilang misterius', *Pikiran Rakyat* (Bandung) 19 August 1978. Nasution, *SPKI* IV, 238–41.

8. File: Sukardjo Wiriopranoto, *Proc.Gen.* 245; 'Verslag over de tweede besprekingen te Bekasi', *Alg.Sec. I* box I, file 33. A. van Sprang, *Wij Werden Geroepen: de Geschiedenis van de 7 December Divisie* (The Hague, 1949), 46–8. Interviews: Dr Eri Soedewo, Jakarta, 14 February 1983; Sadikin, Jakarta, 28 March 1983; Daan Jahja, Jakarta, 2 December 1982.

9. Nasution, *SPKI* IV, 202. Interviews: Daan Jahja, Jakarta, 7, 10, August, 2 December 1982; Sadikin, Jakarta, 28 March 1983; Sidik Brotoatmodjo, Bandung, 16 March 1983; Johar Nur, Jakarta, 13 February 1983; Kusnandar Partowisastro, Bogor, 21 February 1983.

10. Overdijkink, *op.cit.*, 39. *Kedaulatan Rakjat* (Yogyakarta) 19 March 1947; *Repoeblik* (Cirebon) 28 February 1947. The second congress of Sakirman's Lasykar Rakyat, now closely associated with Amir Syarifuddin, was held in Magelang on 28 April 1947 and approved the proposal to form the TNI, suggesting that this was no anti-LR move. See NEFIS, Verkort politiek situatie-overzicht van Nederlandsch Indië [hereafter VPSONI] no. 11 (19 May 1947), *Proc.Gen.* 3.

11. Overdijkink, *op.cit.*, 38–9. M. S. Soemaatmadja, 'Kisah nyata sukaduka pengalaman pada masa revolusi physic tahun 1945', *Perpustakaan 45* no. 832/XLII. Nasution, *SPKI* III 449–454, *SPKI* IV, 65. NEFIS, Terate-signalement, 25 August 1947, *MvD/CAD*, HKGS/ NOI, Inv. nr. GG 16, 1946/47, bundel 1519. Interview: Abdul Karim Abbas, Jakarta, 2 November 1982. A. H. Nasution in interview with John Smail, 9 December 1960 (information kindly made available by Dr Smail).

12. Interviews: Sadikin, Jakarta, 28 March 1983; Johar Nur, Jakarta, 13 February 1983; Sidik Brotoatmodjo, Bandung, 16 March 1983. *Nieuwsgier* 22 April 1947; *Kedaulatan Rakjat* 2 April 1947; *Ra'jat* 3 April 1947. Overdijkink, *op.cit.*, 148–9, 168–9. Mohd Soiz, 'Jalan-jalan yang kususuri', *Perpustakaan 45* no. 157/VIII. Sedjarah Militer Kodam VI Siliwangi, [hereafter Semdam VI], *Siliwangi Dari Masa Kemasa* (Jakarta: 1968), 185, describes as a major source of tension a meeting between army and LRJR leaders in March 1947, in which LRJR leaders demanded control of the Jakarta front. It is probable, however, that this refers to the LRJR-TRI conferences of mid-1946 mentioned in the previous chapter. Dates provided by *Siliwangi Dari Masa Kemasa* are frequently inaccurate and I have discovered no other reference to a meeting along these lines in 1947.

13. Both Nasution's memoirs and the official history of the Siliwangi Division gloss over this delay, making the army operation appear to be a direct response to Suroto's disappearance, when in fact there was a gap of nearly five months between the two events. See A. H. Nasution, *Memenuhi Panggilan Tugas, jilid 1: Kenangan Masa Muda* (Jakarta: 1982), 161–2; Semdam VI, *op.cit.*, 186–7.

14. Semdam VI, *op.cit.*, 187–7; J. R. W. Smail, *Bandung in the Early Revolution, 1945–1946: a Study in the Social History of the Indonesia Revolution* (Ithaca, N.Y., 1964), 133. E. Madli Hasan, 'Perjoangan 45 untuk pembangunan bangsa', *Perpustakaan 45* no. 118/VI. Interviews:

Sidik Brotoatmodjo, Bandung, 16 March 1983; Kusnandar Partowisastro, Bogor, 3 February 1983; Sadikin, Jakarta, 28 March 1983.

15. Stafkwartier I Divisie, 'Overzicht en ontwikkeling van den toestand van 17 April '47 . . . tot 24 April '47', *MvD/CAD*, HKGS-NOI, Krijgsgescheidkundige Sectie, AA24, 1947, bundel 1, stuk 33.

16. Interview: Sidik Brotoatmodjo, Bandung, 16 March 1983. In some Dutch military circles, the idea of cooperation with the TRI against the lasykar was popular and the Dutch watched keenly for indications that this might be possible. See, for example, the report of April 1946 in which Nasution is quoted as saying to a Dutch official, 'It would be splendid if together we could eliminate these extremists', NEFIS, Contact tussen T. R. I. en S. Z. Groep, 30 April 1946, Minog verbaal no. P 25, 29 May 1946; see also Spoor's public statement suggesting TRI-KNIL cooperation against the lasykar, *Nieuwsgier*, 10 December 1946.

17. NEFIS, VPSONI 10 (30 April 1947), *Proc.Gen.* 3; Dagoverzicht van de plaats gehad hebbende gebeurtenissen, 17–26 April 1947, *Proc.Gen.* 147 no. 1. *Sin Po* 23 April 1947. Interviews: Sidik Brotoatmodjo, Bandung, 16 March 1983; Hasjim K. Notokoesoemo, Jakarta, 11 November 1982; Firmansyah, Jakarta, 18 November 1982. For the official government statement on the affair, see *Kedaulatan Rakjat* 3 May 1947; *Ra'jat* 2 May 1947. According to a Dutch report, Sutan Akbar was arrested in Central Java at this time but released soon after; see 'De Bamboe Roentjing—Beweging in West-Java, *NEFIS Bulletin* no. 29 (23 August 1948), *MvD/CAD* HKGS-NOI, Inv.nr. GG 40, 1948, bundel 16577. For the official statement of the Republican Ministry of Defence on the clash, see *Soeara Oemoem* 3 May 1947.

18. Nasution, *SPKI* IV, 442. *Ra'jat* 22 April 1947; *Repoeblik* 21, 23 April, 8 May 1947. Interview: Kusnandar Partowisastro, Bogor, 3 February 1983.

19. Madli Hasan, *op.cit.*; NEFIS, Terate-signalement, *loc.cit.*; Nasution, *SPKI* III, 195–7, *SPKI* IV, 452; Semdam VI, *op.cit.*, 188–9; *Biografi Prof. dr. Moestopo* (n.p., 1980), 8–9. Interviews: Kusnandar Partowisastro, Bogor, 20 January, 3 February 1946; Sidik Kardi, Jakarta, 15 February 1983; Sidik Samsi, Jakarta, 17 November 1982; Hasan Gayo, Jakarta, 1 March 1983; Moh. Soepardi Shimbat, Jakarta, 18 November 1982.

20. NEFIS, 'Tewerkstelling Noerdin Pasariboe', 15 November 1947, *Proc. Gen.* 309. Pasaribu subsequently applied for a job in the Netherlands Indies Foreign Exchange Bureau.

21. Interviews: Supardi Mangkuyuwono, Jakarta, 19 October 1982; Sidik Kardi, Jakarta, 15 February 1983; Sidik Samsi, Jakarta, 11 October, 17 November 1982; K. H. Hasboelah, Klender, 19 October 1982; Johar Nur, Jakarta, 27 October 1982; Hasjim K. Notokoesoemo, Jakarta, 11 November 1982; K. H. Nurali, Babelan, Bekasi, 17 January 1983; Sidik Brotoatmodjo, Bandung, 16 March 1983.

22. Territoriaal Ondercommando Batavia, Uitoefening politiek-politioneel taak, 18 February 1947, *Proc.Gen.* 470; see also Territoriaal Onder-

commando Batavia, Diverse gegevens, 3 January 1947, *ibid.*; Rapp. Alg.Politie Batavia over September 1948, *Proc.Gen.* 875 no. 5; Korps Algemene Politie, Beknopt politiek-politioneel verslag, 30 September 1948, *Proc.Gen.* 192. Interview: Sidik Samsi, Jakarta, 17 November 1982. Akhmad Indin Natapraja, who had led the LRJR underground in Jakarta immediately after the withdrawal to Karawang, was killed in a clash near Bekasi in June 1946 and his place was taken by Oto Soewandi and Endang Soerawan. *Merdeka* 18 June 1946. Interview: Abdul Karim Abbas, Jakarta, 30 October 1982; Sidik Samsi, Jakarta, 1 November 1982.

IV
NEW ADVENTURES

11

Her Majesty's Irregular Troops

In colonial times, the local bosses of the Karawang plain had aspired to join the establishment, either as legitimised hitmen of the authorities or as wealthy retirees. When the revolution broke out, they saw a vast array of new opportunities for satisfying their social aspirations through taking official positions in local government and participating in the lasykar. As these opportunities steadily shrank, some of the local bosses began to look for new patrons. Scenting the changing wind of revolutionary fortune, it was to the Dutch that some groups turned. Panji, Fakhruddin and their followers, together with Harun Umar and Sujono, took the remarkable step of taking service with a local Dutch unit as a kind of auxiliary force. The circumstances which led to this desertion help to illustrate the nature of gangster participation in the revolution.

Panji, a son-in-law of Haji Darip, was a local boss in his own right. According to a Dutch report, before the war he had been sentenced to twelve years' jail for robbery but had escaped during the Japanese occupation and had coordinated an operation supplying rice to the Japanese. Like other local bosses, he had put together an armed band at the start of the revolution, and his unit was a rather loosely gathered collection of about three hundred patriots, toughs and opportunists which he held together both with the strength of his personality and magic powers—like his father-in-law he was believed to be able to produce charms for invulnerability—and by the careful distribution of patronage. He followed Darip, too, into the LRJR but was displaced from his Klender power base early in 1946 by the gradual expansion of the Allied perimeter east of the city. The prospects for such displaced gangs on the Karawang plain were poor. Away from the territory and people they knew well, and facing competition from established local gangs, they were often merely surviving. The power of Haji Darip, for instance, declined dramatically after he was forced from Klender, and he quickly became one of the less significant minor unit commanders in the LRJR. Panji's gang held together better—perhaps he was a more competent military commander than Darip—but by early 1947 he had had enough and he took his unit quietly over the demarcation line, back into his old haunts.

Panji's return to Klender may have been welcomed by some of the local population as a restoration of the Republican presence, but after his prolonged absence from the region Panji found his power base there attenuated. To restore his prestige and authority, re-establish his local networks of influence and create an economic base, Panji found that a good deal of determined and heavy-handed action was needed, and reports of extortion, robbery, arson and intimidation in the area increased dramatically after January 1947, as he removed or cowed Dutch-appointed village officials and collected the money and goods needed to pay his followers.[1]

This flare-up of lasykar activity behind the front lines alarmed the Dutch authorities, and in March 1947, after unsuccessfully inviting Panji's followers to betray him by offering a f500 reward for his death, they posted a full battalion to Klender to take charge of the situation. This battalion was the 3rd battalion of the 9th Infantry Regiment of the 7 December Division, known as 3–9 RI. This division, which consisted of conscripts from the Netherlands, was named for Queen Wilhelmina's speech of 6 December 1941 (heard in Indonesia, because of time-zone differences, on 7 December) in which she had promised thoroughgoing review of the constitutional relationship of the Netherlands to its colonies after the war. This speech, seen by many Indonesian nationalists as a Dutch attempt to delay dealing with the colonial question, was seen conversely by the Dutch as a token of their good faith, a pledging of the national word that change would come. The naming of an army division after this speech was thus a reaffirmation of the Dutch determination to allow change, though only at a pace which they had fixed. The division went to Indonesia not as part of the KNIL but as part of the Dutch army, the KL (*Koninklijke Landmacht*). 3–9 RI arrived there in late October 1946 and subsequently saw little more than garrison duty in Tanggerang before it was posted to Klender.

On its arrival in Klender, the battalion found a tense atmosphere gripping the town and surrounding countryside. Most people avoided contact with the Dutch and Dutch patrols found their progress through the countryside accompanied by the flashing of lights and the beating of warning drums. The occupiers were also aware of the

existence of a Republican shadow government in the region, especially by virtue of the fact that their own village administration
appeared to be barely functioning.[2] In attempting to meet the challenge presented by Panji and his lasykar, the 3–9 RI discovered
quickly that conventional military techniques were ineffective. In the
flat countryside with its tangle of forests and swamps, its network of
paths and streams and its scattering of villages and hamlets there
were no strategic points to be occupied and Panji's lasykar never
stayed long enough in any one place to present a clear target for
military action. Instead, the battalion developed a counter-guerrilla
strategy. Village guard units were established, first in a limited region
around the major army barracks, and later more widely through the
countryside north of Klender. The guards were armed only with
knives and clubs, but the Dutch also developed an alarm system
which enabled them to call rapidly for help from the army. Small
units of eight to ten Dutch troops were scattered about the countryside as a further hindrance to lasykar movement, while a special rapid
response team of about ten men was put together. These were men
familiar with the region as a whole, who kept themselves ready
twenty-four hours a day to respond to calls for help from village
guards, and they prided themselves on being organised so that they
could be in their jeeps and on their way within two minutes of getting
a call. If only a small lasykar group was involved, the rapid response
team might, with the village guards, be able to fight them off. More
often, however, they simply kept the attackers engaged until regular
units of the battalion arrived. Commander of this team was the
battalion's intelligence officer, a young 2nd Lieutenant, Koert Bavinck. He had been in Indonesia as a child, spoke good Malay and
had had some experience of clandestine warfare in the Dutch resistance to the German occupation. As intelligence officer, he was
particularly aware of the need to guarantee the safety of the network
of informers he was gradually building up, and he used the rapid
response team as a means of achieving this.[3]

The strategy worked and, as the area covered was extended,
increasing numbers of troops from Panji's units were captured.
Rather than simply questioning them for information and then keeping them out of circulation, the battalion decided to make use of the
prisoners, sending them back to their units, some as informers,
others with the task of persuading their colleagues to surrender. The
release of prisoners in this way was not as risky as it might appear. In
the first place, the very act of releasing prisoners was a supremely
self-confident gesture likely to give lasykar the impression that the
Dutch were well in control of things. Second, the Dutch generally
took the precaution of releasing only lasykar whose wives and chil-

dren they held hostage. Although not all Dutch units were scrupulous in their treatment of captured Indonesians, it was probably unlikely that the 3–9 RI would have harmed the hostages. Nonetheless, the threat was a real one from the lasykar point of view.[4]

As the number of lasykar deserting or being captured increased, Panji faced a mounting leadership crisis. No gang leader of his kind could retain his position for long in the face of so clear a demonstration of his receding power. He could of course have fled and joined Wahidin Nasution in the Sanggabuana foothills, but that would have meant running the double gauntlet of the Dutch frontline troops and the TNI. It would also have meant abandoning his local power base altogether. The only way for Panji to preserve his authority seemed to be to follow his men into the Dutch camp, and to do so while he still had enough followers to be seen clearly as leader. The gang leaders of the Jakarta region were accustomed to recognising political and military realities, and it was now clear where the balance of power in Klender lay. Hearing rumours that Panji was on the point of surrender, the Dutch redoubled their military pressure on him. On 4 May, then, Panji sent his wife and his mother to Bavinck's office to discuss the terms of a surrender to the Dutch. An understanding was reached that surrendering lasykar would not be handed over under arrest to the civilian authorities and almost at once Panji issued orders to his followers to surrender to the Dutch. On 8 May he himself was en route to Jakarta to surrender when he was arrested by the redoubtable Lt-Colonel Agerbeek. He was immediately, however, handed over to Bavinck and was taken to Klender on the same day. There Panji was brought in front of his assembled men, whom he ordered to give up their weapons and to obey the orders of Bavinck. The men dispersed, and within hours had returned with some ninety weapons, a motley collection of rifles, pistols and old Japanese machineguns, many of them without any ammunition at all.[5]

Having captured Panji and substantial numbers of lasykar, however, the Dutch faced the problem of what to do with them. The prisoners could not simply be released, since they had no other means of support and would be likely to return to banditry. Moreover, in the eyes of the Dutch civil authorities these men, as members of irregular units, were in no way entitled to prisoner-of-war status. Some in fact had been on Dutch wanted lists since the revolutionary violence of late 1945 in Jakarta, and most were regarded as criminals by virtue of their units' reputation for murder and robbery. Putting them on trial, however, was likely to be risky from the Dutch army's point of view, since this would discourage other lasykar still at large in Klender and other regions from surrendering. Nor was it easy simply to detain them, partly because of the expense and drain on manpower, partly because extensive prison camps of any kind were vulnerable to unfavourable publicity, especially close to Jakarta, and partly because the lasykar were likely to become restless and troublesome if given nothing to do. A protest amongst the lasykar, for instance, flared up when Panji was transferred from Klender to the jail at Bukit Duri, and although it died down rapidly it was a sign that lasykar tolerance was limited.[6]

Bavinck, of course, continued to use reliable, or at least controllable, lasykar both to persuade the small, scattered bands of lasykar still operating to surrender, and for the gathering of intelligence, especially from across the demarcation line. But with some 225 lasykar under his command, only a relatively small proportion could be used in this way. From conversations with lasykar, however, it soon became clear to the Dutch that many of Panji's followers nurtured an impressive hatred for the TNI, as well as a fair degree of disillusionment with the Republic as a whole. It also emerged that on 8 May, the day of the great surrender, surrendering lasykar had clashed with a smaller group of their former colleagues under Arbi, who disagreed with the abandonment of the struggle. The idea thus arose in Dutch circles that the lasykar might be used not just for intelligence purposes but as auxiliary soldiers. The idea was particularly attractive to the Dutch as a way of saving the lives of the conscripts in the 7 December Division. Bavinck took the notion to the army commander, General Spoor, who approved it, and then to the Prosecutor-General, H. W. Felderhof, who was persuaded to grant immunity from prosecution to those who volunteered for service with the Dutch. Just as important, he was given a budget for the venture, separate from battalion funds, to provide uniforms, modern weapons, payment and food for the lasykar, and he coined for his new unit the name *Hare Majesteit's Ongeregelde Troepen* (Her Majesty's Irregular Troops) or HAMOTs.[7]

The line of descent from LRJR to HAMOT became clearer with the arrival in camp of the former LRJR unit commanders Harun Umar and Sujono, whose units had apparently disappeared after the Karawang affair. Both were recognised by the Dutch as prominent ideological as well as military figures in the LRJR and, fearing a plot, the Dutch were hesitant to allow them full access to the HAMOTs. It will probably never be clear, however, why these two men surrendered to the Dutch. While weariness with the struggle may have played a role, both apparently expected to enter Dutch service in some capacity such as the HAMOTs. Bitterness towards the TNI may also have led them to this step, and they may have been attracted by the prospect of recognition, training and equipment.

Surviving lasykar, on the other hand, stress the tactical nature of the move, as a ploy to obtain equipment and intelligence from the Dutch while avoiding unnecessary conflict with the TNI, in order to be able to turn later against the Dutch.

The HAMOTs were quartered in a camp at Kampung Sumur near Klender, where they were given light arms and began to receive military training. Bavinck used them primarily for espionage, especially across the demarcation line into Republican territory. This was of course an area with which they were familiar, and where they could make use of at least some of their old contacts. He also employed them in attempting to choke off the trade in contraband and strategic goods across the demarcation line. Again, since the lasykar had recently been engaged in this trade themselves they were well-placed to hinder it. As their experience grew, they were used for sabotage and agitation behind Republican lines, but they also became caught up in a distinctly political venture by a group of middle-ranking Dutch civilian and military figures.[8]

In conservative Dutch circles in Batavia and in West Java in general there was considerable concern not only with the Linggajati Agreement in general but with the first article, in particular. The agreement proposed an independent federal Indonesia, to consist of the Republic on Java and Sumatra and two new federal states of East Indonesia and Borneo (Kalimantan). The first article read, in part,

> The areas [on Java and Sumatra] occupied by Allied or Netherlands forces shall be included gradually, through mutual cooperation, in Republican territory. To this end, the necessary measures shall at once be taken in order that this inclusion shall be completed at the latest on [1 January 1949].[9]

Reluctant to see such major cities as Jakarta and Bandung, not to mention the rich plantation areas of West Java, consigned permanently to the Republic, a small group of conservative Dutchmen began to encourage the idea of a fourth federal state of West Java, or Pasundan, alongside Borneo, East Indonesia and the Republic, based on the distinct ethnicity of the Sundanese people. With a population of perhaps twelve million at the time, West Java offered economies of scale which made the idea of a federal state feasible, while it was common belief amongst Dutch officials in Indonesia that the regional identity of the Sundanese was particularly strong and that they would be keen not to be incorporated into the Republic along with the Javanese, the only ethnic group in the archipelago to exceed them in numbers.[10]

The movement for a federal state of Pasundan was spearheaded publicly by a Sundanese aristocrat, R.A.A.M.M. Suria Karialegawa, the former regent of Garut. His *Partai Rakyat Pasundan* (PRP, Pasundan People's Party), however, founded on 20 November 1946, enjoyed the protection of local Dutch civil and military officials, notably Colonel Thomson in Bogor, the Resident of the Priangan, M. Klaassen, and the acting governor of Batavia, C. W. A. Abbenhuis. These authorities gave active assistance to the Pasundan movement, and supported and encouraged Suria Kartalegawa when he proclaimed the Negara Pasundan (State of Pasundan) in public meetings in Bandung and Bogor on 4 May 1947.[11] Aside from its meagre popular support, the problem for the PRP was that large sections of the territory it claimed lay on the Republican side of the demarcation line, and it had no way at all either of seizing them or even of defending the Dutch-controlled territory it claimed. Under these circumstances, it looked with interest to the HAMOT camp at Kampung Sumur. Few of the lasykar there were in fact Sundanese, but the Karawang clashes had given rise to wild rumours of Sundanese being massacred by the Republic, and the lasykar were certainly opposed to the Republic, for the time being at least. Since the lasykar were rather under-employed, the army authorities were happy for them to be recruited in the short term as propagandists for the PRP. It was as a result of their activities that the PRP was able claim some twenty special branches in the Karawang area, but since they also claimed to be negotiating with the rather left-wing, anti-Sundanese Kyai Akhmad Khatib, Republican Resident of Banten, their claims should be met with some scepticism.[12]

This brief excursion into politics aside, the HAMOT experiment was not an immediate success from the Dutch point of view. A major problem was that the operation rapidly grew beyond the modest scope originally envisaged by Bavinck. By early June some three hundred lasykar had joined the HAMOTs, from other groups as well as Panji's. They had brought with them a similar number of women and children and the entire community now settled down in Kampung Sumur. Catering for such a group was far beyond Bavinck's resources; he had sixty mattresses for the entire group and could only afford to buy rice of such poor quality that the lasykar, used to requisitioning good quality Karawang rice, refused to eat it. So cramped were the conditions in the camp that some single lasykar had to live out, coming to the camp only for their meals. Not only was the HAMOT programme beginning to take on the character of a social welfare exercise but it was becoming impossible to maintain close military control over the lasykar. Not only did it appear that Republican propaganda was finding its way into the camp, but suspicions arose that some lasykar were engaging once more in banditry and that their association with the HAMOTs would only compromise the Dutch. Senior Dutch officials were also worried that lasykar employed to cross the demarcation line would be captured and would betray Dutch infringement of the ceasefire which was part of the Linggajati Agreement. News that entire Hizbullah and BPRI units across the demarcation line were planning to desert to the HAMOTs finally prompted a decision to wind down the programme, retaining about thirty of the more reliable lasykar for espionage work, removing the more capable and less guilty of the rest to another area for formal military training, and sending the remainder home with the right to draw rations temporarily as a reward for having surrendered.[13]

Many of the HAMOTs promptly deserted. This was too close to the kind of rationalisation Nasution had been proposing. The increasing likelihood of Dutch military action against the Republic, however, led the army to leave not thirty but seventy-five men in Bavinck's hands, and these men were prepared not for espionage work but for military action, being given training on weapons such as Brens and Lee Enfields. The result was a much tighter more capable unit, and to add to the enthusiasm of the lasykar, Panji was finally brought from Bukit Duri and restored to his followers. With no apparent bitterness for his weeks of detention, he announced that he wanted nothing more than to take part in smashing the Republic.[14]

Although the Linggajati Agreement was formally signed in an atmosphere of festivity in Jakarta on 25 May 1947, the bad will and distrust which the preceding events generated on both sides made impossible the willing cooperation on which implementation of the agreement depended. The agreement foundered, too, on fundamental points of interpretation. The two sides could not agree on whether the federal states of Borneo and East Indonesia should be formed jointly by the Dutch and the Republic or by the Dutch alone. The Dutch regarded the Republic's continued direct dealings with international organisations and sympathetic countries such as India and Egypt as claiming a degree of sovereignty not appropriate for a mere constituent member of a yet-to-be-formed federation.

This stalemate turned Dutch thoughts increasingly in the direction of war. Several things had changed to make military action an attractive proposition for the Dutch. The British finally departed in November 1946, leaving the Dutch free to formulate policies without risk of a British veto and with less risk of unwelcome publicity for surreptitious operations and preparations. Their position, moreover, was greatly strengthened by the arrival of the 7 December Division from the Netherlands in late 1946, which brought the number of Dutch troops in Indonesia to about 100,000.[15] As 1947 drew on, these forces faced a Republic which was increasingly weakened by the

Dutch naval blockade of Java, and which no longer presented the prosperous face on which so many visitors had remarked in 1946. This apparent weakness, together with the strength of political opposition within the Republic to the Linggajati agreement, encouraged the Dutch to think in terms at least of a show of strength to frighten radical opinion in the Republic into accepting Dutch demands.[16] The Dutch, moreover, had pressing economic reasons for wanting to expand their territory on Java and Sumatra. Although their economic position was far better than that of the Republic, they suffered from food shortages, and they eyed the Karawang area in particular as a source of rice for their establishment in Jakarta. The Dutch were also in increasingly desperate need of foreign exchange, and the only way to generate this in the short term was to recover the rich plantation areas of West and East Java and parts of Sumatra. The army, of course, was quicker to think in terms of war than the civilians, and preparations for a large-scale invasion of the Republic which began as early as March 1947 were reportedly complete by May.[17]

Finally, around midnight on 20 July 1947, van Mook called a press conference to announce that the Dutch were resuming 'freedom of operation' in Indonesia, thereby repudiating all previous acknowledgements of and agreements with the Republic. While the conference was under way, some 120 HAMOT troops under Bavinck's command crossed the demarcation line at Tambun on the east Jakarta front in order to break a passage through the Republican front line of defence. Bavinck accompanied them, sitting alongside Panji in a sandbagged jeep as it rode along the main road towards Tambun. The HAMOTs were pitched there against their old enemies, the Beruang Merah, and heavy fighting took place around Tambun. The initial Dutch targets in the area, however, were the road and rail bridges across the river Citarum just before Karawang. Sabotage on any of the river crossings of the Karawang plain would hamper the Dutch attack, but the Citarum was the broadest river in the area and the bridge across it would be the most difficult to repair if damaged by Republican scorched earth actions. The Dutch, therefore, gambled on sending a heavily armoured train along the railway line, loaded with troops of the 7 December Division, while Dutch military aircraft repeatedly strafed the area around the bridges to prevent the TNI from setting off explosive charges. The train crossed the Citarum bridge undamaged at about midday on the first day of the attack. While the Dutch train was still under way, Indonesians in Karawang sent an unmanned locomotive at full throttle along the track to try to ram the Dutch, but it arrived too late and smashed into the Dutch engine after the Dutch troops had safely disembarked on the eastern bank of the Citarum. Republican troops drove off a Dutch attack on Karawang that afternoon, but the town fell the next day, with Bavinck and ten of his HAMOTs still at the front of the Dutch push. The fall of Cikampek followed on the 23rd and that of Purwakarta on the 24th. The army units on the Jakarta front, the Beruang Merah and Hasibuan's ALRI, retreated rapidly to the east. The ALRI made its way to Banyumas, where it joined up with the main ALRI units from Tegal, while the Beruang Merah headed for Tasikmalaya, harassed along the way by remnants of the LRJR who were also trying to hamper the Dutch advance.[18]

The heaviest fighting in the region took place in the Ciater pass area above Subang, between troops of the Purwakarta regiment and Dutch troops attacking from Bandung, but here too the Dutch soon broke through. Highly effective scorched earth tactics were applied by Republican troops in the Cibarusa area, where they destroyed almost all the bridges on the road from Cibinong through Cileungsi and Cibarusa to Karawang and added numerous road-blocks, so that the Dutch troops attacking along that road arrived too late in Karawang to join in any further operations. Much of the town of Subang was also burnt before the Dutch arrived. In general, however, the attack was little short of a disaster for the TNI 3rd Brigade, with defences crumbling sooner than expected, the Resimen Perjuangan of Rambe disintegrating under Dutch pressure, and both Rambe and the brigade commander Sidik Brotoatmojo retreating rapidly eastwards towards Cirebon and Central Java.[19]

The story was only a little better for the Republic in the rest of Java. In few places was the army's collapse as complete as in Jakarta, but everywhere the Dutch advanced rapidly and easily into Republican territory. The Dutch V-Brigade, attacking from Bandung, captured Cirebon on 23 July. Other Dutch troops took Pelabuhan Ratu on the south coast and the town of Sukabumi. In East Java, they took over most of the peninsula east of Malang, an area rich in plantations. Van Mook began to think not only of capturing economically valuable territory but of destroying the Republic by capturing Yogyakarta. He was prevented from this, however, by a resolution of the United Nations Security Council, accepted by the Netherlands government, calling for a cessation of hostilities. The order was issued on 4 August 1947, and the Dutch advance towards Yogyakarta was halted, but the Dutch reserved the right to conduct 'mopping-up' operations within the territory they claimed to have seized, and they launched successful attacks on Tasikmalaya and Garut during the days following the ceasefire.[20]

The sudden expansion of Dutch territory in the military action left the troops of the 7 December Division in charge of the entire, unfamiliar Karawang plain. Although many TNI and lasykar units seemed to have left the region, it quickly became clear that many other small armed groups remained. The experience of 3–9 R.I. and other units before July had suggested that the appropriate technique for dealing with such groups was the dispersal of troops into the countryside and the creation of close connections with villagers. This strategy, however, was vetoed by the divisional commander, General Dürst Britt. As part of the Dutch army rather than the KNIL, the division was destined to be sent back to Europe in 1948 to take up duties under very different conditions on the Rhine, and Dürst Britt wanted to retain the division's structural integrity for this task. Experience and skills gained in patrolling the kampungs and rice fields of Karawang were unlikely to contribute to the division's performance of its tasks in Germany.[21]

Renewed attention was given, therefore, to the HAMOTs as a means of projecting Dutch power into every corner of the region. The performance of the HAMOTs in the military action had dramatically improved their reputation and Bavinck was later awarded the prestigious Militaire Willemsorde for his part in the HAMOT action. Several other Dutch battalions began to imitate the experiment. In the sixth field artillery regiment, a Lt Spier formed his own group of a hundred or so lasykar, called the 'Spiertjes', which he posted in the flat country north of Subang. A further ninety-odd were used on guard duty by 3–10 RI in the area around Purwakarta, while still others were used in the hill country between Subang and Linggajati, and in the Garut and Tasikmalaya areas. Most spectacular of all, however were Bavinck's own operations. He selected what appeared to be the cream of the army and lasykar units which had surrendered after the Military Action and his HAMOTs expanded to six platoons, at least one of them drawn largely from former TNI troops, totalling two to three hundred men. They were used over a wide stretch of country around the battalion headquarters in Cikampek, for patrol and guard duties as well as for the collection of intelligence and the breaking up of smuggling rings. They were also 'lent' occasionally to other Dutch units for similar purposes.[22]

All, however, was not well with the HAMOTs. Harun Umar's desertion shortly after the Military Action had been a minor setback which was barely noticed in the general euphoria. Matters were put aright in any case, in the Dutch view, when he was recaptured in September and shot. Sujono, who had deserted a little later, was killed as a traitor by the people of his own village. More serious was the turning of Panji, shortly after Harun Umar's desertion. Precisely what happened is not clear. Interviews with figures from both sides reported simply that Panji began negotiating with the Republican

resistance and that he was found out by the Dutch and shot, along
with his co-conspirator, Fakhruddin. If this were the case, it suggests
that Panji had perhaps not forgiven his captors for his long incarcer-
ation in Bukit Duri and that, having dealt with one set of enemies,
the Beruang Merah, he turned immediately to deal with another. He
was buoyed, perhaps, by a belief that the HAMOT victory in Tambun had been instrumental in the Dutch military success; or perhaps
he simply found the discipline which Bavinck sought to impose on
him irksome. Documentary evidence is less clear, but suggests that
Panji was kidnapped by the TNI and later killed by them. There must
be some doubt, however, whether the TNI or any other nationalist
group was well-organised enough at this time to pull off such a coup.
It is not impossible that Panji's execution by the Dutch was deliberately concealed at the time to preserve the HAMOT's newly
acquired image of success.[23]

Also disturbing for the Dutch was their inability to establish
effective administrative control in the region. Close to the old demarcation line, where the population had suffered from skirmishes,
blockades, and the at times heavy-handed presence of front-line
army or lasykar forces, the Dutch reported an enthusiastic reception
from local people. Further into Republican territory, however, they
met hostility and occasional resistance: less fruit, more hand grenades, as one Dutch writer put it.[24] It proved correspondingly difficult
to re-establish Dutch administration, despite the defection of senior
Republican officials such as Rubaya and Juarsa. At lower levels of
the administration in the Karawang region, there had been a significant turnover of officials and this new generation was far less inclined
than men such as Juarsa to think of working with the Dutch. The
circumstances, moreover, which had made Bavinck's intelligence
operation in Klender a success were not repeated here. 3–9 RI was
now responsible for a much larger territory and was less free than
before to post its men widely across the region. It therefore found
great difficulty in responding fast enough to calls for help from people
in isolated places.[25] This inability to provide protection at call was a
fatal weakness in its endeavour to build up a reliable local administration, for no village official could afford to ignore the fact that he
might one day have to account to a roving nationalist band for his
dealings with the Dutch.

Added to this was the impressive Karawang rumour market. Like
the Dutch, the lasykar circulated all kinds of rumours calculated to
undermine the position of their opponents. On one occasion, for
instance, troops of the 7 December Division discovered a pamphlet
issued by the 17 August Division announcing in part:

On Wednesday 26.8.47 at 10.00 a.m. the Dutch surrendered to
the Republican government. [Troops from] Australia, India and
Russia have since arrived in Batavia. At 10.00 a.m. the Dutch
flag was struck and then the Republican (red-white) flag was
raised. All radios of the Dutch have been confiscated by the
International powers.[26]

The effect of such rumours, bizarre though they might be, was to
unsettle the region, reinforcing the feeling that any outcome was
possible. This was evident in the local exchange rate between the
Netherlands Indies guilder and the Republican rupiah, which remained at 20:1 a month after the military action, far better for the
rupiah than the rate of exchange in urban Jakarta. The Dutch
accused local Chinese from Cikampek and Jakarta of holding up the
exchange rate artificially so as to be able to dispose of their own
unwanted rupiah, but the high rate was also supported enthusiastically by the nationalists.[27]

So serious was the security problem in the region for the Dutch
that the military authorities decided to post units of the notorious
Special Troops Depot (*Depot Speciale Troepen*) to the region for
brief periods from August to November 1947. This force, commanded by Captain R. P. P. 'Turk' Westerling, had been created
originally as a kind of commando unit for the KNIL. It had gained
notoriety in South Sulawesi in early 1946 as a result of its brutal
counter-revolutionary tactics there. Thereafter, it was quartered at
Jakarta, and after the Military Action was employed in areas of
particular difficulty for conventional Dutch forces. The DST's
achievements in the Karawang area, however, were unimpressive.
Though skilled at killing, the commandos lacked the local knowledge
and intelligence sources to act effectively against the guerillas.[28] By
mid-November, 3–9 RI had decided to abandon altogether the northern part of its region, stretching from just north of Cikampek and
Kosambi all the way down to the northern coast. The tangle of creeks
and swamps in this sparsely-populated area was simply too difficult to
patrol adequately, and the battalion established a defensive demarcation line along a major irrigation canal. It was a severe blow to
Dutch prestige.[29]

The strength of nationalist resistance on the Karawang plain
created further problems for the Dutch with the HAMOTs. From the
start, they had worked the HAMOTs hard, using them extensively
and on difficult military patrols and dangerous intelligence operations. The result had been a high casualty rate, about fifty HAMOTs
being killed in the two and a half months after the Military Action.[30]
While most lasykar accepted death as one of the risks of their

occupation, an attrition rate at this level was disturbing to say the least. The continued inability of the Dutch forces to establish order throughout the region, too, made the Dutch victory in July seem less decisive as time went on, and with their traditional inclination to stick closely only to proven winners, the lasykar began to consider other possibilities. On the night of 26/27 November 1947, the HAMOT platoon of former TNI soldiers, twenty-seven men in all, deserted from their post at Rengasdengklok, taking with them their twenty-seven rifles and a mortar, but leaving their no doubt relieved Dutch NCO asleep and unharmed. The deserters had not left their families as hostages in Dutch camps, but the greater military discipline which their TNI background had given them had encouraged the Dutch nonetheless to use them on patrols. Their defection was thus a blow to Dutch hopes that the HAMOTs might be the basis for a reliable auxiliary force.[31]

Within two months, however, the Dutch had been able to turn the military situation in their favour. Even while on the defensive they had managed to book some minor achievements such as the capture and execution of Bantir, one-time local boss of Bekasi. The major breakthrough arose, however, when Dürst Britt finally gave into pressure from the KNIL generals Spoor and Buurman van Vreeden to adopt the counter-guerilla tactics needed in the Karawang region. This enabled the 3–9 RI to launch an intensive series of armed patrols through most of its region from early December. The patrolling increased the number of casualties and was as physically exhausting for the Dutch troops as it had been for the HAMOT, but it kept the nationalist resistance off balance and on the defensive, so that the Dutch civil administration could at last begin to be established in the countryside.[32]

The result of this success, however, was that the posting of a full KL battalion to the Karawang area ceased to be necessary. Plans were under way, too, to return the 7 December Division to Europe, and the 3–9 RI was thus withdrawn from the Karawang region, along with other KL units. The KNIL units which succeeded them were perhaps better trained for counter-guerrilla warfare, and their arrival was accompanied by a determination on the Dutch part not to repeat the HAMOT experiment. Effective though the HAMOT had been from time to time in the hands of Bavinck, the Dutch military leadership realised that such a unit, dependent on the personal energy and charisma of one man, and liable at any time to break into some or other unpredictable action, could not be incorporated into the army on any long-term basis. It had to be seen simply as an imaginative and temporary measure. The military authorities did not seek to disband the existing HAMOT-style units outright, but they made it clear that they should not be expanded. This decision was heartily endorsed by the KNIL, which had on the whole viewed the HAMOTs with an abiding suspicion. Although a few KNIL units had worked well with HAMOT-style auxiliaries recruited from the lasykar, most rejected the idea. European regulars of the KL and the indigenous auxiliaries of the HAMOT could co-exist happily, but the indigenous regulars of the KNIL generally had little but contempt and distrust for the like of HAMOTs.

1. Territoriaal Ondercommando Batavia, 'Uitoefening politiek-pol. taak', 18 February 1947, *MvD/CAD*, HKGS-NOI, GG 6, bundel 117, 1947, stuk 78; Oorlogs-dagboek, Staf 2e Inf.Brig.I Div. '7 December' February-March 1947, and bijlage 37, 'Bijzonder inlichtingenrapport (gegevens Pandji)', 12 May 1947, *MvD/CAD*, archief Staf IIe Inf.Brig.Groep, doos GG7.
2. Territoriaal Ondercommando Inlichtingendienst, 'Gegevens O. front', 2 February 1947, *Proc.Gen.* 309; Oorlogsdagboek III-9 RI, October-November 1946, March 1947, archief Staf IIe Inf.Brig.Groep, *MvD/CAD*, archief Staf IIe Inf.Brig. Groep, GG12, doos 14. Interview: Lt-Col. K. Bavinck, The Hague, 14 February 1984.
3. Oorlogs-dagboek Staf 2e Inf.Brig.I Div., bijlage 37, *loc.cit.* Interview: Lt-Col. K. Bavinck, The Hague, 14 February 1984.
4. Oorlogs-dagboek Staf 2e Inf.Brig.I Div., bijlage 37, *loc.cit.*; Oorlogsdagboek III–9 RI, April-May 1947, *loc.cit.* Interview: Lt-Kol. K. Bavinck.
5. Oorlogs-dagboek Staf 2e Inf.Brig.I Div., Map IV, Bijlage 37, Bijzonder inlichtingenrapport over de arrestatie van Pandji', 12 May 1947, *loc. cit.*
6. Oorlogsdagboek III–9 RI, June 1947, *loc.cit.*
7. *Ibid.*, May-June 1947. Interview: Lt-Kol. K. Bavinck, The Hague, 14 February 1984.
8. Buurman van Vreeden to Spoor, 'Behandeling Lasjkar Rajats', 11 June 1947, *MvD/CAD*, HKGS-NOI, GG18, bundel 7158, 1947, ongen.
9. For the text of the Linggajati Agreement, see Charles Wolf, *The Indonesian Story: the Birth, Growth and Structure of the Indonesian Republic* (New York, 1948), 175–178.
10. For the development of Dutch ideas on federalism, see Robert Bridson Cribb, 'Jakarta in the Indonesian Revolution 1945–1949', (Ph.D. dissertation, University of London, 1984), 170–174, 191–3.
11. Yong Mun Cheong, *H. J. van Mook and Indonesian Independence: a Study of his Role in Dutch-Indonesian Relations, 1945–48*, (The Hague, 1982), 105–107. For a contemporary and highly critical Dutch assessment of the PRP, see the report 'Partai Ra'jat Pasundan', n.d. (ca May 1947), *Proc.Gen.* 3.
12. Oorlogs-dagboek 2e Inf.Brig.I Div., 21 May 1947, *loc.cit.*; NEFIS,

VPSONI no 11, 19 May 1947; no. 12, 4 June 1947, *Proc.Gen.* 3; NEFIS, VPSONI no 14, 7 July 1947, *Proc.Gen.* 142. *Dagblad* 1 May 1947. Nasution, *SPKI* IV, 451.

13. Staf IIe Inf.Brig.Groep Commandant (Uylenburg) to Buurman van Vreeden, 'L. R. Kamp', 9 June 1947, *MvD/CAD*, HKGS-NOI, GG18, bundel 7158, 1947, stuk 676; KNIL, K & P to Buurman van Vreeden, 'Lasjkar-Rajat kamp', 11 June 1947, *ibid.*; Buurman van Vreeden, 'Behandeling Lasjkar Rajats', *loc.cit.*

14. Cdt 3–9 RI, 'Geschiedenis HAMOT', 20 June 1948, *MvD/CAD*, archief Staf IIe Inf.Brig. Groep doos GG7; Oorlogsdagboek III–9 RI, June, July 1947, *ibid.*; NEFIS, VPSONI no. 12 (4 June 1947), *Proc.Gen.* 3; Dagoverzicht van de plaats gehad hebbende gebeurtenissen, 12, 14 May 1947, *Proc.Gen.* 147/1. Operatief rapport van het KNIL en de KL over het tijdvak 9–5–1947 t/m 15–5–1947, *OBB* X, 645 n. 2. A. van Sprang, *Wij werden Geroepen: de Geschiedenis van de 7 December Divisie* (The Hague, 1949), 57; A. van Sprang, *Laatste acte: een cocktail van soldatenleven en politiek in Indonesië* (The Hague, 1947), 23–24. Situatierapport nr. 64, 24–31 May 1947, *OBB* IX, 213. *Ra'jat*, 29 May 1947. Interviews: Sidik Samsi, Jakarta, 11 October, 1, 17 November 1982; Abdul Karim Abbas, Jakarta, 30 October 1982; K. H. Hasboelah, Klender, 19 October 1982; Camat Nata, Cibitung, Bekasi, 26 January 1983; Hasjim K. Notokoesoemo, Jakarta, 11 November 1982; Kusnandar Partowisastro, 20 January, 3 February 1983.

15. Pierre Heijboer, *De Politionele Acties: de Strijd om 'Indië' 1945/1949* (Haarlem, 1979), 21.

16. Yong, *op.cit.*, 127.

17. *Ibid.*, 126–31; C. Smit, *De Dekolonisatie van Indonesië: Feiten en Beschouwingen* (Groningen, 1976), 19–20; Paul van 't Veer, ed., *Drees: Neerslag van een Werkzaam Leven: een Keuze uit Geschriften, Redevoeringen, Interviews en Brieven uit de Jaren 1902–1972* (Assen, 1972), 217; Heijboer, *op.cit.*, 71.

18. Nasution, *SPKI* V, 107, 118–27, 159–70, *SPKI* VI, 266–71, 338; K. Helder, *Tiga Doeabelas: Gedenkboek 3–12 R. I.* (Groningen, 1951), 86–9; Heijboer, *op.cit.*, 34–6; van Sprang, *Wij Werden Geroepen*, 77–87. *Berita Indonesia* 24, 26 July 1947.

19. Nasution, *SPKI* V, 150–73; Heijboer, *op.cit.*, 34–9. Masnika Yusuf, 'Sekelumit pengalaman saya pada tiga zaman, khususnya pada masa revolusi', Perpustakaan 45 no. 224/XIII; Suliani Zumhan, 'Kisah nyata perjuangan kemerdekaan R. I. periode 1945–1950', Perpustakaan 45 no. 489/XXV. Interviews: Eri Soedewo, Jakarta, 14 February 1983; H. Moh. Supardi Shimbat, Jakarta, 15 November 1983; Sidik Kardi, Jakarta, 15 February 1983.

20. Heijboer, *op.cit.*, 37–83; G. McT. Kahin, *Nationalism and Revolution in Indonesia* (Ithaca, N.Y., 1952), 213–6.

21. Oorlogsdagboek III–9 RI, July 1947, *MvD/CAD*, archief Staf IIe Inf. Brig. Groep, doos GG7.

22. *Ibid.*, 27–28 August 1947; 'Inheemse vrijwilligers 2e Inf. Brig. Groep', 2 June 1948, and 'Geschiedenis HAMOT', 20 June 1948, Oorlogsdag-

boek Staf IIe Inf. Brig. Groep, map XII, bijlage II, *MvD/CAD*, archief Staf IIe Inf. Brig. Groep, doos GG7; Staf 2e Inf. Brig. Groep, Afd. Operatien, 'Voorstel org. Laskar-Rajat-eenheden', 28 November 1947, *MvD/CAD*, HKGS-NOI, GG 18, bundel 7158, 1947, ongen. *ANETA-Nieuws*, 4 August 1948. Interview: Lt.Col. K. Bavinck, The Hague, 14 February 1984.
23. Oorlogsdagboek III–9 RI, 15 August 1947, *loc.cit.*; *Berita Indonesia*, 24 September 1947; Interviews: Lt.Col. K. Bavinck, The Hague, 14 February 1984; confidential interviews with former lasykar.
24. Heijboer, *op.cit.*, 94.
25. Oorlogsdagboek III–9. RI, October & November 1947, *loc.cit.*,
26. Van Sprang, *Wij Werden Geroepen*, 122.
27. Oorlogsdagboek III–9 RI, 21 August, 4 October 1947, *loc.cit.*
28. J. A. de Moor, 'Het Korps Speciale Troepen: tussen Marechaussee-formule en Politionele Actie', in G. Teitler and P. H. M. Groen, eds, *De Politionele Acties* (Amsterdam, 1987), 129–131; Heijboer, *op.cit.*, 115–6.
29. Oorlogsdagboek III–9 RI, 13 November 1947, *loc.cit.*; Oorlogsdagboek Staf IIe Inf. Brig. Groep, 4 September, 15 November. 1947, *loc.cit.*
30. Oorlogsdagboek III–9 RI, 2 October 1947, *loc.cit.*.
31. Dagelijks operatief rapport 27 November 1947, Oorlogsdagboek III–9 RI, *loc.cit.*; Interview: Lt Col. K. Bavinck, The Hague, 14 February 1984.
32. Oorlogsdagboek III–9 RI, December 1947, January 1948, *loc.cit.* Nasution, *SPKI* VI, 228–9, 325, 341. *Nieuwsgier* 23 December 1947.

12

The Guerrilla Division
of the Bamboo Spears

The Karawang affair of April 1947 left the Republican army for the first time in undisputed charge of the east Jakarta front. Since one of the purposes of the suppression of the LRJR had been to ensure that ceasefires could be maintained on the front, it is ironic that the army's victory coincided with an increase in the Dutch determination to seek a military solution to the conflict. The air of competence and professionalism which the Karawang affair had created was to be shattered in the Dutch Military Action three months later, giving the lasykar an unexpected opportunity to re-assert themselves.

Dutch preparations for military action were watched by the TNI with foreboding. None of those who knew the army's weakness held out any hope that it could withstand a frontal attack by the Dutch. On the Jakarta front the prospects were particularly dismal, for the armed forces were in disarray after their clash with the lasykar. The Cikampek regiment was extensively reorganised after the clash and its numbers were reduced by about a third as part of Nasution's rationalisation plans. Most of those who remained were posted under Sadikin to Tasikmalaya to recuperate after the clash, and the Jakarta region was left to the Purwakarta regiment, the Resimen Perjuangan in Subang, the Beruang Merah, Hasibuan's ALRI in the northern swamps and a few smaller units of the old Cikampek regiment. The Beruang Merah was posted to the front line and reportedly soon lost its enthusiasm for fighting as it enjoyed the material benefits of trade with Jakarta. It quickly came to be referred to as *ber-uang merah* (having red, i.e. Dutch, money).[1]

Army strategists in Yogyakarta thus began to develop plans for a new line of defence running approximately from Cirebon to Garut, leaving the rest of West Java to the Dutch, and extensive preparations were made for scorched earth tactics in the territories being evacuated.[2] A withdrawal along these lines was perfectly consistent with the Republic's strategy of sacrificing outlying regions to preserve the centre. Nasution had earlier approved this strategy, but he was not disposed to accept it when it was applied to the whole of West Java. He made preparations instead for army units in the area to retreat into what became known as 'pockets' (*kantong*) from which they could attack the Dutch once the initial momentum of their thrust was lost. Nasution divided West Java into six zones, using brigades rather than regiments as his basic unit of organisation. Each brigade was intended to be administratively self-sufficient and to face the Dutch along a front line or a major arterial route along which they might be expected to attack. Each, moreover, was close to a mountainous region into which it could retreat. Although there was much talk of guerrilla warfare, Nasution's instructions were emergency measures to avoid total destruction in a Dutch attack rather than a conscious choice of guerrilla strategy. Their emphasis on the self-sufficiency of brigades and the use of secure and inaccessible bases, however, ran in many respects counter to the earlier emphasis on mobility and hierarchical control, and they foreshadowed Nasution's later guerrilla strategies.[3]

It was the TNI which bore the brunt of the Dutch attack of July 1947 on most of the front lines. Although the army fought heavily in many areas, its general retreat did serious damage to its reputation and thereby bolstered the position of its military rivals. In Central Java Amir Syarifuddin, who had succeeded Syahrir as prime minister just a week before the Dutch attack, felt strong enough to take another step in the creation of a second army within the Republic by announcing the establishment of a *Bagian Masyarakat* (Social Section) of the TNI, generally known as the *TNI Masyarakat*. Units of the TNI Masyarakat were formed as early as 23 July and they consisted almost entirely of former units of the Dewan Kelasykaran. Sakirman, who had since joined the PKI, was principal commander of the TNI Masyarakat, but appointments in the new force were in the hands of Syarifuddin, who retained the post of defence minister in his own cabinet.[4]

The Siliwangi Division in West Java, although still more or less allied with Syarifuddin, faced an even more serious setback in the military organisation of the Republic. When reports reached Yogyakarta of Dutch success in West Java, it appeared at first that the Siliwangi Division had totally collapsed. This impression was reinforced by Dutch pamphlets and radio broadcasts purporting to carry messages from Nasution announcing that the Siliwangi had surrendered and urging all troops in West Java to give themselves up to the

Dutch. This, it must be admitted, was news which some sections of
the army in Central Java were not wholly displeased to hear. The
apparent easy defeat of the Siliwangi Division with its much-vaunted
hierarchy, technical skill and international orientation confirmed the
belief of Central Javanese military in the superiority of spirit and
morale for fighting the Dutch. The Siliwangi defeat also gave an
opportunity to Sutan Akbar, still in Yogyakarta and now backed by a
small but fairly well supplied unit of refugees from the Siliwangi
razzias in West Java. Akbar apparently assured Sudirman that elements of the West Java Lasykar Rakyat were still operating effectively in the region and urged that responsibility for the recovery of
the region be handed to them. Sudirman, who had little affection for
the Siliwangi, agreed and appointed Akbar commander of a new
Divisi Gerilya Bambu Runcing (Guerrilla Division of the Bamboo
Spears).[5]

The term *gerilya* was not a new one in Indonesian military thinking. Since shortly after the declaration of independence the word had
been in circulation as a kind of shorthand for military struggle which
engaged the people, as opposed to the purely technological conduct
of warfare which supposedly characterised the Dutch. Figures such as
Mao and Tito were recognised practitioners of guerrilla warfare, but
little detail of their thought or practice seems to have reached
Indonesia at this stage, and since every military commander, including Nasution, claimed to be engaging the people in the struggle, the
term had little theoretical content. In any case, there had been little
scope on Java for the practice of guerrilla warfare: until the Military
Action, the Dutch controlled little territory outside the perimeters of
the larger cities, and Indonesian operations in Dutch controlled
regions inevitably had the character of commando raids, rather than
true guerrilla struggle.

Akbar at once made broadcasts over a special 'Radio of the River
Citarum' and sent messengers out to his old colleagues in West Java,
instructing them in general terms to carry on the struggle and in-
forming them of their new official status. He also divided them into
five notional brigades, covering Banten, Bogor, Jakarta, the Priangan and Cirebon. In Banten, which the Dutch left largely untouched
in their attack, Akbar dealt particularly with Kyai Akhmad Khatib,
whose conflicts with the local Siliwangi officers have already been
mentioned. In the Bogor-Sukabumi area, the dominant lasykar force
in the early revolution had been the Pesindo, led by Wikana's cousin
Waluyo, who became head of the local Biro Perjuangan. He was
later joined by Armansyah from Karawang and by Muhidin Nasution, who had come to West Java as an officer of the Biro Perjuangan
after the arrest of Tan Malaka. Waluyo represented the Bogor-

Sukabumi Lasykar Rakyat at the West Java LR conference in November 1946 but played only a minor role in it, since a large part of his unit had been forcibly incorporated into Kawilarang's Sukabumi regiment of the TRI earlier in 1946. Many of these, however, were demobilised by Kawilarang in about May 1947 during Nasution's rationalisation of the Siliwangi Division, and after the Dutch attack many of these demobilised lasykar rejoined Waluyo and Muhidin in a new unit operating in the hills around Sukabumi and as far east as the Cianjur area. It was this unit which became the B or Bogor Brigade of the Bambu Runcing.[6]

In the Jakarta area, Wahidin Nasution had escaped from detention in Purwakarta during the chaos of the Dutch attack and had made his way to Mt Sanggabuana, where he joined with remnants of the Karawang Lasykar Rakyat and commanded the Bambu Runcing C-Brigade. The D-Brigade in the eastern Priangan was headed by Akhmad Astrawinata, who had been released from jail in Tasikmalaya just before Dutch troops reached the town. The strongest Bambu Runcing unit, however, was the E-Brigade in Ciwaru, southeast of Cirebon, where Sastrosuwiryo and Khamdi of the Cirebon Lasykar Rakyat were joined by Maulana, former secretary of the West Java Lasykar Rakyat, and by Sutan Akbar himself, who arrived there in about August 1947 with his armed unit in Central Java. Ciwaru was an ideal point from which to conduct an armed struggle in West Java, since it lay in the heart of a mountainous area relatively safe from Dutch attack and it controlled the Republic's main overland line of communications between Central and West Java now that the Dutch had occupied most of the lowlands and main roads. With Alizar Thaib still in Central Java, and Hasan Gayo also there, having been released from jail along with Akhmad Astrawinata, Sutan Akbar was in a position to receive a constant stream of supplies and information from Yogyakarta. In practice, however, Akbar exercised little real authority over the other Bambu Runcing brigades. Communications were difficult, and his own personal authority had been diminished by his long absence in Central Java. His supply routes from Yogyakarta possibly gave him some control over the weaker Priangan brigade, but with the Bambu Runcing in Jakarta, Bogor and Banten the relationship was one of the distant alliance rather than subordination.[7]

Wahidin's C-Brigade was possibly the strongest of the Bambu Runcing brigades after that in Ciwaru. The brigade also commonly referred to itself as the 17 August Division in pointed opposition to the KL's 7 December Division down on the plains.[8] Wahidin established his headquarters near the town of Pangkalan on the slopes of Mt Sanggabuana and he was joined there shortly after his arrival by

Syamsuddin Can from Jakarta. Harun Umar turned up, too, having deserted from the HAMOTs soon after the Dutch attack. As noted earlier, however, he was soon to be re-captured and shot by the Dutch. The links between lasykar units on the northern coastal plain had been thoroughly disrupted by the clash with the TNI and the Dutch attack, so the Bambu Runcing's first task was to draw together the surviving lasykar into another broad military alliance. Leaders of the old LRJR such as Wim Mangelep northeast of Karawang quickly agreed to cooperate, though the Bambu Runcing had greater difficulty with some of the local bosses such as Pa' Macem, who had re-established himself southwest of Karawang. Macem toyed for a time with the idea of joining a kind of territorial militia sponsored by the Dutch somewhat along HAMOT lines, but clandestine appeals by the Bambu Runcing to his nationalism helped to win him back.[9]

Wahidin's re-establishment of the lasykar in the Jakarta region was considerably facilitated by the fact that there were now no significant army units in the area. The nearest TNI concentration consisted of remnants of the Purwakarta regiment at Buah Dua in the Sumedang area, led by Major Akhmad Sukarmadijaya, former Chief of Staff of the 3rd Brigade, who formed a so-called Guerrilla Staff for Nothern West Java. Eri Sudewo, who had been appointed Purwakarta garrison commander just before the attack, led a similar organisation in the Indramayu area, while remnants of the Resimen Perjuangan, including troops under Imam Syafe'i, gathered still further east around Majalengka.[10]

As important as rebuilding the old military alliance of the LRJR was the reconstruction of Syamsuddin Can's village defence system which had given the lasykar administrative control of much of the Jakarta region before the clashes of April 1947. Many of the old components of this organisation were still present and, although it required a good deal of coordination and persuasion to bring them together again, they gradually coalesced to form a shadow administration in the region. The Bambu Runcing also established around Pangkalan a zone where Republican currency remained the legal tender, despite Dutch success in replacing it with Dutch currency in many other parts of West Java. The village defence system became the basis for a campaign of guerrilla warfare in the Karawang area, providing food and shelter for the lasykar in their running battles with the Dutch. Bambu Runcing guerrilla tactics were known locally as *systeem lumpur* (mud system): a foot disappears when it is put into the mud, and the mud closes behind it when it is removed.[11]

The rebuilding of the village defence system had to be done, however, not only in the face of severe communications difficulties in an area frequently patrolled by Dutch troops, but against a lack of enthusiastic cooperation by parts of the civil administration. There had been no clear instructions from Yogyakarta to local officials concerning their duties if the Dutch attacked. Some stayed at their posts, announcing that they would continue to serve the people while refusing to cooperate with the Dutch, while others followed a policy of burning all their records and retreating from the towns which were the immediate target of the Dutch troops into the forests and mountains where lasykar and local bosses still maintained control. Those officials, such as Bantir of Bekasi, who had come to power early in the revolution as local bosses in their own right slipped back easily into their old role. Officials, on the other hand, who had served in the administrative corps under the Dutch, Japanese and Republican governments found, outside their offices and without any possibility of support from the central government, that they were thoroughly eclipsed by the guerrillas. Lacking enthusiasm for a struggle in which they had little role to play and which they saw as being unlikely to succeed, many, including Rubaya and Juarsa, regents of Karawang and Purwakarta respectively, allowed themselves to be captured by the Dutch.[12]

In his attempts to establish a broad coalition of resistance in the Jakarta region, Wahidin also turned to the Purwakarta area, where LRJR influence had traditionally been weak. In particular he made contact with the Hizbullah of Tabrani Idris in Plered, and with the Field Preparation in the area south of Cikampek, led locally by Usman Sumantri, Setianegara and Wagianto. He also contacted the leaders of the Masyumi in Purwakarta, Mohammad Syafe'i and Oya Sumantri. With the regent Juarsa joining the Dutch, and the Resident Kosasih having retreated from the Jakarta to Buah Dua in Sumedang regency to join Akhmad Sukarmadijaya's Guerrilla Staff for Northern West Java, Syafe'i and Oya sought to maintain a Republican civil government in the Purwakarta area on the basis of their membership of the working committee of the local KNI. Both men were religious leaders whose political power dated mainly from the start of the revolution, who enjoyed close links with the local Hizbullah, and who had been leaders of the political opposition to Juarsa and Kosasih before the Dutch attack. Also in the area was a former official of the Jakarta residency office, Muhammad Mu'min, father of the first commander of the Cikampek regiment, Mufreni Mu'min, who apparently took over, with the Subang labour leader Karlan, practical leadership of the remnants of the Jakarta residency administration from Kosasih in mid-October 1947. He and Karlan divided the residency into two, with Mu'min taking the western section based in the Purwakarta area. Mu'min, however, almost immediately appointed Syafe'i as acting regent ('coordinator') of Karawang-Purwakarta and was thereafter more or less eclipsed by him.[13]

Despite the Dutch operations, therefore, and the use of the HAMOTs, Bambu Runcing activity in the Karawang area made the region highly insecure, particularly for the PRP supporters and Chinese. In a period of fifteen days in October 1947, twelve local leaders of the PRP in the Karawang area were allegedly killed and thirty-two were kidnapped. Those who survived thought it better to go into hiding. Many local village officials who had once cooperated with the Dutch now appeared to be working with or for the nationalists. Those who stayed faithful to the Dutch were intimidated, kidnapped or killed; a Dutch planter complained that of seventy village heads in the Purwakarta district only twenty remained faithful to the Dutch.[14]

Sabotage against economic targets continued, particularly those owned by local Chinese. In early September, Spoor had given permission for the Chinese militia Pao An Tui to establish units in the Karawang area for the protection of Chinese property, but the task was beyond it. In the three weeks to 10 November 1947, six rice mills were burnt in the Karawang-Cikampek area. Roads were frequently blocked, the transport of rice from the countryside into the towns was hindered, telephone lines were cut, the railway lines were sabotaged. Of twenty-eight rubber plantations in the mountain regions around Purwakarta which re-opened after the Dutch attack, twenty-five had closed again by the end of the year, either because sabotage and the destruction of trees made them uneconomical, or simply because they were no longer safe for their European personnel. Both the lasykar and later the army carried the struggle into Jakarta, and there were frequent grenade attacks on Dutch posts in the city and numerous reports of intimidation of Indonesians working for the Dutch.[15]

After miserable defeat and humiliating defection, thus, the lasykar appeared by October 1947 to have reconstituted themselves as the major nationalist armed force in the Jakarta region. It was an impressive achievement on Wahidin's part, but it was to be short-lived. The Bambu Runcing derived its authority and sense of purpose from the mandate which Sudirman had given it via Sutan Akbar. In mid-October 1947, however, the first units of the old Cikampek regiment returned to the Jakarta area, and with them came the conflict over status which had led to the Karawang affair.

Despite the military debacle in the Jakarta region, and the capture by the Dutch of the main town in West Java, many units of the Siliwangi division had retreated into the pockets more or less in order. When the Dutch attacked, the Cikampek regiment under

Sadikin had pulled back from Tasikmalaya into the hills around Sumedang, where it harassed Dutch troops using the main road between Bandung and Cirebon. There were many other Republican troops in this area, and the Bandung-Cirebon-Tasikmalaya triangle, where important Dutch lines of communication ran through rugged mountain area ideal for guerrilla warfare, saw some of the heaviest fighting in West Java during the later months of 1947.[16]

TNI strength was also concentrated in the mountains south of Sukabumi, Cianjur and Bandung, where Dutch troops barely penetrated, and from this base the energetic Nasution began to re-establish coordination and cooperation between army units. By the middle of October, three months after the Dutch attack, he was able to announce the creation of five *Wehrkreise* (military regions) in West Java. The Wehrkreise were a device to restore the idea of a single military command in each region without attempting the messy task of formally reorganising the Siliwangi Division's order of battle. They corresponded generally to the old brigade regions, which had become unworkable with the large-scale movement of units after the Dutch attack.[17] Nasution also sought to establish a single joint military-civilian leadership for the struggle in West Java, so that the facilities and authority of the civil government would be available to the army in the military struggle. The regional defence councils established in 1946 more or less filled this role at residency level, but Nasution's idea was that there should be a single such council for West Java, led by the governor Sewaka and Nasution himself. Sewaka apparently cooperated with Nasution, but his own authority was limited, and the central government never ratified the creation of a provincial defence council. Some time later, in December 1947, Nasution extended the Wehrkreis structure downwards, creating Sub-Wehrkreise, District Military Commands (*Komando Distrik Militer*, KDM) and Sub-district Military Commands (*Komando Onder Distrik Militer*, KODM), corresponding roughly to regiment, battalion and company units. The structure was intended to match the hierarchy of civil administration divisions, regency, kewedanaan and kecamatan, and military commanders at each level were instructed to work closely with the local civilian authorities, particularly in obtaining supplies for the troops. In practice, however, the structure was established only in a few areas where Nasution's influence was strong.[18]

It was as part of this general reorganisation that Nasution appointed Sadikin as head of the 5th Wehrkreis, covering the Jakarta region, and instructed him to return there. Sadikin had earlier been appointed commander of the 3rd Brigade to replace Sidik Brotoat-mojo, but his effective command was limited to four or five battalions in the Sumedang area. He was also hampered by food shortages in his area of operations which limited his troops' ability to combine living off the land with retaining the support of the local population. During the months after the Dutch attack, enthusiasm for returning to the Jakarta area grew amongst the officers and men of the Cikampek regiment, and they saw Nasution's instruction of October 1947 more as permission to return than as a command. Small units of the regiment arrived in Subang in mid-October but Sadikin and the bulk of his troops did not reach their old territory until mid-November.[19]

The Wehrkreis system, which placed all Indonesian armed forces in occupied West Java under the operational command of army officers, was a direct challenge to the Bambu Runcing. One of Nasution's first moves after the dust of the Dutch military action had begun to settle was to obtain with the help of his allies on the general staff in Yogyakarta the withdrawal of Sutan Akbar's mandate to lead the struggle in West Java. This took place on 25 September 1947. Not surprisingly, Akbar ignored this change in status and continued to organise his guerrilla base around Ciwaru.[20] Akbar's presence was an irritation to the army for several reasons. In the first place his control of the area left a large gap in the middle of the 4th Wehrkreis of Colonel Abimanyu. Akbar's claim to be responsible for the armed struggle in West Java and his propaganda campaign to the effect that the Siliwangi Division was an agent of the Dutch was also extremely irritating to Siliwangi officers sensitive to the charge that the poor Siliwangi performance during the Dutch attack was the result of a lack of enthusiasm for independence, rather than of purely military factors. Akbar, moreover, apparently had the cooperation of the Resident of Cirebon, Hamdani, thereby leaving Abimanyu's Wehrkreis without a significant civilian component. According to a Dutch intelligence report, Hamdani joined the propaganda battle against the TNI, accusing the army of senseless murders, plunder and arson. He added that it appeared from his inspection tours that the army's heroic deeds were fantasy and that the population had more trouble from the TNI than from the Dutch.[21] Akbar's position on the main line of communications to Central Java, too, gave him access to resources unavailable to the Siliwangi Division and he began to extend his influence by recruiting army units into the Bambu Runcing. He was successful on one occasion in winning over a member of Nasution's personal staff. Especially serious from the army's point of view, moreover, was his confiscation of supplies being brought through the Ciwaru region for the Siliwangi Division, and his arrest of Rukman, one of Abimanyu's company commanders.[22]

Nasution, of course, could only tolerate this for so long. He had lost none of his enthusiasm for disarming lasykar, and in early January 1948 he authorised Abimanyu to move against Sutan Akbar's forces. Units under Rukman, who had since escaped from detention in Ciwaru, and Umar Wirahadikusumah surrounded the Bambu Runcing position and after four days' fighting finally entered Ciwaru. Those leaders of the organisation who were captured, including Sastrosuwiryo and Maulana, were shot on the spot. Estimates of the number of Bambu Runcing officers executed range from seventeen to sixty-four, but there is no question that the leadership of the Bambu Runcing E-Brigade was virtually wiped out. Sutan Akbar reportedly escaped the Ciwaru massacres, but is said to have been shot soon afterwards while swimming across a river in the mountains.[23]

In the Karawang area, tension between the army and the lasykar did not reach the point of armed clashes. When elements of the old Cikampek regiment began to arrive in the Jakarta region in October and November 1947, Wahidin reportedly invited them to join the struggle under his general leadership. For reasons of prestige, and because army officers still suspected Wahidin of complicity in the disappearance of Suroto Kunto, these overtures were rejected. The army concentrated on creating its own bases and building its own network of communications in the area. The support which the Bambu Runcing and Hizbullah commanded amongst village officials made this difficult at times, but the authority of the Bambu Runcing in areas not controlled by the Dutch was still sufficiently loose to give the army room to re-establish itself, and to live in a state of wary co-existence with the lasykar. Wahidin's stronghold on Mt Sanggabuana was far enough from the army's centres of power and lines of communication for Wahidin to present no serious threat, except to the local regiment, which was in no position to challenge him yet. There was little cooperation, but conflict was postponed and avoided.[24] Relations between the army and the lasykar began to reflect a pattern set before the Dutch attack, with the lasykar maintaining a vigorous and provocative opposition to the army, Nasution organising operations to disarm them where possible, and hostility between the two being limited primarily by their common opposition to the Dutch. In Ciwaru, where army and lasykar were relatively safe from Dutch attack, they could afford to clash. Elsewhere, pressure from the Dutch forced them to bury their differences for the time being.

By late 1947, in fact, the Dutch military campaign in West Java was beginning to bite deeply and Nasution reported to Yogyakarta that the Siliwangi Division could not fight on indefinitely at its current level. The Bambu Runcing for that matter was also badly hit by Dutch operations in Karawang in December 1947. Dutch intelligence also allegedly captured a letter from Nasution to his chief of

staff written in November 1947 deploring the army's lack of authority
and discipline. The Siliwangi Division was continuing to do a great
deal of damage to the Dutch in West Java, but there was an increasingly serious risk that all semblance of central coordination and
direction would disappear under Dutch pressure and that the division, having dissolved into a number of independent and vulnerable
guerrilla units, would not be able to fight on long enough to defeat
the Dutch. In November 1947, army leaders in West Java reportedly
discussed reaching a compromise with the Dutch by transforming the
Siliwangi Division into a kind of militarised police force. Nasution
also reported that sympathy of Sundanese separatism was strong
within the division.[25] It is not improbable that Nasution exaggerated
these reports of the Siliwangi's difficulties in order to attract government attention; he had developed plans for a new offensive in West
Java, involving a change of emphasis from the defence of sanctuaries
to a more mobile strategy paying greater attention to winning popular support and disrupting the Dutch in the occupied territories.
There is no doubt, however, that both army and lasykar in West Java
were in a parlous state.

Events in West Java, however, were overtaken in early 1948 by the
signing of another agreement between the Republic and the Dutch
aboard the United States naval vessel *Renville*, anchored in Jakarta
Bay. Unlike Linggajati, which had unsuccessfully lain down the
terms of a settlement, Renville merely foreshadowed a comprehen-
sive agreement and established a framework for the detailed discussions which would produce it. Both sides, however, bound
themselves to a number of actions. In particular, they agreed to
recognise the so-called van Mook line, which linked the furthest
points to which Dutch troops had advanced in the Military Action,
and to withdraw all troops to their respective sides of that line. With
the exception of Banten, all of West Java fell on the Dutch side of the
line. This abandonment of West Java was later bitterly criticised by
Nasution, though his pessimistic reports had probably been amongst
the factors leading to his government's willingness to give up the
region. Other TNI units were less disappointed. The Renville Agreement, like Syahrir's order to the army and lasykar to abandon Jakarta
in November 1945, gave the army in West Java an opportunity to
avoid a fight which it was now far from winning.

The final dismantling of the Republic's apparatus of government in
West Java was the work of only a few weeks. TNI headquarters in
Central Java issued orders to the Siliwangi troops in the pockets to
report to processing centres at various places in West Java. From
there the troops were taken by road, rail and sea to Republican
territory. Some who distrusted the Dutch marched instead overland

to Central Java or into Banten. Others stayed behind, either because they did not wish to leave West Java or because they had received secret orders from the army command to remain behind and organise underground resistance. The Dutch indeed suspected that a good proportion of the evacuating troops consisted of non-military villagers enticed by the prospect of a visit to Central Java to make up the numbers for Siliwangi troops ordered to stay behind. In the weeks to 20 February, however, approximately 20,000 guerrilla troops departed for Republican territory and the Republic's effective military presence in West Java was ended.[26] The lasykar once more had the Jakarta region to themselves.

1. Nasution, *SPKI* IV, 329, 362; Nasution, *SPKI* V, 152–6; Soerjono, 'Kumpulan humor revolusi', in D. Marpaung, ed., *Bingkisan Nasional: Kenangan 10 Tahun Revolusi Indonesia* (Jakarta, 1955), 170. Interviews: Saleh Tedjakusumah, Jakarta, 28 March 1983; Sadikin, Jakarta, 28 March 1983; Daan Jahja, Jakarta, 1 September 1982; Suhendro, Bekasi, 22 January 1983. At about this time Nasution replaced the strong-willed Umar Bahsan as commander of the Purwakarta regiment with Omon Abdurrakhman.
2. NEFIS, VPSONI no. 12 (4 June 1947), *Proc.Gen.* 3. Nasution, *SPKI* IV, 330, 452, *SPKI* V, 154. Interviews: Daan Jahja, Jakarta, 1 September 1982; Sidik Brotoatmodjo, Bandung, 16 March 1983. See also Pierre Heijboer, *De Politionele Acties: de Strijd om 'Indië' 1945/1949* (Haarlem, 1979), 36. Nasution to brigade and regiment commanders, 5 April 1947, DOBIN no. 487, 13 November 1947, *Alg.Sec.I* box III file 9.
3. Nasution, *SPKI* III, 450, 474–477, *SPKI* IV, 329–31, 451–3. Interview: Daan Jahja, Jakarta, 1 September 1982.
4. George McTurnan Kahin, *Nationalism and Revolution in Indonesia* (Ithaca, N.Y., 1952), 261; A. J. S. Reid, *The Indonesian National Revolution 1945–1950* (Hawthorn, Vic., 1974), 99; D. C. Anderson, 'The Military Aspects of the Madiun Affair', *Indonesia* 21 (1976), 23.
5. Nasution, *SPKI* V, 178–9, 182. E. Madli Hasan, 'Perjoangan 45 untuk pembangunan bangsa', Perpustakaan 45 no. 118/VI. 'De Bamboe Roentjing-Beweging in West-Java', NEFIS Bulletin No. 9, 23 August 1948, *MvD/CAD*, HKGS-NOI, Inv. nr. GG40, 1948, bundel 16577.
6. Interviews: Muhidin Nasution, Ciluer, 14, 31 October 1982; Subarna, Jakarta, 27 October 1982.
7. De Bamboe Roentjing-Beweging, *loc.cit.*; Tan Malaka, *Dari Pendjara ke Pendjara* III (Jakarta, n.d.), iv; Nasution, *SPKI* VI, 350. *Berita Indonesia*, 28 July 1947. Interviews: Moh. Hasan Gayo, Jakarta, 1 March 1983; Sidik Samsi, Jakarta, 1 November 1982; Subarna, Jakarta, 27 October 1982; Alizar Thaib, Jakarta, 28 February 1983; Pitoyo Wardi,

168 GANGSTERS AND REVOLUTIONARIES

Jakarta, 16 November 1982; Sidik Kardi, Jakarta, 15 February 1983.
8. See TNI Divisi Agustus, Makloemat, n.d., DOBIN no. 477, 1 November 1947, *Alg.Sec.I* box III, file 9. According to Wahidin's *Riwayat hidup* held by the Angkatan 45 in Jakarta, he founded the 17 August Division on personal instructions from Sudirman.
9. 'De Bamboe Roentjing-Beweging', *loc.cit.* Interviews: Sidik Kardi, Jakarta, 11 October 1982; Abdul Karim Abbas, Jakarta, 30 October 1982."
10. Nasution, *SPKI* V, 168, 458; VI, 113, 148, 154. Interviews: Soepardi Shimbat, Jakarta, 18 November 1982; Sidik Kardi, Jakarta, 15 February 1983; Eri Soedewo, Jakarta, 14 February 1983.
11. Verslag van den Recomba West-Java over de periode Juli tot en met September 1947' [hereafter *Verslag Recomba Juli-September 1947*], *Alg.Sec.I* box IV, file 29; Korps Algemeene Politie, Detachement Veldpolitie Krawang, Inlichtingen Rapport no. 41, 31 December 1947, *Proc.Gen.* 3. *Berita Indonesia*, 29 August, 1 September, 23 October 1947; *Nieuwsgier*, 16 August 1947. Interview: Abdul Karim Abbas, Jakarta, 2 November 1982; Sidik Samsi, Jakarta, 1 November 1947.
12. *Verslag Recomba Juli-September 1947*; Brief no. 223, *Alg.Sec.I* box XXIII, file 4. Nasution, *SPKI* V, 173; VI, 234–235. Gani, 'Kebayoran Lama—tahun 1945', Perpustakaan 45 no. 848/XLIII. *Dagblad* 26 July, 5 August 1947. Interviews: H. Moh. Damsjik, Bekasi, 18 January 1983; Moh. Husein Kamaly, Bekasi, 17 January 1983.
13. Nasution, *SPKI* V, 458; VI, 113, 343–4. 'Initiatief Sdr. Sapei Koordinator Kaboepaten Krawang Barat', 22 December 1947, *Proc.Gen.* 138. S. Abdurrachman (pseud.), 'Riwajat singkat pemerintahan sipil Republik Indonesia di Djawa-Barat', 15 October 1949 (in my possession). Interviews: Kosasih Purwanegara, Jakarta, 18, 30 August 1982; Sidik Samsi, Jakarta, 11 October, 17 November 1982. *Berita Indonesia* 23 October 1947; *Nieuwsgier* 5 August 1947.
14. Situatie-rapport nr. 80 (29–30 July 1947), *OBB* X, 130.
15. NEFIS, VPSONI no. 26 (31 December 1947), 8–9, 22–3, *Alg.Sec.II* 681; Recomba West-Java, Afdeling Politie, Beknopt Politiek-politioneel verslag van de regentschappen, November 1947, *Alg.Sec.I* box III, file 9; Korps Algemeene Politie, Batavia, Geheim Generaal Rapport der Criminele Recherche, 11–20 December 1947, *Proc.Gen.* 192; Recomba West-Java, AILO, Terrorisme in het ressort Krawang, 27 December 1947, *Proc.Gen.* 784; *idem*, Opgave van plaats gehad hebbende feitelijkheden in het gebied Poerwakarta, November 1947, *Proc.Gen.* 784; Lt-Kol. Soeria Santoso, 'Politiek situatie in W. Java', 24 December 1947, *Proc.Gen.* 782; 'Barisan Gadjah Mada', 23 June 1948, *Proc.Gen.* 83; Mailrapport 16/Geh/48, 6 January 1948, *Rapportage Indonesië* file E5. Nasution, *SPKI* I, 58, 336, *SPKI* VI, 228–9, 325, 341; Heijboer, *op.cit.*, 115–6; A. van Sprang, *Wij werden Geroepen: de Geschiedenis van de 7 December Divisie* (The Hague, 1949), 122–25. *Berita Indonesia* 24 September, 23, 28, 30 October, 6 November 1947; *Nieuwsgier* 19, 22 November, 23 December 1947. Interviews: Zainal Simbangan, Jakarta, 11 January 1983; Sidik Samsi, Jakarta, 1 November 1982.

16. Verslag Recomba Juli-September 1947. Heijboer, *op.cit.*, 94–99; Nasu-
    tion, *SPKI* V, 196–8. Interviews: Sadikin and Saleh Tedjakusumah,
    Jakarta, 28 March 1983.
17. Nasution *SPKI* VI, 144–9, 273–7. Nasution (*SPKI* V, 65) states that the
    Wehrkreise were originally formed by a decision of the then Chief of
    Staff, General Urip, of 31 May 1947, but it seems that nothing was
    done to implement this decision.
18. Nasution, *SPKI* VI, 57, 153–4, 258–64, 278–86.
19. Nasution, *SPKI* V, 458–459; VI, 104–5, 108–13, 145–8. Mohd
    Soiz, 'Jalan-jalan yang kususuri', Perpustakaan 45 no. 157/VII. Inter-
    view: Sadikin, Jakarta, 28 March 1983.
20. 'De Bamboe Roentjing-Beweging', *loc.cit.* See also S. M. McKem-
    mish, 'A political biography of General A. H. Nasution' (M.A. disser-
    tation, Monash University, 1976), 37.
21. DOBIN no. 483, 8 November 1947, *Alg.Sec.I* box III, file 9. According
    to this and the preceeding report (DOBIN no. 482, 7 November 1947,
    ibid.) these accusations accompanied Hamdani's resignation or dis-
    missal from the post of Resident of Cirebon and his replacement by
    Sastrosuwiryo. It is not entirely certain that Hamdani was cooperating
    willingly with the Bambu Runcing. Nasution (*SPKI* VI, 346, 349)
    suggests he was more or less a prisoner of the lasykar. He was
    subsequently appointed as a member of the Republican delegation for
    negotiations with the Dutch, which suggests his sympathies were not
    thought to lie with the hard line of the Bambu Runcing, though in fact
    he never took up his appointment.
22. 'De Bamboe Roentjing-Beweging', *loc.cit.* Iwa Kusumasumantri, *Sed-
    jarah Revolusi Indonesia, Djilid ke-dua: Masa Revolusi Bersendjata*
    (n.p., n.d.), 176; Nasution, *SPKI* VI, 158–9, 346–51.
23. R. E. Sulaeman Kartasumitra, ed., *Catatan-catatan dari Beberapa Ex-
    Anggota Batalion 400 Tentara Pelajar XVII* (Jakarta, 1977), 16–17; R.
    E. Sulaeman Kartasumitra, *Dokumentasi Batalion 400 Tentara Pelajar
    Brigade XVII* (Jakarta, 1977?), 72–73; Nasution, *SPKI* VI, 351–2.
    Interviews: Moh. Hasan Gayo, Jakarta, 1 March 1983; Johar Nur,
    Jakarta, 11 October 1983; Sidik Kardi, Jakarta, 15 February 1983. It
    has been alleged that Sutan Akbar survived the Ciwaru massacre, and
    Dutch military reports occasionally mention his name after his sup-
    posed death, but as far as can be made out he played no further role in
    the history of the Jakarta region.
24. Korps Algemeene Politie, Detachement Veldpolitie Krawang, Verslag-
    Rapport, 27 December 1947, *Proc.Gen.* 3. Nasution, *SPKI* VI, 228.
25. Simatupang to Kawilarang and Daan Yahya, *loc.cit.*; Oorlogsbevel Cdt.
    Div. Slw., *loc.cit.*; Militair overzicht, 16–30 December 1947, *Alg.Sec.II*
    1223; NEFIS, VPSONI no. 27 (15 January 1947), 4, *Alg. Sec. II* 681;
    Commander Brigade Tirtayasa, Banten, to General Staff Section I, 8
    December 1947, *Alg.Sec.II* 1161; DOBIN no. 477 & 482, 1, 7 Novem-
    ber 1947, *Alg.Sec. I* box III, file 9; Kahin, *op.cit.*, 228–9; Nasution,
    SPKI VI, 151–2, 257–8, 261–2, 278, 288–9; U. Sundhaussen, 'The
    Political Orientations and Political Involvement of the Indonesian

Officer Corps 1945–1966: the Siliwangi Division and the Army Headquarters' (Ph.D. dissertation, Monash University, 1971), 121–2, 161. *Nieuwsgier* 23 December 1947, 6 January 1948. Interview: Sidik Samsi, Jakarta, 1 November 1982.
26. Heijboer, *op.cit.*, 106; K. Helder, *Tiga Doeabelas: Gedenkboek 3–12 R. I.* (Groningen, 1951), 210, 213; Nasution, *SPKI* VI, 505–11.

13

Towards Extinction

The Republic's agreement to evacuate West Java applied to all armed forces, regular and irregular. A few lasykar, such as Dulkair from Cileungsi, joined the TNI units at the assembly points in Lemahabang,[1] but most contemptuously rejected the order to withdraw and dug in for a protracted struggle. Convinced as before of the need for unity, Wahidin forged into a federation the three major irregular units operating in the area: his own Bambu Runcing, Tabrani Idris' Hizbullah and Usman Sumantri's Field Preparation, which changed its name shortly after the signing of the *Renville* Agreement to SP88 (*Satuan Pemberontakan 88*, Revolution Unit 88).[2] This federation adopted the name 17 August Division previously used by the Jakarta Bambu Runcing alone. The term division, however, exaggerated the size and organisation of Wahidin's following. The 17 August Division encompassed perhaps a couple of thousand men, not all of them armed, grouped in units which ranged from a few hardened and relatively well-trained descendants of the LRJR to many small bands led by local bosses such as Pa' Macem. The SP88 was also active amongst trade unions in the Jakarta area, particularly in the railways system, a harking back to Haji Darip's old connections.[3]

It was of course congenial for the 17 August Division to be free of interference from the TNI, but this freedom contributed little to the ability of the lasykar to fight the Dutch. Indeed, the absence of Siliwangi troops enabled the Dutch to concentrate their efforts against lasykar strongholds. The guerrillas found that they had little room to manoeuvre. Although their sphere of influence extended well beyond the slopes of Mount Sanggabuana, they actually controlled very little territory and they were forced to move their headquarters repeatedly from one small settlement to another to avoid attack by Dutch mobile columns whose access to aerial surveillance compensated somewhat for their shortage of local intelligence sources.

Tight organisational discipline had never been the strong point of the lasykar, but the dispersal of authority was now especially pronounced. Dutch military action broke up large lasykar concentrations, making it difficult for the lasykar units to assemble for conferences on strategy as they had done in the old days in Karawang. Wahidin, moreover, found it virtually impossible to assemble the forces necessary to impose discipline on unruly followers. The result was a proliferation of small units barely distinguishable from the pre-war gangs, but claiming some allegiance to the Bambu Runcing, often through the SP88. These units took on names which frequently had much in common with the grandiloquent nomenclature of the pre-war gangs. They bore names such as *Pasukan Siluman* (Ghost Squad), *Srigala Hitam* (Black Jackal), *Pemotong Leher* (Neck Cutters) and *Garuda Putih* (White Eagle). Their equally colourfully-named commanders included figures such as Phantom Bomb. Most units were nominally set as raiding parties especially for operations into Jakarta and the larger towns of the region, but their activities included a good deal of simply plundering, alongside more patriotic actions. Outside the core units loyal to Wahidin, few of these gangs survived long. Unlike the well-established ommelanden gangs of the colonial period, these gangs never had the opportunity to develop firm bases in the areas where they operated, and it often took no more than a well-directed Dutch *zuiveringsoperatie* ('mopping-up operation') to discredit their leaders and disperse their members.

Although the Dutch were often successful in eliminating gangs, there was little they could do to stop them from re-forming around other bosses and leaders. The social disruption of the Karawang area had generated a large reserve of men willing to follow a local leader to death or glory and the defeated gangs were soon replaced by others. The SP88 was in its element here. Whereas Wahidin still worked for military successes, the SP88 focused on psychological warfare, which it called the war of ideas (*perang pikiran*). Its aim was to keep the Dutch off balance, and it imposed little discipline on its associated gangs. Changes of name and organisation were part of its tactic to confuse the Dutch, and many of its leaders accumulated long strings of noms de guerre. Intimidation was its stock in trade, and it distributed posters such as the following:

> Anyone who dares to work for the Dutch is a traitor; every traitor should be killed.
> Those who have become the henchmen of the Nica and the

Nica-appointed lurahs and their deputies must be killed; also
those sons of Indonesia who serve in the Dutch forces and the
police
Take care, bung [brother]! You may have received high
positions, you may have been appointed camat or bupati, but
you will not feel at ease!
Remember, sons of Indonesia, that the Dutch are your enemies.
Remember, bung!
Once free, always free!!!
    The Tiger of Jakarta, the Broom of the World,
    alias the Thunderbolt.[4]

Although unsuccessful in controlling territory, therefore, the combined effect of the scattered gangs and the guerrilla warfare campaign
of the 17 August Division was to tie down Dutch troops and prevent
the re-establishment of Dutch administrative authority in the region.
Dutch military posts were attacked and travel in the Karawang region
was still unsafe for Europeans, Indonesians and Chinese working for
the Dutch. Numerous local Indonesian officials working for the
Dutch or for the private estates were killed. In some areas virtually
the entire lower administrative cadre was wiped out, while the SP88
even managed to wound the regent of Karawang in one attack. The
guerrillas were also able to hamper the restoration of life on the
estates by burning factories and warehouses and ambushing trucks as
they carried produce from outlying regions. It soon became clear,
however, that the guerrilla campaign could not go beyond such
attacks to challenge the Dutch in other parts of West Java.[5]

The guerrillas, however, faced a difficult problem of choosing a
framework for their struggle. Their refusal to evacuate had made
them once more publicly defiant of the Republican authorities. The
Republic, for its part, had publicly disowned them by its signing of
the Renville Agreement. The agreement had included a de facto
recognition by the Republic of Dutch authority in West Java. A
plebiscite was foreshadowed for the region to decide whether it
would form a negara in its own right or would revert to the Republic,
but the Republic's acceptance of this amounted to an abdication of its
sovereign claim over West Java. Before Renville, the Republic had
publicly and aggressively asserted its sovereignty over West Java;
after the agreement, Republicans still believed that the region was
rightfully theirs but they could no longer assert this openly at the risk
of appearing to show bad faith. Renville thus effectively orphaned
not only the lasykar but the Republic's own officials in the region.

By October 1948, the lasykar had constructed a formula to cope
with this mutual rejection. In an announcement backdated to 17
August 1948, the anniversary of the declaration of independence,

and issued in the name of 'the people of the Dutch-occupied territory of West Java who have faith in the proclamation of 17 August 1945', they publicly proclaimed the establishment of what they called the *Pemerintah Republik Jawa Barat* (PRJB).[6] This term permits several translations into English, but most appropriate is probably 'Republican Government of West Java'. The PRJB claimed to be loyal to the original principles of the declaration of independence and to Sukarno and Hatta. It rejected, however, all subordination to the Republic and especially rejected the Renville Agreement. In selecting the term, *pemerintah* (government) rather than *negara* (state), the PRJB signalled, like the PRRI a decade later, that it was not secessionist but rather advocated a different government within the Indonesian Republic. This distinction was an important one, since the Dutch had gone ahead in March 1948 with the establishment of the Negara Pasundan in West Java. Wahidin chose Oya Sumantri to head the new government, hoping that a Sundanese would neutralise some of the appeal of the Negara Pasundan. The PRJB stood in stark contrast to the Muslim guerrillas of the *Darul Islam* (abode of Islam) movement in the mountains of southern West Java. While consolidating their military positions in guerrilla struggle against the Dutch, these fighters also distanced themselves progressively from the Republic, finally declaring an Islamic State of Indonesia (*Negara Islam Indonesia*, NII) in August 1949.[7]

Beyond this purpose, however, the declaration of the PRJB was a highly ambiguous gesture. On the one hand it was a gesture of profound hostility to the Republic. Renville had magnified the disgust of the lasykar with what they saw as the Republic's timidity and they abhorred the Republic's willingness to accept a sub-national status within the new Indonesian federation. As sentiment in lasykar circles grew that the Republic had been hijacked by politicians unfaithful to its original ideals, they began to ask themselves whether this was still the Republic they had fought for in 1945. Increasingly, therefore, the Republic of 1945 assumed the status of an icon amongst the lasykar, and the PRJB was invested with the status of bearer of the ideals of that Republic. Conversely, however, for many others the PRJB was a gesture of deep loyalty to the Republic. A West Java underground or shadow government which was avowedly of the Indonesian Republic would have opened the Republic to accusations of bad faith of unwillingness to accept the will of the people as expressed in the plebiscite. A government that was Republican but not of the Republic, by contrast, offered a format for keeping a Republican administrative network alive while avoiding embarrassment to the Republic.[8]

The PRJB called itself a government, but its administrative structure was rudimentary. With the signing of the Renville Agreement, there had been a fresh wave of defections by civil servants in the countryside. Until the Renville Agreement, the 'coordinator' movement had maintained at least a skeleton Republican administration in the Jakarta region. Shortly after the signing of Renville, however, on 3 February 1948, the Republican government had announced an amnesty for those civil servants who had gone over to the Dutch. Although it did not explicitly permit still-loyal Republican officials to follow them, it was read immediately as doing so. As news of this release reached the Karawang hinterland, nearly three quarters of the Republican administrative apparatus gratefully left their uncomfortable mountain posts. Mu'min announced that he was going to Jakarta to investigate and would report back with instructions. His message, when it finally arrived, was that the Republican administration in West Java had been abolished. These defections soured the atmosphere amongst those who remained, as officials and fighters eyed each other suspiciously. Several defectors were killed as they tried to make their way to Jakarta. Those who remained led a tenuous existence moving from village to small village – Pasirtanjung, Kutatandingan—to avoid Dutch bombing and strafing raids. The PRJB managed to keep Dutch currency out of circulation but in the impoverished uplands there was little enough money of any sort available. The only taxation which the PRJB could levy was an informal collection of food contributions: people were supposed to put aside a little rice for the PRJB each time they cooked and this was collected once a week.[9]

The PRJB was thus more of a political statement and a forum for military coordination than an administration. Military figures from the old LRJR and religious politicians from the Masyumi comprised its seven-man governing committee. Wahidin was Oya's deputy as well as defence commander of the PRJB. Nunung Syamsulbahri of the Masyumi was 2nd deputy chairman and head of religious affairs, while Syamsuddin Can, Kyai Haji Nurali, Usman Sumantri and Mohamad Syafe'i made up the remaining members. Only Suwanta, a former wedana in Cibarusa who was government secretary, represented the old civil service in the upper levels of the PRJB, and he had no staff at all to help him in his tasks. He was forced, like the armed units of the 17 August Division, to lead a difficult peripatetic existence, shifting through the hills from village to village.[10]

The contradiction between the pro- and anti-Republican views of the PRJB suddenly became acute when the Dutch launched a second military action against the Republic on 19 December 1948. Although the attack saw the capital Yogyakarta fall into Dutch hands, along with most of the Republic's cabinet, it released the Republic from any legal obligation or political need to continue to accept the Renville Agreement's partition of Java. A conference of the PRJB was held in the village of Ciririp on 26–27 January 1948 to review the situation. On one side it was argued that now was the time to come forward and to support the Republic's struggle by declaring a Republican administration over the region once more. On the other side it was asserted that the Republic had brought the crisis on its own head by its pusillanimity and that the PRJB should proceed with the struggle alone. After much debate, the conference decided to change the PRJB's name to *Pemerintah Negara Kesatuan Republik Indonesia* (Government of the Unitary Republic of Indonesia), in effect a declaration of loyalty to the existing Republic, and it seemed as though the lasykar would return once more to the Republican fold.

The lasykar opposing this move, however, were reinforced shortly after the Ciririp conference by the arrival from Central Java of a small group of old LRJR associates, including Khaerul Saleh, Hasan Gayo, Johar Nur and about seventeen others.

The new arrivals were experienced politicians and all had been deeply involved in the tangled politics of the Republic during 1948. Amir Syarifuddin had fallen from office shortly after signing the Renville Agreement and political parties in the Republic abruptly changed their public policy towards the negotiations. The new government of Vice-President Hatta, which included some of the fiercest opponents of previous negotiations, now became the upholders of the Renville Agreement, while the new opposition, which had been responsible for signing the agreement, became its bitter opponents. As former opponents of Amir Syarifuddin, Tan Malaka and his followers, many of whom were in jail or in hiding, were suddenly viewed with considerably more favour by the government. Tan Malaka and Khaerul Saleh were released from jail and others emerged from hiding to form the *Gerakan Rakyat Revolusioner* (GRR, Revolutionary People's Movement), whose primary aims were to block any return to power by the socialists and to push the Republic towards a more vigorous defence policy. In the former, they were enthusiastic partners of the government and the Siliwangi Division and GRR members took part in the crushing the PKI during the Madiun affair of September 1948. Their rejection of the negotiations, however, put them once more in opposition to the government, and with the fall of Yogyakarta and the loss of the cabinet they sought to take charge of the national struggle. Khaerul Saleh and his colleagues had tried to persuade Tan Malaka to join them in West Java, but he chose East Java and was subsequently captured and executed there by the TNI. Thus, when the party reached Mt Sangga-buana in February 1949, they brought the lasykar a strong message of the need to fight on without relying on the Republic. Khaerul Saleh persuaded Wahidin and Oya to call another conference in the village of Serna, and after much debate the assembled nationalists agreed to preserve the PRJB and the 17 August Division. The administrative structure of the PRJB was strengthened by the installation of Hasan Gayo as head of an information or propaganda section and Johar Nur as head of economic affairs.[11]

The PRJB, however, no longer had the Jakarta region to itself. Aware of the possibility of a second Dutch military action, Republican planners, notably Nasution as head of the new Java Territorial Command, had prepared and equipped the Siliwangi Division to return to West Java and carry on guerrilla war there if the attack came. When the Dutch did indeed attack the Republic, the exodus to West Java began, with five waves of Siliwangi troops making their long way along the mountainous spine of central Java, parting company close to the West Java border, and proceeding to their old brigade areas. Units were harassed along the way by both Dutch and Darul Islam troops, and Daan Yahya, Nasution's successor as commander of the Siliwangi Division, was captured en route by the Dutch and interned on Nusa Kambangan. After six weeks to two months, however, most units were back in their old territories, with battalions under Lukas Kustaryo, Darsono and Sentot Iskandardinata based in the Cikampek, Karawang and Purwakarta regions respectively, under the general command of Sambas Atmadinata as territorial commander for the Jakarta region.[12]

Back in familiar territory, the Siliwangi troops moved to implement Nasution's guerrilla strategies. They re-established the Wehrkreise and the District and Sub-district Military Commands, and sought once again to bring the civilian administration under their authority, creating a third rival administration in the Jakarta region, alongside the PRJB and Pasundan. Like the PRJB, the TNI actually controlled relatively little territory, but it was able to deny control over much of the Jakarta region to its rivals.[13]

After an uneasy initial contact, the PRJB and the Siliwangi Division seem to have avoided conflict. Having worked with the Siliwangi Division in Central Java against the PKI, Khaerul Saleh and his colleagues were able to cooperate effectively with the local army units, at least when it came to keeping out of each other's way. Khaerul Saleh, Wahidin, and other leaders of the 17 August Division joined the regional TNI commander Sambas on a coordinating committee which supposedly regulated relations between the two groups. A few of the army officers such as Lukas Kustaryo were charismatic figures in their own right and their style of bravado and daring soon became popular with the lasykar. Even as relations became less friendly, the presence of the Dutch made further clashes out of the question. It is clear, on the other hand, that the army had only scant respect for the lasykar and was not inclined to see itself in any way as a partner with them in securing victory. Khaerul Saleh's rather premature suggestion that the army and lasykar should join together for a victory parade in Jakarta was rejected out of hand by the army.[14]

At last, however, war-weariness was growing amongst the lasykar. Although their activities made the Dutch insecure, Dutch counter insurgency had made the existence of the lasykar increasingly difficult. The guerrillas were short of weapons and were kept constantly on the move across the high ridges of Mt Sanggabuana. Forced to live off the jungle, they suffered from malnutrition which led in turn to disease and despondency. Shooting a tiger was a major occasion for one unit; they feasted on its meat for days and discovered that their skin diseases were cured as well. More debilitating, though, than the physical conditions in the hills was the growing conviction on the part of the lasykar that their struggle had become irrelevant. The performance of the Siliwangi troops in the field now far outshone that of the 17 August Division. It became steadily clearer that the great issues of the day were once more being resolved politically rather than militarily. With the resumption of negotiations between the Republic and the Dutch and the prospect of some kind of transfer of sovereignty in the near future, many of the political leaders of the PRJB decided that priority lay in influencing the policies of the Republican government rather than in continuing to fight the Dutch in the field. Like the API leaders who chose in 1945 to retreat to Central Java and to join the political campaigns of Tan Malaka and the PP, many of the political leaders of the PRJB who had made the long march from Central Java slipped into Jakarta to organise political rather than military action.[15]

Then, on 7 May 1949, the Republic and the Dutch signed yet another agreement, generally called the Rum-van Royen Agreement, after the principal negotiators. This time the Dutch, under heavy American pressure, were ready to hand over power to a sanitised federal Indonesia headed by Hatta. High on Mt Sanggabuana, the PRJB leaders met to discuss the new agreement. At issue in particular was whether the 17 August Division would adhere to the ceasefire which was a part of the agreement. Details of the proceedings are sketchy, but it appears that, as in Ciririp and Serna, opinions were thoroughly divided between those who saw the agreement as marking the final victory of the Republic and those who saw it as yet another betrayal by the Republic of the nationalist principles of the revolution. The latter group suspected, too, that the agreement, like

Linggajati and Renville, would simply be a prelude to another military action by the Dutch. After much discussion, the matter was postponed. Finally, on 1 September, when the reality of the Dutch retreat was incontrovertible, the PRJB agreed to dissolve itself and to recognise that the Republic was once again sovereign in West Java. Wahidin disbanded the 17 August division, giving its members a free choice on where they might go. Mu'min bobbed up once more as Republican resident of Jakarta and Oya Sumantri formally handed over power to the new Republican governor of West Java, Ukar Bratakusumah, in the village of Taringgal on 17 November 1949.[16]

1. Rapport nr 13 [Cileungsi and Klapanunggal], 5–7 February 1948, archief Michiels-Arnold Landen 110.
2. 'SP88' stood, according to one report, for 'HH' or *hati-hati* ('beware'). Another report has it that the first 8 stood for S, the eighth letter of the Javanese alphabet, the second 8 for H, the eighth letter of the Roman alphabet; '88', therefore, was a concealed reference to Sukarno and Hatta. Interview: A. S. Wagijanto, Karawang, 1 November 1982.
3. Veldpolitie Krawang, Inlichtingenrapporten, 6, 24 March 1948, *Proc. Gen.* 3; 'Activiteit S. P. 88 (SOBSI "88") onder SS personeel', 20 December 1948, CMI Document no. 5019, *Alg. Sec. I* box XXII, file 6. *Nieuwsgier*, 30 January 1948. *Republik Indonesia Kotapradja Djakarta Raya, op. cit.*, 554–555. Interview: Sidik Samsi, Jakarta, 11 October, 1 November 1982.
4. Quoted in Netherlands Delegation to Committee of Good Offices, 17 March 1948, *Proc. Gen.* 792
5. Dienst der Staatspolitie, Jogjakarta, 'Darul Islam c.s. in het gewest West-Java', 9 June 1948, CMI Document no 5495, *Alg.Sec.I* box XXII, file 6; Rapport nr 14 [Cileungsi and Klapanunggal], *loc.cit.*. Rapport nr 16, 14–17 December 1948, archief Michiels Arnold Landen 110; Rapport inzake het gebeurde te Tjibeureum in de nacht van 28 op 29 September 1948, archief Michiels-Arnold Landen 110. Oorlogsdag-boek III–9 RI, *MvD/CAD*, archief Staf IIe Inf. Brig. Groep, doos GG7. A. H. Nasution, *SPKI* IX (Bandung, 1979), 84; P. Heijboer, *De Politionele Acties: de Strijd om Indië 1945/1949* (Haarlem, 1979), 110; K. Helder, *Tiga Doeabelas: Gedenkboek 3–12 R. I.* (Groningen, 1951), 211. *Nieuwsgier*, 5 March 1948. Interview: Sidik Samsi, Jakarta, 1 November 1982.
6. 'Samenvatting omtrent het wezen van het schijnbestuur "Pemerintah Republik Djawa Barat" (P. R. D. B.)', *Proc.Gen.* 138. O. Wanakusu-manegara, 'Bekendmaking', 17 August 1948, CMI Doc. no 5540, *MvD/CAD*, HKGS-NOI, GG 58, bundel 6323 G, stuk 15070. Warsa Djajakusumah, 'Api '45 dari Masa ke Masa', *Aku Akan Teruskan* (Jakarta, 1976), 123. Interviews: Johar Nur, Jakarta 4 October 1982,

13 April 1983; Subarna, Jakarta, 27 October 1982; H. Moh. Damsjik, Bekasi, 18 January 1982.

7. C. van Dijk, *Rebellion under the Banner of Islam: the Darul Islam in Indonesia* (The Hague, 1981), 81–97; Hersri S. and Joebaar Ajoeb, 'S. M. Kartosuwiryo, Orang Seiring Bertukar Jalan', *Prisma* 11, 5 (1982), 89–91.

8. S. Abdurrachman [pseud.], 'Riwajat singkat pemerintahan sipil Republik Indonesia di Djawa-Barat', 15 October 1949 (in my possession). Wanakusumanegara, 'Bekendmaking', *loc.cit.*; Politiek manifest van de 'Pemerintah Republik Djawa Barat', 17 August 1948, CMI Doc. 5540, *MvD/CAD*, HKGS-NOI, GG 58, bundel 6323 G, stuk 15070. Confidential interviews.

9. Recomba West-Java, Afd. Politieke Zaken, [Rapport], 7 April 1948, *Proc.Gen.* 747. Abdurrachman, 'Riwajat singkat', *loc.cit.*. Confidential interviews.

10. Abdurrachman, 'Riwajat singkat', *loc.cit.*; 'Samenvatting omtrent het schijnbestuur', *loc.cit.*. Confidential interviews.

11. Abdurrachman, 'Riwajat singkat', *loc.cit.* Warsa Djajakusumah, *op. cit.*, 124. Helen Jarvis, personal communication. Interviews: Moh. Hasan Gayo, Jakarta, 1 March 1983; Kusnandar Partowisastro, Bogor, 3 February 1983; Johar Nur, Jakarta, 3 December 1982. Confidential interviews.

12. Sedjarah Militer Kodam VI Siliwangi, *Siliwangi dari Masa ke Masa* (Jakarta, 1968), 145–157, 177–189, 198–302; *Album Kenangan Kodam VI/Siliwangi* (Bandung, 1977), 27–28; Nasution, *SPKI* IX, 229, 281–324; A. H. Nasution, *Fundamentals of Guerilla Warfare* (London, 1965), 108–115. Interviews: Daan Jahja, Jakarta, 7 August 1982; Suhendro, Bekasi, 19 January 1983.

13. 'Rapport nopens K. D. M. (Kommando Daerah Militair) of K. O. D. M. (Kommando Onderdistrict Militair)', September 1949, *Proc.Gen.* 124; Politiek politioneel maandverslag (uittreksels), December 1948 – May 1949, *ibid.* Interviews: Sadikin, Jakarta, 28 March 1983.

14. Nasution, *SPKI* X (Bandung, 1979), 217–225. Interviews: Moh. Hasan Gayo, Jakarta, 1 March 1983; Johar Nur, Jakarta, 4 October 1982; Sidik Samsi, Jakarta, 11 October, 17 November 1982; Alizar Thaib, Jakarta, 28 February 1983.

15. Warsa Djajakusumah, *op.cit.*, 125; Heijboer, *op.cit.*, 151. C-Divisie 7 December, Overzicht ontstaan en organisatie der 'Divisie Guerrilla 17 Augustus', 13 May 1949, *Alg.Sec.II* 300. Interviews: Johar Nur, Jakarta, 4 October 1982; Kusnandar Partowisastro, Bogor, 3 February 1983; Moh. Hasan Gayo, Jakarta, 1 March 1983.

16. 'Riwajat singkat', *loc.cit.* Interviews: Johar Nur, Jakarta, 19 October 1982; confidential interviews.

V
EPILOGUE

14

The Survivors

The Jakarta lasykar dispersed. Wahidin's dissolution of the 17 August Division set a symbolic seal on the Jakarta underworld's drive for power in the region, and the last vestiges of a common purpose amongst the lasykar disappeared. It only remains here to trace briefly the careers of those who did not disappear totally from view. Wahidin and many of the lasykar 'returned to society' (*kembali ke masyarakat*), either taking up their old criminal pursuits in their home territories or moving on to new occupations, criminal or otherwise, in Jakarta. Usman Sumantri was allowed, according to some reports, to join the TNI; in other accounts he was killed by them. Pa' Utom, a local boss from Cianjur who had been one of the minor unit commanders of the Division, joined the Darul Islam. Many of the political leaders of the lasykar found a tenuous existence in the national capital as journalists. Imam Syafe'i, the one-time boss of Senen who had been amongst the few gang leaders to move successfully into the army, remained an officer in the Siliwangi Division while continuing to manage his criminal fief. He acquired a reputation as one who could produce the necessary crowds on the streets of Jakarta for political demonstrations and is said to have assembled many of those who demonstrated for the dismissal of parliament in the 17 October 1952 Affair.[1] He later made a brief appearance in Sukarno's so-called 'Cabinet of 100 Ministers' installed on 21 February 1966, as Minister of State for People's Security. He died in 1982. According to reports which can probably never be confirmed, other ex-lasykar joined the Siliwangi Division in suppressing the Darul Islam rebellion in other parts of West Java, while one or two took part in an uprising against the Portuguese in East Timor.[2]

A few of the HAMOTs were able to find brief careers in the

so-called security battalions which the Dutch set up in 1948 and 1949. In considering military arrangements for Indonesia, the Dutch were concerned not simply with immediate security problems but also with political issues. Fervent Republicans may have found the Renville and Rum-van Royen Agreements highly unpalatable, but they nonetheless envisaged and ultimately led to a fairly rapid transfer of power to a federated republic in which the Republic of Indonesia was one of the more powerful constituents. One of the principal thrusts of Dutch diplomacy in the post-Renville negotiations had been to reduce the size of the TNI component which the new federal army would have to take into itself, but they were also keen to boost the military strength of the federalists as a bulwark for the agreement. Many Dutch feared that the leaders of the Republic would sign almost any list of guarantees if that were necessary to remove the colonialists, but would then repudiate those guarantees once Dutch power to enforce them was gone.

To guard against this, the Dutch military authorities began the ambitious task of creating an indigenous military apparatus. As early as October 1947, when the movement towards Renville was already clear, advisers to General Spoor had recommended as a first step the creation of 'security battalions' (*veiligheidsbataljons*), territorially-oriented units trained not for external defence but for 'the cleaning out of trouble-making groups and the maintenance of law and security'.[3] The proposal was quickly supported by the senior civil authorities in the colony, who saw political advantage in the Netherlands if demands on Dutch troops could be reduced in Indonesia by increasing the indigenous profile of the colonial side. Given the predictable antagonism of the KNIL to such plans, it was decided to separate the new units administratively. They were to be directly under the Lieutenant Governor-General in his capacity as commander-in-chief and were to be posted on a permanent basis to assist the governments of the negara and other federal regions. In the short term, they were to be under the operational command of Dutch regional military commanders, but their organisational structure gave them the potential to become provincial armies of the negara if the need arose. And at a planned strength of 13,200 by the end of 1948, they would have been a substantial addition to the military equation.[4]

The first security battalions were established in November 1947 in North Sumatra, another region where the Dutch were trying hard to strengthen the federal order. The first West Java battalion followed in February 1948, and was quartered at Cimahi, near Bandung in the Sundanese heartland of the Priangan. Aversion to the HAMOT model showed in Dutch recruitment and training patterns: rather than taking an existing irregular unit and attempting to shape it as a whole into something usable, the security battalions began with individual recruits and gave them prolonged and intensive training intended to turn them into reliable soldiers. It was as individuals, therefore, that a few of the surviving HAMOTs joined the Cimahi battalion. Because of the extended training period, it was not until the second half of 1948 that they began to be employed militarily.[5]

While the prospect of legitimacy in the Veiligheidsbataljons attracted some lasykar, others were drawn into a different kind of venture. The Dutch counter-terrorist Raymond Westerling, who had led the DST in the Karawang region in 1947, had been dismissed from the Dutch army just before the second military action. He shared the concerns over Pasundan's weakness which led to the formation of the Veiligheidsbataljons—West Java was his old stamping ground and he was reputed to be the lover of one of the daughters of the Pasundan head of state, R. A. A. M. Wiranatakusumah—and he was able to assemble a small armed unit of demobilised KNIL soldiers, TNI deserters and former lasykar. His intention was to use this force to defend federalism in Indonesia. J. Rapar, a former leader of the Jakarta KRIS, was amongst those who joined Westerling. Few of the lasykar survived this venture and their reasons for joining Westerling must remain obscure. The counter-terrorist, however, was a man of considerable charisma and charm who revelled in the sense of power which came from commanding violence. Calling his units APRA (*Angkatan Perang Ratu Adil*, Armed Forces of the Just Prince), he attempted to place himself in a line of descent from the legendary liberator princes of Java. As a Menadonese, on the other hand, Rapar may have been more attracted by Westerling's commitment to staving off alleged Javanese imperialism in the outer islands. As the lasykar contemplated the shrinking opportunities available to them in post-revolutionary Indonesia, Westerling must have been an attractive figure.

Westerling issued an ultimatum to the new federal government, demanding guarantees of the maintenance of the federal system. When the federal government remained unintimidated, he launched a coup of sorts in Bandung on 22 January 1950 and in Jakarta on 26 January. Bandung, where the strongest elements of the APRA were concentrated, fell briefly into the rebels' hands, but the putsch in Jakarta was a fiasco. Rapar and many of his followers were killed in a brief skirmish with TNI troops and the city was barely ruffled by the incident. The sheer improbability of a successful coup in Jakarta by a small gang of lasykar and the relative unimportance of the plotters' principal target, Bandung, in national politics has led to speculation that Westerling and his followers may have been duped into an easily suppressed putsch which would compromise the federalists, but this remains obscure. Certainly Rapar's former colleagues saw him as a dupe of Westerling rather than a traitor to the Republic.[6]

The closest to the tradition of the old LRJR were those who refused to accept Wahidin's decision to disband the 17 August Division. This group contained many of those who had fiercely resisted the dissolution of the PRJB during 1948 and 1949, and they were led by Khaerul Saleh. Even after it had become abundantly clear that the Dutch were indeed leaving, this group remained highly dissatisfied with the terms of the Dutch withdrawal. The new United States of Indonesia left the original Republic as one amongst sixteen negara and other federal territories, the federation was burdened with the foreign debt of the old Netherlands Indies (part of which had been acquired in the struggle to suppress the Republic), a large Dutch military mission was to be maintained, and a Dutch-style parliamentary system of government was installed. All of these provisions were viewed with some hostility throughout the Republic, and Khaerul Saleh aimed to channel this hostility into direct political pressure on the new government.

Saleh re-assembled lasykar units under the command of Sidik Samsi, Pa' Macem, Camat Nata, Wim Mangelep and Saridil in the hills south of Karawang, setting up a command headquarters in Pangkalan. Initially the TNI seemed to be willing to tolerate them there, but the army's patience with the lasykar soon wore thin. After some clashes in which many lasykar were killed and the headquarters was driven from Pangkalan, Saleh decided to move the scene of his operations. In the words of one of his followers, there was not enough forest in the Karawang region to be able to hide from the Siliwangi Division. In a meeting near Jonggol, Saleh and his colleagues decided to move towards the peninsula of Ujung Kulon on the far southwestern corner of the island, an isolated spot where a few Javan rhinoceros could still be found in the thick lowland jungle. Like many rebels on Java in earlier times, they had the idea of crossing the Sunda Straits to set up a more secure base in the wilder regions of southern Sumatra. Johar Nur was sent to Jakarta to act as lasykar spokesman in the capital. The lasykar were joined en route by remnants of the Bogor Brigade of the Bambu Runcing under Muhidin Nasution and Banten units under K. H. A. Khatib and Mohamad Khusnun, and on 11 October 1949, they announced the formation of a new *Tentara Rakyat* (People's Army).[7]

The announcement was a bitter one:

> . . . on 15 August, the Indonesian people forced their will on
> the national leaders Sukarno and Hatta, to whom they entrusted
> the declaration of the Indonesian people's freedom in the form

of the proclamation of independence of 17 August 1945. But in the course of the struggle which followed the Indonesian people have experienced sadness and bitterness.

In the end it must be said that the fate, the interests and the needs of the Indonesian people can no longer be entrusted to weak leaders who lack confidence in the strength of the people themselves. The people in struggle have realised that they cannot rely on anyone but themselves to defend and guarantee their principals and their interests.[8]

Khaerul Saleh reconstructed a smaller version of the old PRJB political council, consisting of himself, Johar Nur, Syamsuddin Can and Eikin. Before they could reach the coast, however, they were intercepted by Siliwangi Division forces under Major Sudarsono and dispersed. Again many lasykar were killed, though on this occasion the leaders all escaped. Khaerul Saleh, Syamsuddin Can and Muhidin Nasution, however, were all arrested soon afterwards and placed in jail. Mangelep returned to his old haunts along the lower reaches of the Citarum but was killed soon after in a clash with the army. Sidik Samsi and Camat Nata survived to establish themselves once more in the foothills of Mt Sanggabuana. They revived the name Bambu Runcing and their troops were active for a time in the countryside of Karawang. Military operations by the Siliwangi Division, however, quickly reduced their numbers. Warsad in north Karawang, Tajuddin in Pasirtanjung and Sukenda in Cikampek were all attacked and killed by the army. Amongst the survivors, many decided to abandon the struggle when the last of the negara was dissolved and the federal Republic was replaced by a unitary Republic of Indonesia in August 1950. With commendable lack of malice, the Republican government organised for them to receive agricultural training in Serang and Tasikmalaya, though they were given neither land nor money. Camat Nata in Cibitung responded to an official amnesty in March 1954 and returned to civilian life, leaving only a few small Bambu Runcing units under Cece Subrata south of Sukabumi and Haji Usman Debot in the limestone hills around Cibinong. Caves in the limestone provided Debot's forces not only with shelter but with a useful income from the lucrative sale of edible birds' nests. Debot's fief seems to have become an accepted part of the local political landscape, to the extent that Bambu Runcing members campaigned openly for the Nationalist Party (PNI) and the left-wing Murba and Akoma parties in the 1955 general elections. These parties in turn encouraged the government not to move forcefully against the rebels. In 1959, however, Debot also descended from the hills when Sukarno abandoned the Republic's 1950 provisional constitution, which provided for Dutch-style parliamentary democ-

racy, and restored the revolutionary 1945 constitution, thereby eras-
ing the last of the political concessions made to the Dutch with the
transfer of sovereignty in 1949.[9]

1. Ulf, Sundhaussen, *The Road to Power* (Kuala Lumpur, 1982), 70–73.
2. My informant dated this uprising to 1965, but the incident referred to may
   well be the earlier 'movement' of 1959, described by Jill Jolliffe. In this
   episode, fourteen Indonesians arrived in Timor claiming to be refugees
   from the Permesta movement in Sulawesi. Whether they were opponents of Permesta fleeing its areas of control, supporters fleeing the
   destruction of Permesta at the hands of the central government, or
   agents provocateurs using a plausible excuse to enter the colony is not
   clear. See J. Jolliffe, *East Timor: Nationalism and Colonialism* (St
   Lucia, 1978), 48–49.
3. KNIL/KL, Kabinet van den Legercommandant, 'Memorandum betreffende de instelling van het instituut van "veiligheidsbataljons"', 22
   October 1947, *MvD/CAD*, HKGS-NOI, GG 20, 1947, stuk 16325.
4. Jonkman to van Mook, 15 December 1947, *MvD/CAD*, HKGS-NOI,
   Inv.nr. GG 29, 1948, bundel 244, stuk 900; Buurman van Vreeden to
   Spoor, 27 July 1948, *MvD/CAD*, HKGS-NOI, Inv.nr. GG 29, 1948,
   bundel 244, stuk 926; *OBB* XII, 765–766, nn. 4–5.
5. KNIL/KL, Directoraat Centrale Opleidingen, 'Oprichting Veiligheidsbataljons', 31 July 1948, *MvD/CAD*, HKGS-NOI, Inv.nr. GG 29,
   1948, bundel 244, stuk 15624; 'Geschiedenis HAMOT', 20 June 1948,
   Oorlogsdagboek 3–9 RI, *MvD/CAD*, archief Staf IIe Inf. Brig. Groep,
   doos GG7; Spoor to van Mook, 15 December 1947, *OBB* XII, 197.
6. L. I. Graf, 'Verslag dienstreis naar Bandung van 8–10 December 1949',
   Alg.Sec.II 278. George McTurnan Kahin, *Nationalism and Revolution
   in Indonesia* (Ithaca, N. Y., 1952), 454; O. White, *Time Now, Time
   Before* (London and Melbourne, 1967), 147, 193–199; P. Schumacher,
   'Raymond Westerling en de jungle van het verleden', *NRC Handelsblad* 18 September 1981; W. Ijzereef, 'Westerling en zijn poging tot
   rehabilitatie', *Vrij Nederland* 5 February 1983; R. P. P. Westerling,
   Mijn Memoires (Antwerp and Amsterdam, 1952), 204–262; D. Venner
   and R. P. P. Westerling, *Westerling: de Eenling* (Amsterdam 1982),
   331–362; W. Merghart, 'De APRA-Affaire . . . een Enorme Bedrog?'
   (n.d. [1983?], photocopy in my possession). Interviews: Djilis Tahir,
   Jakarta, 2 February 1983; Sidik Samsi, Jakarta, 1 November 1982; R.
   P. P. Westerling, Amsterdam, 20 February 1984; confidential inter-
   views.
7. H. Feith, *The Decline of Constitutional Democracy in Indonesia*
   (Ithaca, N. Y., 1962), 81. Khaerul Saleh to Sadikin, 9 April 1949,
   Proc.Gen. 658. Interviews: Johar Nur, Jakarta, 19 October 1982; Sidik
   Samsi, Jakarta, 17 November 1982; Abdul Karim Abbas, Jakarta, 2
   November 1982; confidential interview.

8. *Sin Po*, 18 November 1949, in *Alg.Sec.I* X–30–47. The twenty-four
   signatories of the declaration included Khatib, Khaerul Saleh, Syamsuddin Can, Mangelep, Muhidin Nasution, Tajuddin, and Sidik Samsi.
9. Lt.Col. Eri Sudewo to Kommando Jawa, 2 November 1949, *Proc.Gen.*
   658. Sedjarah Militer Kodam VI Siliwangi, *Siliwangi dari Masa Kemasa* (Jakarta, 1968), 370–372; C. van Dijk, *Rebellion under the
   Banner of Islam: the Darul Islam in Indonesia* (The Hague, 1981), 110.
   Sumber (Jakarta) 18 March 1954; *Indonesia Raya* (Jakarta) 18 March
   1954. Interviews: Sidik Samsi, Jakarta, 17 November 1982; Muhidin
   Nasution, Ciluer, 14, 30 October 1982; Ma'riful, Jakarta, 23 August
   1982; Supardi Mangkuyuwono, Jakarta, 19 October 1982; Camat
   Nata, Cibitung, Bekasi, 26 January 1983; confidential interviews.

Conclusion: Gangsters and Revolutionaries

The coalition between the Jakarta underworld and a group of younger radical nationalists which reached its peak in the People's Militia of Greater Jakarta was a product of unusual circumstances. The nationalists and gangsters had established important contacts before the Second World War, partly because they shared an opposition to Dutch rule, partly because they had skills to offer each other—the nationalists saw value in the gangsters as one of the few sections of Indonesian society under colonialism which still commanded some expertise in violence, while the gangsters, whose criminal subculture contained elements of social banditry, saw nationalism as offering a future in which they might be recognised and respected as legitimate power-holders in their communities. This association might never have become more than the vague contact which disparate groups excluded from political power sometimes maintain for the sake of mutual encouragement, but for the formalisation of these contacts during the Japanese occupation and the sudden need for close cooperation during the Indonesian national revolution.

The young nationalists lacked the political stature and political base to claim power within the Republic in their own right, but they held strong views on the way in which the revolution against the Dutch should be fought. They wanted the Republic to mobilise all its human resources in a concerted attack on colonialism and, although their primary aim was thus a political one directed at the Republican leadership, they were also prepared to put their conviction into practice by taking up arms against the Dutch and their allies. For both goals they needed a constituency, a basis for claiming to speak in the name of the people and an armed force to fight. The under-

world of Jakarta served them well, though ultimately not well
enough, for both purposes.

The Jakarta underworld for its part was deeply interested in its
future in the changing political environment. The end of the Japanese
occupation and the start of the revolution had left the gangster
leaders of Jakarta and the surrounding countryside in a position of
unprecedented power, a position, however, which was under threat
from all sides. The Jakarta gangsters found much that made sense in
the fiery rhetoric of the younger nationalists which claimed that the
Republic was under dire threat and they had no doubt, at least
initially, that the defeat of the Republic would see them driven back
into outlawry. They joined the young nationalists, therefore, in a
determination to fight the Dutch and to oppose what they saw as the
misguided policies of the Republican leadership. Both the gangsters
and the nationalists, too, shared an increasing hostility towards the
Republican government which not only rejected their demands but
sought to remove them from the political and military equation, and
their sense of being beset by enemies on all sides helped to preserve
their alliance.

What made this coalition more than a simple alliance of expedi-
ency was the surprising congruence between the values of the two
groups, and it was this which made the lasykar a distinct phenomenon
in Indonesian history. They possessed only vague notions of the
meaning of independence beyond believing that it would give them
power and eliminate the Dutch, but they nourished populist and
patriotic impulses which gave them deep roots in the societies of the
countryside east of Jakarta. They held a naive enthusiasm for action,
especially fighting, and an abundant readiness to believe themselves
betrayed, together with a surprising resilience in the face of ad-
versity. And they shared an exaggerated sense of their own importance and power, and let this lead them into adventures—Her Majesty's Irregular Troops and the Bambu Runcing—which were
doomed to fail from the start.

The excursion of the lasykar into national politics came to an end.
They did not disappear entirely, but, as we have seen, their footprints
in Indonesian history became progressively shallower and less distinct. The turbulent history of the lasykar nonetheless tells us important things about Indonesia's war of independence. First, the sudden
prominence of the Jakarta underworld enables us to focus scholarly
attention on a group whose social organisation and ways of thought
would otherwise be more difficult to trace. Autobiography is uncommon in Indonesia, and none of the local bosses of the colonial era
have left personal records of any kind. We know something of them

because of the attention they attracted from colonial police forces, but we know a good deal more about them because they chose a political cause which demanded communication with the rest of the community.

Second, the study helps us to demonstrate, as has been suspected for some time, that the social roots of the Indonesian revolution were more complex than the intellectual history of the nationalist movement might suggest. The nationalist movement was certainly in many ways a consequence of contradictions in the evolving Dutch colonial system. Colonialism created the extensive grievances which fuelled the nationalist movement, established the geographical and political scope of the movement and trained, in one way or another, many of the people who were to lead the struggle against it. Yet the nationalist struggle drew also on existing social formations, of which the Jakarta underworld was one.

And third, this study enables us to trace the consolidation of the Republican state, its transformation from little more than a state of mind in 1945 to a state which, though desperately weak by contemporary standards, was nonetheless strong enough to establish authority over its most troublesome subjects. The Jakarta lasykar were not alone in finding themselves attacked by the state they had helped bring into being—the Tiga Daerah revolutionaries in north central Java and many others found a similar fate—but their relations with the Republic were amongst the most tempestuous. We can see in this story the swift adjustment of nationalist leaders of the centre to the priorities of state-formation and the rapid transition they made from mainting a broad nationalist coalition in colonial times, to preserving a more powerful but narrower political base in the form of the Indonesian Republic.

Bibliography

I. Archival Materials

1. Algemeen Rijksarchief, The Hague:
Algemene Secretarie te Batavia
Michiels-Arnold Landen
Ministerie van Kolonien (Ministerie van Overzeese Gebiedsdelen)
Ministerie van Kolonien—Supplement
Procureur-Generaal bij het Hooggerechtshof van Nederlandsch-Indië
Regeringsvoorlichtingsdienst
Personal archives:
C. W. A. Abbenhuis
P. J. Koets
H. J. van Mook
P. Sanders
2. Archieven Hulpdepot, Ministerie van Binnenlandse Zaken, The Hague:
Rapportage Indonesië
3. Arsip Jayakarta, Jakarta:
Dokumentasi Pemerintah Nasional Kota Djakarta
Dokumentasi Kantoor voor Gemeentezaken, Batavia
4. Centraal Archievendepot, Ministerie van Defensie, The Hague:
Assistent Adjudant-Generaal
Hoofdkwartier Generaal Staf, Nederlandsch Oost Indië
Staf IIe Infanterie Brigade Groep
5. India Office Library and Records, London:
L/P&S series
L/WS series
6. Public Record Office, London:
Foreign Office series
War Office series
7. Rijksinstituut voor Oorlogsdocumentatie, Amsterdam:
Indische Collectie

8. Waseda University, Tokyo:
Nishijima Collection
9. Private collections:
R. Abdulkadir Widjojoatmodjo
P. J. Koets
Ruth T. McVey
Shigetada Nishijima
John R. W. Smail
Moh. Tarekat Prawirowijoto
T. R. Tjoet Rachman

II. Unpublished Reminiscences, Perpustakaan 45, Jakarta

Moehamad Dja'man, 'Naskah revolosi perjuangan kemerdekaan: Negara
Republik Indonesia (Pengalaman selama tahun 1945 s/d 1949)', 206/XI
Suwarsih Djojopoespito, 'Yang tak dapat kulupakan', 317/XVI
Gani, 'Kebayoran Lama — tahun 1945', 848/XLIII
E. Madli Hasan, 'Perjoangan 45 untuk pembangunan bangsa', 118/VI
Radjimin Moenawi, 'Pengalamanku selama 1945–1950', 636/XXXII
Titik Pamudjo, 'Nyimah Srikandhi "Patok Besi" yang buta huruf', 701/
XXXVI
Tom Pasarminggu, 'Kisah nyata perjuangan kemerdekaan R.I. periode
1945–1950', 742/XXXVIII
Rachyadi, 'Kisah perjuangan antara tahun 1945 s/d 1950', 165/IX
M. Sani, 'Yatim dan perjuangan bangsa', 10/I
Sanusi W. S., 'Perjuangan 45 untuk pembangunan bangsa', 823/XLII
M. Siradz, 'Pertempoeran', 764/XXXIX
Mohd Soiz, 'Jalan-jalan yang kususuri', 157/VIII
M. S. Soemaatmadja, 'Kisah nyata suka-duka pengalaman pada masa revo-
lusi physic tahun 1945', 832/XLII
R. M. Soleh Suriaamijaya, 'Pasar Minggu waktu subuh', 166/IX
Didi Tanuwidjaja, 'Setitik ujung-pena pengorbanan bagi perjuangan bang-
saku periode 1945–1950', 289/XV
Wakrim Wahyudi, 'Kisah nyata perjoangan kemerdekaan Republik In-
donesia, periode 1945–1950', 504/XXVI
Masnika Yusuf, 'Sekelumit pengalaman saya pada tiga zaman, khususnya
pada masa revolusi', 244/XIII
Suliani Zumhan, 'Zisah nyata perjuangan kemerdekaan R.I. periode 1945–
1950', 489/XXV

III. Newspapers and Periodicals

Antara (Jakarta & Yogyakarta), 1946
Asia Raya (Jakarta), 2602, 2605 [i.e. 1942, 1945]
Benteng (Malang), 1947
Berdjoeang (Malang), 1946

Berita Indonesia (Jakarta), 1945–1948
Het Dagblad (Batavia), 1945–1948
Djakarta Raya (Jakarta), 1945
Economic Review of Indonesia, 1947–1949
The Fighting Cock (Jakarta), 1945
Harian Indonesia (Bandung), 1948
Independent (Jakarta), 1945–1946
Kan Po (Berita Pemerintah) (Jakarta), 2602, 2603, 2604 [1942–1944]
Kedaulatan Rakjat (Yogyakarta), 1945–1947
Masa Indonesia (Jakarta), 1947
Merdeka (Jakarta), 1945–1948
Min Pao (Jakarta), 1945
Negara Baroe (Jakarta & Yogyakarta), 1946
Netherlands News, 1946
Het Nieuwsblad (Batavia), 1946, 1947
Nieuwsgier (Batavia), 1945–1948
Ra'jat (Jakarta), 1945–1947
De Ronde Tafel (Batavia), 1946
Sari Pers (Jakarta), 1948
Sin Min (Semarang), 1947
Soeara Merdeka (Bandung), 1945
Soeara Oemoem (Jakarta), 1947
Star Weekly (Jakarta), 1946–1947

IV. Books and Articles

Abeyasekere, Susan. 'Colonial Urban Politics: the Municipal Council of Batavia', *Kabar Seberang* 13–14 (1984), 17–24
——. ed. *From Batavia to Jakarta: Indonesia's Capital 1930s to 1980s*. Clayton, Vic.: Centre of Southeast Asian Studies, Monash University, 1985
——. *Jakarta: a history*. Singapore: Oxford University Press, 1987
Adas, Michael. 'From Avoidance to Confrontation: Peasant Protest in Precolonial and Colonial Southeast Asia', *Comparative Studies in Society and History* 23, 1 (1981), 217–47
Agustaman, Harry. *5 Tahun Melawan SAC: Subandrio Aidit Chaerul*. [Bandung: Badar, 1966]
Aku Akan Teruskan, Jakarta: Dewan Nasional Angkatan 45, Pusat Dokumentasi Sejarah Perjoangan 45, 1976
Album Kenangan Kodam VI/Siliwangi 1946–1977. Bandung: Markas Kodam VI/Siliwangi, 1977
Alers, Henri J. H. *Om een Rode of Groene Merdeka: 10 Jaren Binnenlandse Politiek Indonesië 1943–1953*. Eindhoven: De Pelgrim, 1956
Anderson, Benedict R. O'G. *Java in a Time of Revolution: Occupation and Resistance, 1944–1946*. Ithaca, N.Y.: Cornell University Press, 1972
——. *Some Aspects of Indonesian Politics Under the Japanese Occupation, 1944–1945*. Ithaca, N.Y.: Cornell University Modern Indonesia Project, 1961

Ansems, H. J. Een Jaar 'W'-Brigade: Gedenkboek Uitg. ter Gelegenheid van het Eenjarige Bestaan der 'W'-Brigade. Cianjur: n.p., 1947

Anwar, H. Rosihan. Kisah-kisah Jakarta Menjelang Clash ke-I. Jakarta: Pustaka Jaya, 1979

——. Kisah-kisah Jakarta Setelah Proklamasi. Jakarta: Pustaka Jaya, 1977

——. Kisah-kisah Jakarta Zaman Revolusi: Kenang-kenangan Seorang Wartawan 1946–1949. Jakarta: Pustaka Jaya, 1975

Arlacchi, Pino. 'The Mafioso: From Man of Honour to Entrepreneur', New Left Review 118 (November-December 1979), 53–72

Aziz, M. A. Japan's Colonialism and Indonesia. The Hague: Martinus Nijhoff, 1955

'Back to the "P. & T." Lands', Java Gazette 1, 5 (March 1948), 117

Bahsan, Oemar. Tjatatan Ringkas Tentang: PETA ('Pembela Tanah-Air') dan Peristiwa Rengasdengklok. Bandung: Melati Bandung, 1955

Ball, Desmond J. 'Allied Intelligence Cooperation Involving Australia during World War II', Australian Outlook 32, 3 (December 1978) 299–309

Baudet, H., and I. J. Brugmans, eds. Balans van Beleid: Terugblik op de Laatste Halve Eeuw van Nederlandsch-Indië. Assen, 1961

Beets. 'Rapport over de Tanggerangsche Ratoe Adil Beweging: rapport van het bestuursonderzoek naar de feiten en toestanden, welke oorzaak zijn geweest of aanleiding hebben gegeven tot de gewapende verzetsactie te Tanggerang tegen de overheid op den 10den Februari 1914'. Photocopy in John M. Echols Collection, Cornell University Library.

Benda, Harry J. The Crescent and the Rising Sun: Indonesian Islam under the Japanese Occupation, 1942–1945. The Hague: W. van Hoeve, 1958

'Bevolkingssterkte en Grootte van de Federale Gebieden Volgens Naoorlogse Gegevens', Bestuursvraagstukken/Soal-soal Pemerintahan 1, 4 (October 1949), 494–495

Biografi Prof. dr. Moestopo. N.p.: n.p., 1980

Biro Pemuda, Departemen P.D. & K. Sedjarah Perdjuangan Pemuda Indonesia. Jakarta: Balai Pustaka, 1965

Blok, Anton. The Mafia of a Sicilian Village 1860–1960: a Study of Violent Peasant Entrepreneurs. Oxford: Basil Blackwell, 1974

——. 'The Peasant and the Brigand: Social Banditry Reconsidered', Comparative Studies in Society and History 14, 4 (1972), 494–503

Blumberger, J. Th. Petrus. De Communistische Beweging in Nederlandsch-Indië. Haarlem: Tjeenk Willink, 1928

——. De Nationalistische Beweging in Nederlandsch-Indië. Haarlem: Tjeenk Willink, 1931

Blussé, Leonard. Strange Company: Chinese Settlers, Mestizo Women and the Dutch in VOC Batavia. Leiden: Koninklijk Instituut voor Taal-, Land- en Volkenkunde, 1986

Braudel, Fernand. The Mediterranean and the Mediterranean World in the Age of Philip II. London: Fontana, 1975

Breman, Jan. The Village in Nineteenth Century Java and the Colonial State. Rotterdam: CASP, 1980

Brugmans, I. J. et al., eds. Nederlandsch-Indië onder Japanse Bezetting: Gegevens en Documenten over de Jaren 1942–1945. Franeker: T. Wever, 2nd ed., 1960

Cahaya Dari Medan Laga. Jakarta: Dewan Harian Nasional Angkatan 45, Pusat Dokumentasi Sejarah Perjoangan 45, 1976

Campbell, Donald Maclaine. *Java Past & Present: a Description of the Most Beautiful Country in the World, its Ancient History, People, Antiquities, and Products*. 2v. London: Heinemann, 1915

Castles, Lance. 'The Ethnic Profile of Djakarta', *Indonesia* 1 (April 1967), 153–204

Chaeruddin, Entol. *Proklamasi 17 Agustus dan Pemindahan Kekuasaan*. [Jakarta]: n.p., [1973]

Cheah Boon Kheng. 'Hobsbawm's Social Banditry, Myth and Historical Reality: a Case in the Malaysian State of Kedah, 1915–1920', *Bulletin of Concerned Asian Scholars* 17, 4 (October-December 1985), 34–51

Cobban, James L. 'The City on Java: an Essay in Historical Geography'. Ph.D. dissertation, University of California, 1970

Coedès, G. *The Indianized States of Southeast Asia*. Canberra: Australian National University Press, 1975

Cohen, S. 'Herstel der Veldpolitie', *Koloniaal Tijdschrift* 27 (1938), 116–123

Cohn, Norman. *The Pursuit of the Millennium: Revolutionary Millenarians and Mystical Anarchists of the Middle Ages*. London: Paladin, 1970

Comber, L. F. *Chinese Secret Societies in Malaya: a Survey of Triad Societies from 1800 to 1900*. New York: J. J. Augustin, 1959

Cribb, Robert Bridson. 'Jakarta in the Indonesian Revolution 1945–1949'. Ph.D. dissertation, University of London, 1984

——. 'Opium and the Indonesian revolution', *Modern Asian Studies* 28, 4 (1988), 701–722

——. 'Political Dimensions of the Currency Question, 1945–1947', *Indonesia* 31 (April 1981), 113–136

——. 'A Revolution Delayed: the Indonesian Republic and the Netherlands Indies, August-December 1945', *Australian Journal of Politics and History* 32, 1 (1986), 72–85

Davis, Fei-ling. *Primitive Revolutionaries of China: a Study of Secret Societies of the Late Nineteenth Century*. Honolulu: University of Hawaii Press, 1977

Di Antara Hempasan dan Benturan: Kenang-kenangan dr. Abdul Halim 1942–1950. Jakarta: Arsip Nasional Republik Indonesia, 1981

Diah, B. M. 'Transition of power and responsibility: the young generation is not prepared', *Prisma: the Indonesian Indicator* 6 (June 1977), 43–46

van Dijk, C. *Rebellion under the Banner of Islam: the Darul Islam in Indonesia*. The Hague: Martinus Nijhoff, 1981

Dinas Sejarah Militer Kodam V/Jaya. *Sejarah Perjuangan Rakyat Jakarta, Tanggerang dan Bekasi dalam Menegakkan Kemerdekaan R.I.* [Jakarta]: Virgo Sari, [1975]

Djojohadikusumo, Margono. *Herinneringen uit 3 Tijdperken: een Geschreven Familie Overlevering*. Amsterdam: Gé Nabrink, 1970

'Dokumentasi ikhtisar singkat sejarah perjuangan rakyat pemuda Senen Shiku Jakarta-Raya dalam mempertahankan Proklamasi Kemerdekaan Republik Indonesia 17–8–'45'. Jakarta: Dewan Harian 'Angkatan 45' Ranting Kecamatan Senen, 1982

van Doorn, J. A. A. and W. J. Hendrix. *Ontsporing van Geweld: over het*

Nederlands/Indisch/Indonesisch Conflict. Rotterdam: Universitaire Pers Rotterdam, 1970

Doulton, A. J. F. *The Fighting Cock: being a History of the Twenty-Third Indian Division, 1942–1947.* Aldershot: Gale and Polden, 1951

Egmond, Florike. *Banditisme in de Franse Tijd: Profiel van de Grote Nederlandse Bende 1790–1799.* Dieren: De Bataafsche Leeuw, 1986

Encyclopaedie van Nederlandsch-Indië. 4v. and 4 supplements. The Hague and Leiden: Martinus Nijhoff and E. J. Brill, 1917–1939

Fabricius, Johan. *Hoe Ik Indië Terug Vond.* The Hague: H. P. Leupold, 1947

Feith, Herbert. *The Decline of Constitutional Democracy in Indonesia.* Ithaca, N.Y.: Cornell University Press, 1970

——, and Lance Castles, eds. *Indonesian Political Thinking 1945–1965.* Ithaca, N.Y.: Cornell University Press, 1970

Fisher, Charles A. *South-east Asia: a Social, Economic and Political Geography.* London: Methuen, 2nd ed., 1966

Frederick, William Hayward. 'Indonesian Urban Society in Transition: Surabaya, 1926–1946'. Ph.D. dissertation, University of Hawaii, 1978

Fryer, D. W. 'The "Million City" in Southeast Asia', *Geographical Review* 43, 4 (October 1953), 474–494

Furnivall, J. S. *Netherlands India: a Study of Plural Economy.* Cambridge: Cambridge University Press, 1939

Geertz, Clifford. *The Religion of Java.* Glencoe: Free Press, 1960

van Gheel Gildemeester, F. P. A. 'Marechaussees', *Indisch Militair Tijdschrift* 51, 1 (1920), 642–6

Gifford, Barbara S., and Guy Hobbs, trans. *The Kenpeitai in Java and Sumatra.* Ithaca, N.Y.: Cornell University Modern Indonesia Project, 1986

Go Gien Tjwan. *Eenheid in Verscheidenheid in een Indonesisch Dorp.* Amsterdam: Universiteit van Amsterdam, Sociologisch-Historisch Seminarium voor Zuidoost Azië, 1966

Great Britain. Naval Intelligence Division. Netherlands East Indies. 2v. [London]: HMSO, 1944

Gunawan, Rijadi. 'Jagoan dalam Revolusi Kita', *Prisma* 10, 8 (August 1981) 41–50

Guntingan Pers Ibu Kota 30th Kemerdekaan R.I. 17–8–75: Mengungkap Kembali Semangat Perjuangan 1945. Jakarta: Departemen Penerangan, 1975

de Haan, F. *Oud Batavia: Gedenkboek Uitgegeven naar Aanleiding van het Driehonderd Jarig Bestaan van der Stad in 1919.* 2v. Batavia: G. Kolff, 1922–23

——. *Priangan: de Preanger-regentschappen onder het Nederlandsch bestuur tot 1811.* 4v. Batavia: Bataviaasch Genootschap van Kunsten en Wetenschappen, 1901–1912

Hadisutjipto, S. Z. *Bara dan Njala Revolusi Phisik di Djakarta.* Jakarta: Dinas Museum dan Sedjarah D. C. I. Djakarta, 1971

Hall, D. G. E. *A History of South-east Asia.* London: Macmillan, 3rd ed., 1968

Hanifah, Abu. *Tales of a Revolution.* Sydney: Angus & Robertson, 1972

Harahap, Parada. *Saat bersedjarah.* Jakarta: Gapura, 1947

Hardjono, J. *Indonesia, Land and People*. Jakarta: Gunung Agung, 1971
Hatley, Ron, et al. *Other Javas: Away from the Kraton*. Clayton, Vic.: Monash University, 1984
Hatta, Mohammad. *Kumpulan Pidato dari Tahun 1942 s.d. 1949*. Jakarta: Yayasan Idayu, 1981
——. *Memoir*. Jakarta: Tintamas, 1979
——. *Memoirs*. Singapore: Gunung Agung, 1981
Heeren, H. J., ed. 'The Urbanisation of Djakarta', *Ekonomi dan Keuangan Indonesia* 8, 11 (November 1955), 696–736
Heijboer, Pierre. *De Politionele Acties: de Strijd om 'Indië' 1945/1949*. Haarlem: Fibula-Van Dishoeck, 1979
Helbig, Karl. *Am Rand des Pazifik: Studien zur Landes- und Kulturkunde Südostasiens*. Stuttgart: W. Kohlhammer, 1949
——. *Batavia, eine Tropische Stadtlandschaftskunde im Rahmen der Insel Java*. Doctoral dissertation, University of Hamburg, 1931
Helder, K. *Tiga Doeabelas: Gedenkboek 3–12 R.I.*. Groningen: n.p., 1951
Hering, B. B., ed. *The van der Most Report: a P.I.D. view of Sukarno's P.N.I.* Townsville: James Cook University, 1982
Hersri S. and Joebaar Ajoeb. 'S. M. Kartosuwiryo, Orang Seiring Bertukar Jalan', *Prisma* 11, 5 (May 1981), 79–96
Hobsbawm, E. J. *Bandits*. Harmondsworth: Penguin, 1972
——. 'Social Bandits: a Reply', *Comparative Studies in Society and History* 14, 4 (1972), 503–505
van Hogendorp, C. S. W., Graaf. *Tafereelen van Javaansche Zeden: Vier Oorspronkelijke Verhalen*. Amsterdam: C. G. Sulpke, 1837
Holt, Claire, ed. *Culture and Politics in Indonesia*. Ithaca and London: Cornell University Press, 1972
Ijzereef, Willem. 'Westerling en zijn poging tot rehabilitatie', *Vrij Nederland* 5 February 1983
Indisch Verslag 1939, II: Statistisch Jaaroverzicht van Nederlandsch-Indië over het Jaar 1938. Batavia: Landsdrukkerij, 1939
Indra, W. I. Panji, et al. *Perjuangan Phisik Rakyat Jakarta Mempertahankan Proklamasi 17 Agustus 1945*. Jakarta: Dinas Museum dan Sejarah, Daerah Khusus Ibukota Jakarta, 1982
Ingleson, John. '"Bound Hand and Foot": Railway Workers and the 1923 Strike in Java', *Indonesia* 31 (April 1981), 53–87
——. *Road to Exile: the Indonesian Nationalist Movement 1927–1934*. Singapore: Heinemann, 1979
Iwa Kusumasumantri. *Sedjarah Revolusi Indonesia, Djilid ke-dua: Masa Revolusi Bersendjata*. N.p.: n.p., n.d.
Jaquet, L. G. M. *Aflossing van de Wacht: Bestuurlijke en Politieke Ervaringen in de Nadagen van Nederlandsch-Indië*. Rotterdam: Ad. Donker, 1978
Jassin, H. B. *Chairil Anwar: Pelopor Angkatan 45*. Jakarta: Gunung Agung, 1956
Jellinek, Lea, Chris Manning and Gavin Jones. *The Life of the Poor in Indonesian Cities*. Clayton, Vic.: Monash University Centre of Southeast Asian Studies, 1978

Jolliffe, Jill. *East Timor: Nationalism and Colonialism*. St Lucia: University of Queensland Press, 1978

Kahin, Audrey, ed. *Regional Dynamics of the Indonesian Revolution: Unity from Diversity*. Honolulu: University of Hawaii Press, 1985

——. 'Struggle for Independence: West Sumatra in the Indonesian National Revolution 1945–1950', Ph.D. dissertation, Cornell University, 1979

Kahin, George McTurnan. *Nationalism and Revolution in Indonesia*. Ithaca, N.Y.: Cornell University Press, 1952

Kamaly, M. H. *Rakyat Bekasi Berjuang*. Bekasi: author, 1973

Kanahele, George Sanford. 'The Japanese Occupation of Indonesia: Prelude to Independence'. Ph.D. dissertation, Cornell University, 1967

Karimoeddin, T. 'Pendidikan Dokter Jaman Pendudukan Jepang (Ika-Dai-Gaku), in *125th Pendidikan Dokter di Indonesia 1851–1976*. Jakarta: Panitia Peringatan 125th Pendidikan Dokter di Indonesia, 1976

Kartasumitra, R. E. Sulaeman, ed. *Catatan-catatan dari Beberapa Ex-Anggota Batalion 400 Tentara Pelajar Brigade XVII*. Jakarta: author, 1977

——, ed. *Dokumentasi Batalion 400 Tentara Pelajar Brigade XVII*. Jakarta: author, [1977?]

Karya Jaya: Kenang Kenangan Lima Kepala Daerah Jakarta 1945–1966. Jakarta: Pemerintah Daerah Khusus Ibukota Jakarta, 1977

van der Kemp, P. H. *Oost-Indië's Herstel in 1816*. The Hague: Martinus Nijhoff, 1911

Kenangan Sekilas Perdjuangan Suratkabar: Sedjarah Pers Sebangsa. Jakarta: Serikat Perusahaan Surat Kabar S.P.S., 1958

Kertapati, Sidik. *Sekitar Proklamasi 17 Agustus 1945*. Jakarta: Pembaruan, 3rd ed., 1964.

Keyfitz, Nathan. 'The Ecology of Indonesian Cities', *American Journal of Sociology* 66 no. 4 (1961), pp. 348–354

Koch, D. M. G. *Om de Vrijheid: de Nationalistische Beweging in Indonesië*. Jakarta: Jajasan Pembangunan, 1950

Koesnodiprodjo, ed. *Himpunan Undang2, Peraturan2, Penetapan2 Pemerintah Republik Indonesia, 1946*. Jakarta: S. K. Seno, rev. ed., 1951

van der Kroef, Justus M. '"Petrus": Patterns of Prophylactic Murder in Indonesia', *Asian Survey* 25, 7 (1985), 745–59

Kurasawa, Aiko. 'Mobilization and Control: a Study of Social Change in Rural Java, 1942–1945'. Ph.D. dissertation, Cornell University, 1988

——. 'Social Changes in Javanese Villages, 1942–45: the Forced Delivery System and its Impact', *Southeast Asian Studies* 19, 1 (June 1981), 77 (English abstract of article in Japanese, pp. 77–105)

Kusnandar Partowisastro. 'Daftar Nama-nama Mahasiswa yang Pernah Tinggal di Ashrama BAPERPPI Jalan Raya Cikini 71 Jakarta Raya'. Typescript, Jakarta, 1979

——. 'Sedikit Catatan Saya Pengalaman Selama Dalam Periode Pendudukan Jepang'. Typescript, Jakarta, 1979

——. 'Sekelumit Ungkapan Sejarah dan Peranan Gedung Juang Menteng 31 Jakarta-Raya'. Typescript, Jakarta, 1978

'Laporan D. H. R. Angkatan 45 Ranting Senen dalam Rangka Malam Silaturakhmi tgl. 20 September 1981 di Aula Kelurahan Bungur'. Typescript, Jakarta, 1981

Laporan-laporan tentang Gerakan Protes di Jawa pada Abad-XX. Jakarta: Arsip Nasional Republik Indonesia, 1981

Leclerc, Jacques. 'Underground Activities and their Double: Amir Syarifuddin's Relationship with Communism in Indonesia', *Kabar Seberang* 17 (June 1986), 72–98

——. 'La Condition du Parti: Revolutionnaires Indonésiens à la recherche d'une identité', *Cultures et Développement* 10, 1 (1978), 3–70

Legge, J. D. *Sukarno: a Political Biography*. Harmondsworth: Penguin, 1973

Lekkerkerker, C. 'Het Krawangsche Oproer van Mei 1832', *De Indische Gids* 54, 2 (1932), 577–583

Letusan di Balik Buku. Jakarta: Dewan Harian Nasional Angkatan 45, Pusat Dokumentasi Sejarah Perjoangan, 1976

'Liquidatie der Particuliere Landerijen', *Bestuursvraagstukken/Soal-soal Pemerintahan* 1, 3 (July 1949), 351–353

List of Material and Personal Outrages and Injuries Perpetrated Against Indonesians by Dutch Soldiery in the City of Djakarta (October-December 1945). Jakarta: Ministry of Foreign Affairs, 1946

Lubis, Mochtar. *Bromocorah: Dua Belas Cerita Pendek*. Jakarta: Sinar Harapan, 1983

——. *A Road with no End*. Translated and edited by Anthony H. Johns. London: Hutchinson, 1968

Lucas, Anton E. *Local Opposition and Underground Resistance to the Japanese in Java, 1942–1945*. Clayton, Vic.: Centre of Southeast Asian Studies, Monash University, 1986

——. 'The Bamboo Spear Pierces the Payung: the Revolution against the Bureaucratic Elite in North Central Java in 1945', Ph.D. dissertation, Australian National University, 1981

McCoy, Alfred W., et al. *The Politics of Heroin in Southeast Asia*. New York: Harper, 1972

McKemmish, Susan Marilyn. 'A Political Biography of General A. H. Nasution'. M.A. dissertation, Monash University, 1976

Mackie, Jamie, et al. *Contemporary Indonesia: Political Dimensions*. Clayton, Vic.: Monash University, 1979

——, ed. *Indonesia: the Making of a Nation*. Canberra: Research School of Pacific Studies, Australian National University, 1980

McQuilton, John. *The Kelly Outbreak 1878–1880: the Geographical Dimension of Social Banditry*. Melbourne: Melbourne University Press, 1987

McVey, Ruth T. 'The Post-Revolutionary Transformation of the Indonesian Army', *Indonesia* 11 (April 1971), 131–176; 13 (April 1972), 147–181

——. *The Rise of Indonesian Communism*. Ithaca, N.Y.: Cornell University Press, 1965

——. *Southeast Asian Transitions: Approaches through Social History*. New Haven and London: Yale University Press, 1978

Malik, Adam. *In the Service of the Republic*. Singapore: Gunung Agung, 1980

——. *Mengabdi Republik, jilid II: Angkatan 45*. Jakarta: Gunung Agung, 1978

——. *Riwayat Proklamasi 17 Agustus 1945*. Jakarta: Widjaya, 1975

Mangunwijaya, Y. B. *Burung-burung Manyar*. Jakarta: Djambatan, 1981

Marpaung, Darius, ed. *Bingkisan Nasional: Kenangan 10 Tahun Revolusi Indonesia.* Jakarta: Usaha Pegawai Nasional Indonesia, 1955

Marshall, Jonathan. 'Opium and the Politics of Gangsterism in Nationalist China, 1927–1945', *Bulletin of Concerned Asian Scholars* 8, 3 (1976), 19–48

May, Ron, ed. *Goons, Raskols and Rebels.* Bathurst, NSW: Robert Brown, forthcoming

Memori Serah Jabatan 1921–1930 (Jawa Barat). Jakarta: Arsip Nasional Republik Indonesia, 1976

Merghart, W. 'De APRA-Affaire . . . een Enorme Bedrog?'. Photocopy, n.d

Meyer, D. H. *Japan Wint den Oorlog: Documenten over Java.* Maastricht: Leiter-Nypels, 1946

——. 'Over het Bendewezen op Java', *Indonesië* 3 (1949–1950), 178–189

Milone, Pauline Dublin. 'Queen City of the East: the Metamorphosis of a Colonial Capital'. Ph.D. dissertation, University of California, 1966

——. *Urban Areas of Indonesia.* Berkeley: University of California, 1966

Moertono, Soemarsaid. *State and Statecraft in Old Java: a Study of the Later Mataram Period, 16th to 19th Century.* Ithaca, N.Y.: Cornell University Modern Indonesia Project, 1974

Moestopo. *Memori Pengalaman.* Jakarta: Yayasan Universitas Prof. Dr. Moestopo, 1977

Mohamad Roem 70 Tahun: Pejuang-Perunding. Jakarta: Bulan Bintang, 1978

de Moor, J. A. 'Het Korps Speciale Troepen: tussen Marechaussee Formule en Politionele Actie', in G. Teitler and P. H. M. Groen, eds. *De Politionele Acties.* Amsterdam: De Bataafsche Leeuw, 1987

Nasution, A. H. *Fundamentals of Guerilla Warfare.* London: Pall Mall, 1965

——. *Memenuhi Panggilan Tugas, Jilid I: Kenangan Masa Muda.* Jakarta: Gunung Agung, 1982

——. *Sekitar Perang Kemerdekaan Indonesia.* 11v. Bandung: Angkasa, 1977–1979

——. *Tentara Nasional Indonesia.* 3v. Bandung: Ganaco, 2nd ed., 1963

Nasution, Syarif Alwahidin. 'Titik-titik (Saat-saat) Perjuangan Bersama Syarif Alwahidin Nasution dengan Idris P. Siregar sejak Zaman Mahasiswa Ika Daigaku sampai kepada Tahun 1950'. Typescript, Jakarta, n.d

Netherlands, Staten-Generaal. *Enquêtecommissie Regeringsbeleid 1940– 1945. Verslag Houdende de Uitkomsten van het Onderzoek, deel 8A en B: Militair Beleid 1940–1945: Terugkeer naar Nederlandsch-Indië (Punt P van het Enquêtebesluit): Verslag en Bijlagen.* The Hague: Staatsdrukkerij- en Uitgeverijbedrijf, 1956

Netherlands, Tweede Kamer der Staten Generaal. *Nota Betreffende het Archievenonderzoek naar Gegevens omtrent Excessen in Indonesië Begaan door Nederlandse Militairen in de Periode 1945–1950.* The Hague: 1969

Netherlands Indies, Departement van Landbouw, Nijverheid en Handel. *Volkstelling 1930, deel I: Native Population in West Java.* Batavia: Landsdrukkerij, 1933

Niel, Robert van. *The Emergence of the Modern Indonesian Elite.* The Hague: van Hoeve, 1960

Nish, Ian, ed. *Indonesian Experience: the Role of Japan and Britain, 1943–1948*. London: International Centre for Economics and Related Disciplines, London School of Economics, [1979]

Nishijima, Shigetada, et al., eds. *Japanese Military Administration in Indonesia*. Washington D.C.: Joint Publications Research Service, 1963

Nugroho Notosusanto, ed. *Markas Besar Komando Djawa*. Jakarta: Pusat Sejarah ABRI, 1973

——. 'Jakarta dan Tentara Peta', *Budaya Jaya* 10, 109 (June 1977), 373–379

——. *The PETA Army during the Japanese Occupation of Indonesia*. Tokyo: Waseda University Press, 1979

O'Malley, Pat. 'Social Bandits, Modern Capitalism and the Traditional Peasantry: a Critique of Hobsbawm', *Journal of Peasant Studies* 6, 4 (1979), 489–501

O'Malley, William Joseph. 'Indonesia in the Great Depression: a Study of East Sumatra and Jogjakarta in the 1930s'. Ph.D. dissertation, Cornell University, 1977

'De Onveiligheid op de Particuliere Landen in West-Java', *De Indische Gids* 59 (1937), 532–537

Operations of the Army in the South-western Regions: the Defence of Malaya and the Dutch Indies (Official Japanese war history series vol. 92), type-script translation of ch. 7 section 7, 'Outline of the indonesian [sic] independence question and the demobilization'. N.p., n.d

Orang Indonesia Jang Terkemoeka di Djawa. [Jakarta]: Gunseikanbu, 2604 [i.e. 1944]

Overdijkink, G. W. *Het Indonesische Probleem: de feiten*. The Hague: Martinus Nijhoff, 1946

——. *Het Indonesische Probleem: nieuwe feiten*. Amsterdam: Keizerskroon, 1948

Papanek, Gustav F. 'The Poor of Jakarta', *Prisma* (English ed.) 3 (May 1976), 33–51

Penders, C. L. M. *The Life and Times of Sukarno*. London: Sidgwick & Jackson, 1974

Pengabdian KODAM V/Jaya dalam Tiga Dasa Warsa. Jakarta: Dinas Sejarah Militer, Komando Daerah Militer V Jayakarta, 1979

Perang Kolonial Belanda di Aceh: the Dutch Colonial War in Aceh. Banda Aceh: Pusat Dokumentasi dan Informasi Aceh, 1977

'Pertemoean dengan Oetoesan Repoeblik Indonesia Tentang Perihal Kedjadian di Bekasi'. Typescript, Jakarta, 1945

Poeze, Harry. 'The PKI-Muda 1936–1942', *Kabar Seberang* 13–14 (1984), 157–176

——. *Politiek-Politioneele Overzichten van Nederlandsch-Indië, deel I 1927–1928*. The Hague: Martinus Nijhoff, 1982

——. *Politiek-Politioneele Overzichten van Nederlandsch-Indië*, deel II 1929–1930. Dordrecht: Foris, 1983

Quinn, George. 'The Javanese Science of Burglary', *Review of Indonesian and Malayan Affairs* 9, 1 (1975), 33–54

Raffel, Burton, tr. and ed. *The Complete Poetry of Chairil Anwar*. Albany: State University of New York Press, 1970

——. *The Development of Modern Indonesian Poetry*. Albany: State University of New York Press, 1967

Raffles, Thomas Stamford. *The History of Java*. 2v. Kuala Lumpur: OUP, 1965

Raliby, Osman. *Documenta Historica: Sedjarah Dokumenter dari Pertumbuhan dan Perdjuangan Negara Republik Indonesia*. Jakarta: Bulan Bintang, 1953

Reid, Anthony J. S. *The Blood of the People: Revolution and the End of Traditional Rule in Northern Sumatra*. Kuala Lumpur: OUP, 1979

——. *The Indonesian National Revolution, 1945–1950*. Hawthorn, Vic.: Longmans, 1974

——, and Oki Akira. *The Japanese Experience in Indonesia: Selected Memoirs of 1942–1945*. Athens, Ohio: Ohio University, 1986

Remmelink, W. G. J. 'The Emergence of the New Situation: the Japanese Army on Java after the Surrender', *Kabar Seberang: Sulating Maphilindo* 4 (July 1978), 57–74

Report on the Military Situation in Java-Sumatra-Madura (August 4 – September 4, 1947). Yogyakarta: Ministry of Foreign Affairs, 1947

Republik Indonesia Kotapradja Djakarta Raya. Jakarta: Kementerian Penerangan, 1953

Republik Indonesia Propinsi Djawa Barat. Jakarta: Kementerian Penerangan, 1952

Ricklefs, M. C. *Jogjakarta under Sultan Mangkubumi 1749–1792: a History of the Division of Java*. London: OUP, 1974

'Riwayat hidup Sjarif Wahidin Nasution'. Typescript, Jakarta, n.d

Roem, Mohamad. *Bunga Rampai dari Sejarah*. Jakarta: Bulan Bintang, 1972

Rush, James R. 'Social Control and Influence in Nineteenth Century Indonesia: Opium Farms and the Chinese of Java', *Indonesia* 35 (1983), 53–64

Sadikoen et al. *20 Tahun Perkembangan Angkatan Kepolisian Republik Indonesia*. Jakarta: Inkopak, 1967

Said, Salim. 'The Genesis of Power: Civil-Military Relations in Indonesia during the Revolution for Independence'. Ph.D. dissertation, Ohio State University, 1985

Saleh, Jo Chaerul. 'Peranan Gedung Menteng 31 dalam Perjuangan Kemerdekaan'. Typescript, Jakarta, 1977

Sarekat Islam Lokal. Jakarta: Arsip Nasional Republik Indonesia, 1975

Sartono Kartodirdjo and Anton Lucas. 'Banditry and Political Change in Java', in Sartono Kartodirdjo, *Modern Indonesia: Tradition and Transformation*. Yogyakarta: Gadjah Mada University Press, 1984

Sartono Kartodirdjo. *The Peasants' Revolt of Banten in 1888, its Conditions, Course and Sequel: a Case Study of Social Movements in Indonesia*. The Hague: Martinus Nijhoff, 1966

——. *Protest Movements in Rural Java: a Study of Agrarian Unrest in the Nineteenth and early Twentieth centuries*. Singapore: OUP, 1973

——. 'The Role of Struggle Organizations in the Indonesian Revolution', *Review of Indonesian and Malayan Affairs* 14, 2 (December 1980), 92–110

Schmidt, H. J., and Du Croo, M. H. *Marechaussee in Aceh*. Maastricht: Leiter-Nypels, 1943

Schulte Nordholt, Henk. 'De Jago in de Schaduw: Misdaad en "Orde" in de Koloniale Staat op Java', *De Gids* 146, 8/9 (1983), 664–675

Schumacher, Peter. 'Raymond Westerling en de Jungle van het Verleden', *NRC Handelsblad* (Rotterdam), 18 September 1981

Schutte, Gerrit, and Heather Sutherland, eds. *Papers of the Dutch-Indonesian Historical Conference held at Lage Vuursche, The Netherlands, 23–27 June 1980.* Leiden and Jakarta: Bureau of Indonesian Studies, 1982

Scott, James C. *The Moral Economy of the Peasant: Rebellion and Subsistence in Southeast Asia.* New Haven & London: Yale University Press, 1976

Sedjarah Militer Kodam VI Siliwangi. *Siliwangi dari Masa Kemasa.* Jakarta: Fakta Mahyuma, 1968

Sejarah Kesehatan Nasional Indonesia, I. Jakarta: Departemen Kesehatan, 1978

Sejarah Pertumbuhan dan Perkembangan Kodam V/Jaya: Penyelamat Ibukota Republik Indonesia. [Jakarta: Komando Daerah Militer V Jayakarta, Dinas Sejarah Militer, 1974]

van Setten van der Meer, N. C. *Sawah Cultivation in Ancient Java: Aspects of Development during the Indo-Javanese period, 5th to 15th Century.* Canberra: Australian National University Press, 1979

Sewaka. *Tjorat-tjaret dari Djaman ke Djaman.* Bandung: n.p., [1955]

Simatupang, T. B. *Pelopor dalam Perang, Pelopor dalam Damai.* Jakarta: Sinar Harapan, 2nd ed. 1981

——. *Report from Banaran: Experiences during the People's War.* Ithaca, N.Y.: Cornell University Modern Indonesia Project, 1972

Sjahrir, Sutan. *Our Struggle.* Translated with an introduction by Benedict R. O'G Anderson. Ithaca, N.Y.: Cornell University Modern Indonesia Project, 1968

Smail, John R. W. *Bandung in the Early Revolution, 1945–1946: a Study in the Social History of the Indonesian Revolution.* Ithaca, N.Y.: Cornell University Modern Indonesia Project, 1964

Smit, C. *De Dekolonisatie van Indonesië: Feiten en Beschouwingen.* Groningen: Tjeenk Willink, 1976

Smith, R. B., and W. Watson, eds. *Early South East Asia: Essays in Archaeology, History and Historical Geography.* Kuala Lumpur: OUP, 1979

Soal Beras dan Bahan Makanan Oentoek Kota Djakarta. Siaran Kilat Kementerian Penerangan, Jakarta, November 1946

Soeriaatmadja, Soeparno. *Sedjarah Kepolisian dari Zaman Klasik sampai dengan Zaman Modern.* Jakarta: Perguruan Tinggi Ilmu Kepolisian, 1971

Soerjono, 'On Musso's Return', *Indonesia* 29 (April 1980), 59–90

Soesanto, Soetopo. 'Djakarta Raya pada Masa "Pemerintah Nasional Kota" 17 Agustus 1945 – 21 Djuli 1947'. Skripsi Sarjana, Universitas Indonesia, 1971

Soetanto, Soeranto. 'Pemberontakan PKI Mr. Mohammad Joesoeph Tahun 1946 di Cirebon'. Skripsi Sarjana, Universitas Indonesia, 1981

van Sprang, Alfred. *Laatste Acte: een Cocktail van Soldatenleven en Politiek in Indonesië.* The Hague: W. van Hoeve, 1949

——. *Wij werden Geroepen: de Geschiedenis van de 7 December Divisie.* The Hague: W. van Hoeve, 1949

206 GANGSTERS AND REVOLUTIONARIES

Sudiro. *Pengalaman Saya sekitar 17 Agustus '45*. Jakarta: Yayasan Idayu, 1974

Suleiman, Satyawati. 'The Last Days of Batavia', *Indonesia* 28 (October 1979), 55–64

Sundhaussen, Ulf. 'The Political Orientations and Political Involvement of the Indonesian Officer Corps 1945–1966: the Siliwangi Division and the Army Headquarters'. Ph.D. dissertation, Monash University, 1971

——. *The Road to Power: Indonesian Military Politics 1945–1967*. Kuala Lumpur: OUP, 1982

Suradji, Ngadam. 'Riwayat Singkat Peristiwa "Rengasdengklok"'. Typescript, Karawang, 1976

Surjomihardjo, Abdurrachman. *Pemekaran Kota Jakarta/The Growth of Jakarta*. Jakarta: Djambatan, 1977

'Suroto Kunto Hilang Misterius. Tugu Pahlawannya Kurang Pemiliharaan', *Pikiran Rakyat* (Bandung), 19 August 1978

Suryadinata, Leo. *Eminent Indonesian Chinese: Biographical Sketches*. Singapore: ISEAS, 1978

Sutherland, Heather. *The Making of a Bureaucratic Elite: the Colonial Transformation of the Javanese* **Priyayi**. Singapore: Heinemann, 1979

——. 'Notes on Java's Regent Families', part 1, *Indonesia* 16 (October 1973), 113–147

Sutomo [Bung Tomo]. *The Road to Independence: the History of the Birth of a Free Nation, the Republic of Indonesia*. [Jakarta]: Balapan, [1953]

Sutrisno Kutoyo and Surachman. *Riwayat Hidup dan Perjuangan Mohammad Ramdhan*. Jakarta: Departemen P. dan K., 1977

Sutter, John O. *Indonesianisasi: Politics in a Changing Economy, 1940–1955*. 4v. Ithaca, N.Y.: Cornell University Southeast Asia Program, 1959

Tan Malaka. *Dari Pendjara ke Pendjara*. Vol. III. Jakarta: Widjaya, n.d

Taufik Abdullah, et al., eds. *Manusia dalam Kemelut Sejarah*. Jakarta: Lembaga Penelitian, Pendidikan dan Penerangan Ekonomi dan Sosial, 1978

Taylor, Jean Gelman. *The Social World of Batavia: European and Eurasian in Dutch Asia*. Madison, Wisc.: University of Wisconsin Press, 1983

Teitler, G. *The Dutch Colonial Army in Transition: The Militia Debate, 1900–1921*. Townsville, Qld: James Cook University of North Queensland, 1981

The Liang Gie. *Sedjarah Pemerintahan Kota Djakarta*. Jakarta: Kotapradja Djakarta Raja, 1958

30 Years of Indonesia's Independence (vol 1): 1945–1949. Jakarta: State Secretariat, 1975

Tideman, J. 'De Bevolking van de Regentschappen Batavia, Meester Cornelis en Buitenzorg', *Koloniaal Tijdschrift* 22 (March 1933), 140–168

Tjoet Rachman, T. R., ed. 'Mahasiswa Jakarta Ikadaigaku 1943 – Agustus 1945'. Mimeo, Jakarta, 1975

Toer, Pramoedya Ananta. *Ditepi Kali Bekasi*. Jakarta: Balai Pustaka, 2nd ed., 1957

——. 'Revenge', translated by Ben Anderson, *Indonesia* 26 (October 1978), 43–62

'Toestand op Particuliere Landerijen', *Tijdschrift voor Economische en Sociale Geographie* 5 (1914), 36

Trisnojuwono. *Peristiwa2 Ibukota Pendudukan.* Jakarta: Balai Pustaka, 1970

Turton, Andrew, and Shigeharu Tanabe. *History and Peasant Consciousness in South East Asia.* Osaka: National Museum of Ethnology, 1984

Twang Peck Yang. 'The Indonesian Chinese Business Minority in Transition, 1940–1950'. Ph.D. dissertation, Australian National University, 1987

United States Armed Forces, Far East Head Quarters, Japanese Research Division, Military History Section. *Japanese Monograph no. 165 (army): Java Operations Record, 16 Army, part II.* Washington: 1951

Veenstra, J. H. W. *Diogenes in de Tropen.* Amsterdam: Vrij Nederland, 1947

Veer, Paul van 't, ed. *Drees: neerslag van een werkzaam leven: een keuze uit geschriften, redevoeringen, interviews en brieven uit de jaren 1902–1972.* Assen: van Gorcum, 1972

Venner, Dominique, and R. P. P. Westerling. *Westerling: de Eenling.* Amsterdam: Spoor, 1982

van der Wal, S. L., ed. *Besturen Overzee: Herinneringen van Oud-Ambtenaren bij het Binnenlands Bestuur in Nederlandsch-Indië* Franeker: T. Wever, 1977

——, ed. *Officiële Bescheiden Betreffende de Nederlands-Indonesische Betrekkingen 1945–1950.* 14 v. to date (later volumes edited by P. J. Drooglever and M Schouten). The Hague: Martin Nijhoff, 1971–1988

Wertheim, W. F. *Indonesian society in transition.* The Hague: van Hoeve, 1964

——. *Indonesië: van Vorstenrijk tot Neo-Kolonie.* Amsterdam: Boom, 1978

Westerling, Raymond Paul Pierre. *Mijn Memoires.* Antwerp and Amsterdam: P. Vink, 1952

White, Osmar. *Time Now, Time Before.* London and Melbourne: Heinemann, 1967

Williams, Michael C. *Sickle and Crescent: the Communist Revolt of 1926 in Banten.* Ithaca, N.Y.: Cornell University Modern Indonesia Project, 1982

Wolf, Charles. *The Indonesian Story: the Birth, Growth and Structure of the Indonesian Republic.* New York: John Day, 1948

Wolters, O. W. *Early Indonesian Commerce: a Study of the Origins of Srivijaya.* Ithaca, N.Y.: Cornell University Press, 1967

Wright, Arnold, and Oliver T. Breakspear, eds. *Twentieth Century Impressions of Netherlands India: its History, People, Commerce, Industries, and Resources.* London: Lloyd's Greater Britain Publishing Co., 1909

van Wulfften Palthe, P. M. *Over het Bendewezen op Java.* Amsterdam: van Rossen, 1949

——. *Psychological Aspects of the Indonesian Problem.* Leiden: Brill, 1949

Yang, Anand C. *Crime and Criminality in British India.* Tucson: University of Arizona Press, 1985

Yong Mun Cheong. *H. J. van Mook and Indonesian Independence: a Study of his Role in Dutch-Indonesian Relations, 1945–48.* The Hague: Martinus Nijhoff, 1982

Index